More Praise for
A Romantic Education

"Its prose is strong, at times even brilliant . . . a quarry of richly imagined lines."   —*New York Times Book Review*

"Here is a quiet, meditative passion that brings to mind the voice of Colette in *My Mother's House.* . . . Hampl's ideas are grounded in the instincts and experience of a wise and full heart."   —*Los Angeles Times*

"She writes clearly, beautifully, with penetrating insight, both of her American family and the Czechs, making believable connections between both worlds, between her own and universal concerns, all without strain. This memoir is a treat."

—*Columbus Dispatch*

A
ROMANTIC
EDUCATION

A ROMANTIC EDUCATION

PATRICIA HAMPL

Winner of a Houghton Mifflin
Literary Fellowship Award

W. W. NORTON & COMPANY

NEW YORK · LONDON

Afterword copyright © 1999 by Patricia Hampl
Copyright © 1981 by Patricia Hampl

A portion of this book has appeared in the *Kenyon Review*.

The author is grateful for permission to reprint material from the following sources:
Letter of November 1, 1907, to Clara Rilke, from *The Letters of Rainer Maria Rilke,
1892–1910*, translated by M. D. Herter-Norton. Copyright 1945 by W. W. Norton &
Company, Inc., renewed © 1972 by M. D. Herter Norton. Reprinted with the permission of W. W. Norton & Company, Inc. Excerpts from Petru Popescu's memoir,
from *Index on Censorship* 5, no. 1 (London) 1976. Reprinted by permission. For more
information contact: Tel +44 (171)278 2313, Fax +44 (171)278 1878, Email: contact@in-
dexoncensorship.org, or visit Index on the Web at http://www.oneworld.org/index_oc.
John Berryman, "Mpls, Mother" from *Collected Poems 1937–1971*. Copyright © 1989
by Kate Donahue Berryman. Copyright © 1969 by John Berryman. Reprinted with the
permission of Farrar, Straus & Giroux, Inc. and Faber and Faber, Ltd. James Wright,
"The Minneapolis Poem" from *Above the River: The Complete Poems* (Middletown,
Conn.: Wesleyan University Press, 1990). Copyright © 1966 by James Wright.
Reprinted with the permission of University Press of New England. Milan Kundera,
excerpts from *The Joke* (New York: Coward, McCann & Geoghegan, 1969). Copyright
© 1969 by McDonald & Co., Ltd. Reprinted with the permission of HarperCollins
Publishers, Inc. Osip Mandelstam, lines from a 1930 poem, translated by Clarence
Brown and W. S. Merwin, from *Osip Mandelstam: Selected Poems* (New York:
Atheneum Publishers, 1974). Copyright © 1973 by Clarence Brown and W. S. Mer-
win. Reprinted with the permission of Simon & Schuster, Inc. and Oxford University
Press, Ltd.

Library of Congress Cataloging in Publication Data

Hampl, Patricia, date
A romantic education.

1. Prague—Description. 2. Art—Czechoslovakia.
3. St. Paul—Description. 4. Hampl, Patricia.
I. Title.
DB2614.H35 1981 943.7'12 80-23624

ISBN 0-393-31905-9

W. W. Norton & Company, Inc.
500 Fifth Avenue, New York, NY 10110
www.wwnorton.com

W. W. Norton & Company, Ltd.
10 Coptic Street, London WC1A 1PU

5 6 7 8 9 0

For my father
   STANLEY R. HAMPL
and my mother
   MARY MARUM HAMPL

Contents

I
St. Paul ❧ The Garden

1 ❦

I was five and was sitting on the floor of the vestibule hallway of my grandmother's house where the one bookcase had
been pushed. The bookcase wasn't in the house itself — ours
wasn't a reading family. I was holding in my lap a book of
sepia photographs bound in a soft brown cover, stamped in
flaking gold with the title *Zlatá Praha*. Golden Prague, views
of the nineteenth century.

The album felt good, soft. First, the Hradčany Castle and its
gardens, then a close-up of the astronomical clock, a view of the
baroque jumble of Malá Strana. Then a whole series of photographs of the Vltava River, each showing a different bridge,
photograph after pale photograph like a wild rose that opens
petal by petal, exposing itself effortlessly, as if there were no
such thing as regret. All the buildings in the pictures were hazy,
making it seem that the air, not the stone, held the contour of the
baroque villas intact.

I didn't know how to read yet, and the Czech captions under
the pictures were no more incomprehensible to me than English
would have been. I liked the soft, fleshlike pliancy of the book.
I knew the pictures were of Europe, and that Europe was far
away, unreachable. Still, it had something to do with me, with
my family. I sat in the cold vestibule, turning the pages of the
Prague album. I was flying; I was somewhere else. I was not in
St. Paul, Minnesota, and I was happy.

My grandmother appeared at the doorway. Her hands were

on her stout hips, and she wanted me to come out of the un-heated hallway. She wanted me to eat coffee cake in the kitchen with everybody else, and I had been hard to find. She said, "Come eat," as if this were the family motto.

As she turned to go, she noticed the album. In a second she was down on the floor with me, taking the album carefully in her hands, turning the soft, felt pages. "Oh," she said, "Praha." She looked a long time at one picture, I don't remember which one, and then she took a white handkerchief out of her pinafore apron pocket, and dabbed at the tears under her glasses. She took off the wire-rim glasses and made a full swipe.

Her glasses had made deep hollows on either side of her nose, two small caves. They looked as if, with a poke, the skin would give way like a ripe peach, and an entrance would be exposed into her head, into the skull, a passageway to the core of her brain. I didn't want her head to have such wounds. Yet I liked them, these unexpected dips in a familiar landscape.

"So beautiful," she was crying melodramatically over the album. "So beautiful." I had never seen an adult cry before. I was relieved, in some odd way, that there was crying in adult-hood, that crying would not be taken away.

My grandmother hunched down next to me in the hallway; she held the album, reciting the gold-stamped captions as she turned the pages and dabbed at her eyes. She was having a good cry. I wanted to put my small finger into the two little caves of puckered skin, the eyeless sockets on either side of her large, drooping nose. Strange wounds, I wanted to touch them. I wanted to touch her, my father's mother. She was so *foreign*.

Looking repeatedly into the past, you do not necessarily become fascinated with your own life, but rather with the phenomenon of memory. The act of remembering becomes less autobiographical; it begins to feel tentative, aloof. It becomes blessedly impersonal.

The self-absorption that seems to be the impetus and embarrassment of autobiography turns into (or perhaps always was) a hunger for the world. Actually, it begins as hunger for *a* world, one gone or lost, effaced by time or a more sudden brutality. But in the act of remembering, the personal environment expands, resonates beyond itself, beyond its "subject," into the endless and tragic recollection that is history.

We look at old family photographs in which we stand next to black, boxy Fords and are wearing period costumes, and we do not gaze fascinated because there we are young again, or there we are standing, as we never will again in life, next to our mother. We stare and drift because there we are . . . historical. It is the dress, the black car that dazzle us now and draw us beyond our mother's bright arms which once caught us. We reach into the attractive impersonality of something more significant than ourselves.

We embrace the deathliness and yet we are not dead. We are impersonal and yet ourselves. The astonishing power and authority of memory derive from this paradox. Here, in memory, we live *and* die. We do "live again" in memory, but differently: in history as well as in biography. And when these two come together, forming a narrative, they approach fiction. The imprecision of memory causes us to create, to extend remembrance into narrative. It sometimes seems, therefore, that what we remember is not — could not be — true. And yet it is *accurate*. The imagination, triggered by memory, is satisfied that this is so.

We trust memory against all the evidence: it is selective, subjective, cannily defensive, unreliable as fact. But a single red detail remembered — a hat worn in 1952, the nail polish applied one summer day by an aunt to her toes, separated by balls of cotton, as we watched — has more real blood than the creatures around us on a bus as, for some reason, we think of that day, that hat, those bright feet. That world. This power of memory probably comes from its kinship with the imagination. In memory each of us is an artist: each of us creates. The Kingdom of God, the nuns used to tell us in school, is within you. We may not have made a religion of memory, but it is our passion, and along with (sometimes in opposition to) science, our authority. It is a kingdom of its own.

Psychology, which is somehow *our* science, the claustrophobic discipline of the century, has made us acknowledge the value of remembering — even at the peril of shame. But it is especially difficult to reach back into the merely insignificant, into a family life where, it seemed, nothing happened, where there wasn't the ghost of a pretension. That is a steelier resistance because to break through what is unimportant and as anonymous as dirt a greater sense of worthlessness must be overcome. At least shame is interesting; at least it is hidden, the sign of anything valuable. But for a past to be overlooked, discarded because it was not only useless but simply without interest — that is a harsher heritage. In fact, is it a heritage?

It seems as if I spent most of my twenties holding a lukewarm cup of coffee, hunched over a table, talking. Innumerable cups of coffee, countless tables: the booths of the Gopher Grill at the University of Minnesota where, probably around 1965, I first heard myself use the word *relationship;* a little later, the orange formica table of a federal prison where "the man I live with" (there still is no other term) was serving a sentence for draft resistance; and the second-hand tables of a dozen apartments, the wooden farmhouse table of a short-lived commune — table after table, friend after friend, rehashing our hardly ended (or not ended) childhoods. I may have the tables wrong; maybe the formica one was in the farmhouse, the oak one in the prison, maybe the chairs in the prison were orange and the table gray. But they are fixtures, nailed down, not to be moved: memories.

This generation has written its memoirs early; we squeezed every childhood lemon for all it was worth: my mother this, my father that. Our self-absorption was appalling. But I won't go back — not yet — on that decade. It was also the time when my generation, as "a generation," was most political, most involved.

The people I sat with, picking at our individual pasts, wearing nightgowns till noon as we analyzed within a millimeter our dreams and their meanings (that is, how they proved this or that about our parents), finally put on our clothes, went outside and, in various ways that are too easily forgotten, tried to end a war which we were the first, as a group, to recognize was disastrous. In fact, our protest against the war is what made us a generation, even to ourselves.

Perhaps no American generation — certainly not our parents who were young during the Depression — had a childhood as long as ours. The war kept us young. We stayed in school, endlessly, it seemed, and our protest kept us in the child's position: we alternately "rebelled" against and pestered the grownups for what we wanted — an end to the war. Those who fought the war had no such long, self-reflective youths. Childhood belonged to us, who stayed at home. And we became the "sixties generation."

Our certainty that the war was wrong became entangled with our analysis of our families and our psyches not only because we were given to self-reflection and had a lot of time on our hands. We combed through our dreams and our childhoods with Jung's *Man and His Symbols* at the ready, and were looking for something, I now think, that was neither personal nor familial and perhaps not even psychological. We had lost the national connection and were heartsick in a cultural way. I don't think we knew that; I didn't, anyway. But at home I didn't talk psychology, I talked politics, arguing with a kind of angry misery whose depths confused me and made my family frightened for me, and probably of me. But there was no real argument — I did all the talking; my family, gathered for Sunday dinner, looked glumly at the gravy on their plates as if at liquid Rorschach blots that might suggest why I, the adored child, had come to this strange pass. They weren't "for the war," but the belligerent way I was against it dismayed them and caused them to fall silent, waiting for me to stop. I had opinions, I spoke of my "position" on things.

One night my uncle, trying to meet me halfway, said, "Well, when I was in Italy during the War . . ."

"How do you defend that analogy?" I snapped at him, perhaps partly because for them "the War" was still the Second World War. My family couldn't seem, for a long time, to *focus* on Vietnam. But my uncle retreated in the face of the big guns of my new English-major lingo.

On Thanksgiving one year I left the table to find *I. F. Stone's Weekly* and read parts of it to the assembled family in a ringing, triumphantly angry voice. "But," my father said when I finished, as if I. F. Stone had been compiling evidence about me and not the Johnson administration, "you used to be so *happy* — the happiest person I ever met."

"What does that have to do with anything?" I said.

Yet he was right. My unhappiness (but I didn't think of myself as unhappy) was a confusion of personal and public matters, and it was made more intense by the fact that I had been happy ("the happiest person!") and now I couldn't remember what that happiness had been — just childhood? But many childhoods are miserable. And I couldn't remember exactly how the happiness stopped. I carry from that time the feeling that private memory is not just private and not just memory. Yet the resistances not against memory but against the significance of memory remain strong.

I come from people who have always been polite enough to feel that nothing has ever happened to them. They have worked, raised families, played cards, gone on fishing trips together, risen to grief and admirable bitterness and, then, taken patiently the early death that robbed them of a brother, a son. They have not dwelt on things. To dwell, that appropriate word, as if the past were a residence, faintly morbid and barbaric: the dwellings of prehistoric men. Or, the language of the Bible: "The Word was made flesh, and dwelt amongst us."

I have dwelt, though. To make a metaphor is to make a fuss, and I am a poet, though it seems that is something one cannot claim for oneself; anyway, I write poetry. I am enough of them, my kind family, to be repelled by the significance of things, to find poetry, with its tendency to make connections and to break the barriers between past and present, slightly embarrassing.

It would be impossible to look into the past, even a happy one (especially a happy one), were it not for the impersonality that dwells in the most intimate fragments, the integuments that bind even obscure lives to history and, eventually, history to fiction, to myth.

I will hold up negative after family negative to the light. I will dwell. Dwell in the house of the dead and in the living house of my relatives. I'm after junk. I want to make something out of what my family says is nothing. I suppose that is what I was up to when my grandmother called me out of the vestibule, away from the bookcase and the views of Prague, to eat my dinner with everybody else.

2 🦋

I WANTED TO BE a writer. Didn't everybody? I didn't think this would stop me from also being a doctor, or a microbiologist. (I liked putting something that appeared to be one thing under a lens to see the crammed, multiple life: a strand of hair, for instance, as our biology teacher demonstrated.) I could also see being a teacher, or a nun (the kind that wore sandals and never spoke), or, in a particularly long-lived fantasy, a concert pianist. These occupations and many others — actress, oceanographer, tree surgeon — fascinated me.

Writing, on the other hand, was not fascinating; it was something I just did. In compensation, though, it possessed a reality none of these other occupations, with their glamour, could approach. What after all *was* an oceanographer? A person who . . . looked at oceans? Looked at them hard? And then? *Wrote* about them. And I didn't have to wait until I grew up to be a writer, an advantage over oceanography. I could sit at the dining room table and ask my mother how to spell the hard words.

Later, in college, I was proud to be "majoring in English," which to me was like choosing everything for your subject. The allure of any occupation, anything at all, seemed always to circle back to writing. Because writing, I sensed, *let you in*; it subsumed these other things, oceans and microscopes, teachers, dining room tables. Writing was the soul of everything else. Being a Catholic, I found the word *soul* came easily; it still does. Wanting to be a writer was wanting to be a person.

I wrote poetry: it was easier than prose. In high school I wrote frantically — about the lilacs, about the sunset, about there being no God, about arson and madness. I was phenomenally sane. The fact that people went crazy or were tormented — a favorite word — was a marvelous discovery. It confirmed something, I couldn't say what.

I was breathless with lyricism. It was as if I was clutching in my bare hand a lilac, an arsonist, a tormented lesbian, the reddest sunset (I wrote about all these things) and crying, Me, me, me! It was the most satisfying, exultant message I had.

That was lyricism. It was also adolescence, the personal discovery of everything. Of lilacs, which had always been there in the back yard, down the neighborhood alleys where they cloaked the garbage cans and hugged the sides of old garages too small for the finned fish of that decade's cars. For the first time the lilacs came to me nostalgically because I *noticed* them. Nostalgia and the living, immediate lilac met in a first sensation of adulthood, the knowledge that objects carry their dense bundles of significance out of unconsciousness all the way to — I could almost sense it ahead — the end of the line. To death. I encountered the fragility of the life around me. In this way, objects gradually became images.

As for the arsonists and tormented lesbians, they were creatures of my adolescence the way the figures of Hans Christian Andersen had been in my childhood. Only these were real. A son of a friend of a friend had been picked up, we heard, by the university police for starting a fire in the basement of Ford Hall. "A perfectly ordinary boy" was the phrase. Anything was possible; appearance deceived.

I wrote a sympathetic poem about a crazy boy who burned down a theater; he was caught in his own blaze and "expired." My English teacher, when I showed her the poem, said, "Have you been reading Dostoevsky?" I also wrote a prose poem about a (tormented) lesbian on a train, who was leaving behind the wonderful schoolgirl she had loved but, of course, had not touched. Lesbians didn't do bad things (what things, anyway?);

they only thought them or felt them inside. A lesbian was a heroine to me only if she was tormented; she had to do a lot of silent renouncing. Of happy lesbians I knew nothing at all. Mine was a prose poem that would have appalled — or amused — a real one.

But I wasn't writing about lesbians, and not even about love between women. My heroine, concocted from a moony, inaccurate stereotype, was The Woman Traveling Alone. She was not a lesbian at all: she was a woman on a train who was *going somewhere,* and she was impeded only by her sadness, which gave her an élan I found thrilling. I suppose I made her a lesbian because I believed this made her independent. And I caused her to leave the girl she loved because I was a prude. Not only a sexual prude; I was standoffish about reality itself and sent my heroine on her dim journey (her destination was unclear) as if onto the endless rails of fantasy, away from train rides that end in actual places, away from her own nonexistent biography, away from other people, far from sex of any kind.

This prose poem, I sensed, came closer to some kind of real fire than my story about the arsonist, and I did not show it to my English teacher. My secrecy had little to do with sex, even "forbidden" sex (all sex was forbidden). Like all prudes, I was safeguarding something beyond my discovery of my sexual self. I was holding fast the world of fantasy. I wanted to touch the exotic.

The place I considered my own, the one I went to for several years to write, to sit, to *be* a poet, was a park bench in St. Clair Park, not far from our house in St. Paul. I had tried other places at school, including a tiny box of a room almost completely filled by the grand piano on which I was supposed to be practicing. But this was illegal and therefore nerve-racking. I didn't want to get caught and, being deeply conventional by nature, I did not like my poetry writing to be illicit. In this alone, I was not a romantic.

St. Clair Park was (and still is) set on a bluff of the city, the back yards of the Crocus Hill houses and mansions — I called anything with more than three bedrooms a mansion — rising even higher behind it, and the lowland that fell sharply below the park lying beyond, with its broad plain of working-class houses. From the height of the park I looked down on my grandmother's neighborhood. It had also been my own neighborhood — I was born "down there," baptized at St. Stanislaus, the Czech church. My father still worked there; his greenhouse was only two blocks from where I'd been born, in a house owned by an old Czech couple, our landlords, who hunted mushrooms with Moravian cunning and passion. They gathered them in suburban woods (they took the streetcar) and brought the sinister things — as my mother thought — home to dry. It did not occur to me, when I sat on my park bench, to write about this.

Teta ("Auntie"), as we called her, sliced the perfect, still-wet flesh, and laid the slices of mushroom on a window screen, which her husband Charlie put on the porch table, elevated at the corners by several bricks. The mushrooms lay like this for a couple of weeks, slowly losing their pastels, the lavender of the gills, the bright yellow and red of the more unusual caps. They became stiff, wizened chips. "I don't know, Teta," my mother would say, "that red one — are you sure you know what it is?" And to my father upstairs she said, "She doesn't even own a mushroom book."

"I know, I know," Teta said. "In the winter, when I revive this one, I put it in butter with garlic chopped up, you'll see." But my mother would have none of the mushrooms, fresh or "revived." Nor were my brother and I supposed to have any.

Teta's maiden name had been Žák, an old Moravian name, she said. She was very proud of it. "My name means 'scholar' in Czech," she told me. She believed this indicated that somewhere in her ancestral line there had been a person of great learning. She was interested in her heritage; she was the only one of my grandmother's friends — "the Czech ladies" as even my grandmother called them — who was. Teta told me to pay attention to anything Czech. "You have to learn," she said. But it wasn't clear what it was I must learn or from whom. I ate her illicit food, but I had no questions to ask.

I didn't write about Teta or her mushrooms or about anything "down there." From the park bench I looked down on the immigrant neighborhood, which had become a neighborhood not of immigrants anymore but of old people, ex-immigrants. Here and there new settlers had moved in, new poor people who were, for the most part, American Indians who had left the reservations up north. But they were a distinct minority. The houses still belonged to the Czech and German immigrants who had built them at the beginning of the century. The period had not yet begun when young people, interested in the area's history, would move in, "renovate" the little houses, and "save" the old Czech hall where my grandmother and grandfather had danced and played cards. Everything down there, as I sat above on my park bench, looked simply ordinary.

From the St. Clair hill I looked down on the West Seventh neighborhood, the name of the area taken from its main street. My park bench was situated so that I saw not only the unremarkable houses of the old neighborhood, but the Schmidt Brewery sign, mounted above the nineteenth-century brick factory, that spelled over and over, like an eternal one-word spelling bee, the name S-C-H-M-I-D-T in neon-red chancel-style letters. I looked down on the old neighborhood as if from an airplane, as if on my way to somewhere more important. I was higher, bigger, more life-size than the toy houses and cars and streets, the miniature twig trees and tiny doll people down there. The only thing approaching my dimension was the brewery itself and its blinking sign. Hypnotized, I watched this sign for hours, for whole seasons. I think I sat there just to watch it.

"We know our own rhythms," I read years later in Muriel Rukeyser's book *The Life of Poetry*. "Our rhythms are more recognizably our selves than any of our forms." Yes. And once again, as so many times before and later, the Schmidt sign blinked behind my eyes.

The bedrock of poetry is rhythm. Finding one's "voice" is, essentially, getting to the point where you can say anything. That assurance has everything to do with rhythm, the flow of utterance coming in a familiar, authoritative pattern, lighting its way beat by beat. The Schmidt sign did this. Its repetitive assurance and its intimate knowledge of one thing which, when expressed, illuminated a whole world, found in me a deeply receptive audience. More than an audience — I didn't sit on my bench, often in cold weather, to be edified. I came to be made sluggish, to be stupefied by that beer mantra, a disciple of silence, a seeker after the power behind the voice.

I liked everything about the sign — the way it was hoisted above the brewery which itself seemed to have been converted from a medieval monastery and whose dull orange brick made an appropriate mounting for the sign. I approved too of the style of the letters: the faint overtones of a typeface not so different from the one in Gutenberg's Bible suited my literary taste: I was crazy to be literary. The red neon itself was a red both warm with homeliness and slightly hellish. This satanic quality was emphasized by the thick billows of steam that rose from the underworld of the fake-medieval brewery to the fiery crown of the inferno — the sign spelling out in its diadem its bit of intelligence in unbroken meter.

This meter was not tedious; it did not just beat on and on. It had a snap, it lived:

S-C-H-M-I-D-T (letter by letter)
       pause
SCHMIDT (one great choral voice)
       longer pause
S-C-H-M-I-D-T
       and so, on and on.

I came almost every day to the park, sat on my bench, and watched this basic life-fact impose itself from the Schmidt

Brewery sign, sending out its warm and hellish light in a trance I felt the world might be unaware of but to which it still must be responsive.

This was lyricism. Or was it sentimentality? Only, I think, in the inevitable adolescent reaching for emotional significance. Although my subjects were sentimental (or simply outlandish), my purpose was authentic. Whether a poet is "sentimental" or "difficult," the voice is a cry whose first allegiance is to the authority of rhythm. And rhythm has nothing to do with "feelings," sentimental or otherwise. It is possible that this sense of rhythm in language was heightened for me because I was surrounded by two impenetrable languages, the Latin of church and my grandmother's Czech (though she spoke English too). As an odd result, language, though primarily a means of communication, was also the utterance of things essentially unfathomable. I did not expect the world to make sense: so much of it was consigned to expression in languages I did not know, but whose sound, devoid of meaning, was intimate and reassuring.

Maybe the primacy of rhythm, the longing for it, has to do with the conviction that something is *back there*, poised behind all that rising lyrical steam. And the beat goes *on*, the rock lyric said. It goes on because it is an echo of something.

The red neon dealt its familiar flash cards above St. Paul, over my grandmother's neighborhood, my father's greenhouse, the little houses where everyone I was related to had lived. But it was more than that. At the heart of this lyrical haze that somehow connected everything ("only connect" Forster said, and I believed that when I read it), there was the nugget of autobiography, of history, that gives force to a detail. It was this: Uncle Frank, my father's older brother, had been killed under that red sign. It was a freak industrial accident, "before the War," as everyone said, using that phrase that divided the world in two and separated me from their other half: I was born in 1946, the first year of peace.

I was held by rhythm, entranced as I watched the red letters appear, disappear, reform. My mind moved like lightning and yet was perfectly still. That must be the power of meditation and the appeal of disciplines like Zen. I flew to my sentimental subjects. At the same time I brooded, without knowing it, on the single horror I knew to be mine in some way: Frank, first son of my grandmother, Frank of the dashing mustache, the one who added an e to the end of our name (Frank Hample), who had briefly been a prizefighter (Frankie Campbell), Frank with his antique and therefore fascinating occupation — blacksmith — had burned to death down there in a beer vat, fixing a valve. Someone, not realizing he was there, had turned on the huge, rushing spigots and he had been scalded by boiling water. He lived for three weeks, conscious, knowing it was hopeless.

I watched the reassuring red sign from my bench, thinking I was lost in daydream, thinking I was possibly inspired. In fact I was lost in death, as if I already knew that it, not my lyrical flights, was the real intimate of poetry.

Uncle Frank would have lived, I was told as a child, if the accident had happened after the Second World War because of the advances made then in burn treatment. And so my first confused response to the fact of the War was that it must have been a good thing, and it was too bad it hadn't happened sooner.

But he had died before I was born, long before, during the Depression. I grieved for him, actually wept for this person I'd never known. I sensed this was out of line, not right because I'd never even met the man. Some cooler common sense within me knew that an uncle was not an essential relation and that even my family, who had adored him, would wonder at this excessive grief. His grisly death belonged to them. But I had my private cult.

My grandmother was capable of weeping as melodramatically over Frank's name as she had over the Prague album, but in general everyone, even she, did not cry over him. They reserved for him in death, as they apparently had in life, the glamorous place in their hearts, the spot of unalloyed beauty where he, handsome man, older brother with money in his pocket and a generous heart, was enshrined. He was the foolish past. And they were crazy about the past.

3 ❦

THE SOMETHING missing that informs a life, the absence that sends a person searching and demands the journey which ends up *being* the life: the first missing thing for my family — even before Frank's death — was money. Earning was the earliest romance. The dramatic economic climb out of the Depression was the journey that my generation (of sixties "radicals") came to recognize as our parents' communal biography. The Second World War was not the charnel house of Europe nor was it Hiroshima. (My mother, kind, decent, saying when I brought my history book into the kitchen, "But honey, President Truman *had* to drop the bomb; it saved thousands of lives.") The War was the giant world hospital where the economic wounds were healed at last, the patients sent home to full employment and a boom. The cure effected by the saintly millionaire, FDR.

I listened, as a child, to the quotation of nostalgic hamburger prices ("and hot dogs — they *threw in* a string of hot dogs with your meat order!"), to the carless, collegeless pasts of my aunts and uncles, the business, which as a chocolate freak I had trouble believing, of oranges being a bigger treat than Hershey bars, and the fact that lard had taken the place of butter on the tables of their childhood. Frank had been offered, when he was fourteen or fifteen, to take something from a fruit basket at a friend's house. He grabbed the biggest orange he'd ever seen, pried his way into the monster wedges which turned out to be nastily sour: a grapefruit. He'd never heard of one.

On and on they could go, tacking down the list of differences that settled us on two sides of the world: their magic, lost world wrapped in denial; my pale present of everything-anyone-could-want. I loved it. And begged for more hard luck stories — bring on the lard, bring on the hard times — even at nine stalking my own missing something that was not money but history.

It didn't matter that no one in my family made one of those classic, meteoric rises out of the thirties. We had no millionaires, no one even in the upper middle class, that post-War euphemism that has scrambled the culture and made it harder to recognize economic power. Out of the working class into the petite bourgeoisie I suppose is the correct designation for us. But the fiction, not the documentary, was what mattered. For my family, like characters in a fairy tale, lived representative lives, not wholly personal even to themselves. They spoke of themselves as if they *were* the Great Depression. Their stories, the childhood memories and too-early jobs, were not recited as personal gripes. There wasn't a complainer in the bunch. Theirs was the delighted crowing of people who had been part of something large and significant. They had been historic. "You want to know about the Depression? I'll tell you about the Depression, honey," the principal players of history said as I sat in their laps.

To me they were heroes. They had lived in another country. It was history; it was not just-now. I could not go there, I could not be thrilled by an orange or be humiliated by a grapefruit. But I could hear of such things. I could listen. Sometimes I think what really distinguishes my generation was not only the protests against the Vietnam War, but the almost manic tape-recording of aging relatives that came later and continues. Oral history, it is called, as if we were starved and wanted to wolf down a chunk of the past, not only to make sure it was there, but to make it our own.

Much of history, according to my family, was recorded in quotations to each other of Depression-era prices for household articles, followed by ironic head-shaking over the price of the latest pound of hamburger, the current loaf of bread. "I bought a steak today," Uncle Bill would say. "Sirloin. At the Red Owl. You know how much I paid per pound for that beef?"

Silence for a moment, the cosy anticipatory pause of the rhetorical question drawing us together.

"I paid one dollar and eighty-nine cents for that steak. One dollar eighty-nine cents. What can you do? You pay it. You want a steak" — and we were not a family to question the wanting of a steak — "you pay it."

"And that *same steak*," my father said, "would cost you fifteen cents in 1932. Fifteen cents!" he cried, stirring up in them, in all of us, a vision of the golden age when not only the dollar but the penny was strong.

They traded prices for an hour, lingering over the small change, murmuring the tiny figures of the past to each other. They handled the dry goods of a lifetime, measuring fabric, weighing meat, the heft of cheese by the pound, the cost of beer, the fleeting life of near beer. My father was astonished at his shrewd self every time he recounted the comical price he paid for his first car, as if he'd made a deal with a lunatic. They began to gloat, to admire their cunning at getting things so cheap.

They erased time as they talked, and they walked into the grocery stores of the thirties with their current wallets in their pockets. If only we'd realized how *cheap* everything was, they seemed to be saying, we'd be rich today. Inflation was their life line to the past, the trigger of memory, the tightly woven hemp they shimmied down to reach their lost lives far below them where everything was tiny, antlike, fascinating. They drank Grain Belt from brown bottles in my grandmother's kitchen after Sunday dinner and slid down that long rope of retail prices into whatever gold there is in beer and the contemplation of the past.

"But how much," my father said shrewdly, when they were deep in their nostalgic reckoning and vulnerable, very vulnerable, "how much were you *making* in 1932?" There was a wound in their eyes; his voice was wounded too, the slightly aggrieved tone of one who must bring people to their senses for their own good.

"Well, you put it like that," an uncle said, trailing off. For a moment they rallied with a flurry of incredulity over the dinky wages of the thirties, the minor genius it had taken to live on $35 a week — or was it a month. But the bubble had been popped; the magic trick they played with inflation, with history, in order to get what they wanted — the past, always the past for them — could not be sustained. It wasn't in the nature of magic, it wasn't in the nature of common sense and silence which were the bedrock of their inarticulate honor. They returned to the prosaic equation, to the realistic ratio between 1930s wages and 1930s prices. They steered out of the golden age and back to the golden mean and they embraced the blandness of it with a fervor that was only partly phony.

"You really look at it," Uncle Bill said, alluding to the unnameable thing that comprised the past, the present and any imaginable future, "and things are pretty much the same. Price-wise."

"That steak," my father said, reversing his earlier position completely, "probably would have cost you around fifteen cents during the Depression. You're making more, you're paying more. It's still basically a fifteen-cent steak. You can't get around that."

He placed us in this irrefutable stasis, the changeless world of logic. When things got too alluringly nostalgic, this was the only safety he was sure of. He wanted to save us, I think, from the sheer drop of the imagination. When he saw everyone he loved dangling precariously above life and logic, he was dismayed and yanked everybody back. There is nothing magic down there, he seemed to say. Nothing worth sticking your neck out for.

No one believed him; that is why there was always a break in the conversation, a lull in that loud, everybody-talks-at-once family. They were silent, maybe out of deference to his warning, maybe out of annoyance. But they did not stop buzzing privately.

Their eyes went to their beer bottles where the gold was, and they kept drinking, falling off their steep edges in that pleasant death because everyone has a right to his own view of the past.

Ours is a nostalgic family in the way that others are proud families. We didn't have a sense of history, but an ache for it that had to be assuaged by an act of the imagination — for there, at the head of the family where history should have been with its culture intact, its relation to the nation assumed, was my grandmother, the rootless wonder, our oak that lived in air, not earth. Our immigrant.

They couldn't look to her to satisfy this cultural need. It seemed that to travel as she had in her lifetime through a brisk recapitulation of European history, from a feudal childhood in Bohemia where her brother Rudi was shot in the leg for poaching on "the noble's" estate to the atomic age of my own childhood, it had been necessary for her to jettison memory. She had no stories. She didn't seem to know where she had come from, not even the name of the village. "Europe," she said, when she referred to where she'd emigrated from. Or sometimes, "the Old World." No wonder: the name of the country had not existed when she left. Czechoslovakia came into existence in 1918 when the Austro-Hungarian Empire was dissolved; she had arrived at Ellis Island over twenty years before that.

My family, her children, seemed to look to the American decades for their identity, for a past, as if each turn of ten years had customs, mores, values and episodes of its own like individual countries to which people pledged allegiance. They were the thirties. I was the sixties (although that hadn't quite happened yet). The Depression provided a kind of national, almost racial, identity — theirs. It had various guises, besides poverty and hard luck. There was also the Depression of St. Paul the Gangster Hideaway, the home away from home of John Dillinger, Ma Barker, Alvin Karpis. They were the first historical figures I understood to belong to us. The statues around the city, in parks, were an odd collection that didn't relate much to each other: why did Schiller stand with his small stone book in

Como Park? Who had placed Nathan Hale, and why precisely him, his hands tied with stone cord, in the triangular park on Summit Avenue? Who were these people and why were they and not some other figures set in stone in our midst?

The gangsters, although without statues or plaques, were the real historical figures that lived around us; their dens and hideaways — never just "apartments" — were pointed out to my brother and me as my father drove us downtown.

"You wanted a man killed," my father said as we hung over the front seat, "you just went down to St. Peter Street and there was somebody who'd do it." My father who I think it is accurate to say has never wanted anybody killed in his life, my father who has spent his life growing flowers and who, coming to my house, always goes to my wizened houseplants, checks the soil and, not scolding but frowning, fills the teakettle with water and feeds them, saying, "You know, they're not little statues, they're *alive*" — my father reminded us cheerfully of the time when, he was sure, you could find somebody hanging around St. Peter Street to do in a troublesome person.

"Of course," he said, "the deal was, they could stay here, but they couldn't try anything in St. Paul." It wasn't clear how this squared with the St. Peter Street guns. Maybe the point was they were there but off-duty, so to speak. "They'd come to St. Paul after a . . . a heist or something someplace else. They'd get a house or an apartment and they'd lie low."

Lying low, that St. Paul specialty. "What did they *do?*" I asked.

"They just lived."

Heroes on vacation, desperadoes without a cause. In St. Paul they became people with apartments who had the milk delivered and ordered the newspapers.

"Of course," my mother said, "they lived under assumed names." Of course. I liked the assumed names; they helped erase the homeliness of the rolled paper and the milk bottles outside the door.

"You don't just say, 'Hi, I'm John Dillinger and I'd like that apartment for rent in the paper,' " my father said.

"Naturally not," my mother said. "They moved in, they had their assumed names, they lay low," she said, clasping them easily to the civic bosom, these mannerly gangsters of her youth.

"But," my father said, "they weren't satisfied." How well I understood. "They couldn't let it go at that. They got greedy and they kidnapped Mr. Bremer." This was the grandson of the founder of Schmidt's Brewery. "They ruined it for themselves," my father said. "You couldn't let that go." The police department was given a "shake-up" and "action was taken." The gangsters went elsewhere to lie low, taking with them their bit of reality, as the fifteen-cent sirloin had, but leaving behind a valuable glow, another part of the thirties, the country of my parents.

My family had left something in the thirties and, because they were and remain blessedly prepsychological, jargon-free, with no appetite for self-analysis, they must find their metaphor, the door where they can knock and which will open to let them in where their grieving hearts must go. They go to the thirties, with those nostalgic grocery lists and in the tours through St. Paul the Gangster Hideaway, because Frank is back there still. They want, when they are together, to have him, too.

That's part of it. But it goes beyond plain nostalgia, beyond even the inconsolable grief for Frank. There is also the desire, a cultural instinct, to connect with the spiritual legacy of that time. As I discovered much later in Eastern Europe where people say they are "together" and that is the greatest gift — never mind "repression," never mind not being able to publish, writers said — the Depression has been for people like my family the impersonal hard luck of history, of circumstance, which drew them and the world together in an intimacy they never knew again except in the faulty reconstructions of nostalgia.

We tend to think of nostalgia as soft mush, fake history, a sentimental reference. A lie even. But it was, for my family, not a lie but the life of their desire. It was longing. And if they were "merely" nostalgic, there was accuracy in that melodrama and imprecision. How could such people, just being sliced off from the Old World and not yet rooted in the New, be rigorous about history? Nostalgia, longing, take the place of history in such circumstances, and are as accurate in their acknowledgment of what is not there as history ever is in its recognition of what is.

4 🦋

THE SHARPEST memory I have of a childhood conversation — I don't mean one of those fragments of private perception from childhood that are eloquent with the oddity of life, but rather the only recollection I have of what it was like to be a child talking with other children, a *social* memory of childhood — was really a ritual. Maybe that's why I remember it: we repeated it often.

"What are you?" someone would ask as we walked, four or five of us, up Oxford Street, to St. Luke's School on Summit Avenue. Or the question might come up as we stood in a little knot, shivering on the asphalt playground that on Sundays was the church parking lot.

What are you? And each little girl answered promptly, with satisfaction, as if counting up the family silver: "I'm Norwegian," "I'm German," or the most frequent reply, "I'm Irish," "I'm Irish," "I'm Irish." Occasionally there was a rebel who said, defensively, obviously coached at home, "I'm American." But this was frowned upon and considered an affectation.

"I mean, what are you *really?*" someone would ask impatiently. We waited for the requisite foreignness to be pledged. Our contempt set in soon after our annoyance if the rebel refused to play the game as the implacable rules demanded. What are you *really?* And the girl mumbled something about being a lot of different things — German and French, a little Swiss, a little Irish and partly Finnish. "And so my Mom and Dad say we're

American." This was acceptable, though I found it pretty thin gruel myself.

It is odd that we did this repeatedly and with such relish — we who spoke only English, whose parents were just buying their first television sets, ending forever, it seems now, the ancient art form, night after night filled with gossip. We had so little connection with anything "ethnic" (the word wasn't used) that our little game was all form, no content.

We were natural catechists to whom words were more rhythm and motion than meaning. The *Baltimore Catechism*, that small buff-colored lozenge of Truth, had taught us the satisfaction of recitation, the ready and absolute response:

> *Who made you?*
> God made me.
>
> *Why did God make you?*
> To know, love and serve Him in this world
> in order to be happy with Him forever in the next.

What exactly were we up to when we stood in a circle on the playground of St. Luke's School, huddled in the cold? (I remember all these scenes as winter ones, the crusted snowdrifts and a sharp wind bending us forward into the circle.) Why did we ask that question and what satisfaction came from our answers? It wasn't a process of drawing the self together into "wholeness," to use the current expression. Or if it was, our wholeness was a patch job with all the seams showing. Most of us weren't simply German, or Irish, or any single thing. It took us a while to dissect our reality. "I'm half Irish," I said, sweeping my hand like a cleaver exactly across my midriff, "and half Czech."

It all seems atavistic and even a little morbid. We were, in our way, out for blood. We had very little to say after we'd announced our "nationality." Those of us who had any remnant of foreignness near us (my grandmother, with her accent — I didn't hear it as one — and her inability to write English) were often ashamed of the actual presence of distinctly non-American (I mean non–Irish American) qualities. But we remained proud of, or perhaps it is more accurate to say we were enthralled by, the foreignness that was somehow ours. In a thoroughly unconscious way, we saw ourselves as the authentic products of entire nations which lay, mysteriously but definitely, over there. The Old World.

※

"Terrible little Ellis Island," Henry James called it. My grandmother, in one of her few anecdotes, said that after she got off the boat she was made to stand in a series of long lines at Ellis Island. She got bored with the "prodigious process" (James again, not my grandmother), and slipped under a rope, away from it all, and just let herself into the country, as if with her own key.

Impossible, I know; they must have herded her back, she must have gone through all the regulations, the medical exams, the sortings and siftings, that gave the whole onrush of nations an appearance of order. Nevertheless, as a child I was left with the impression that my grandmother was more foreign than others, not simply an immigrant but an alien who had slipped under a rope when the officials had not been looking. Strictly speaking, she had no business being here at all.

She arrived at Ellis Island about eight years before James toured it in 1904. She was sixteen, alone: her own mother had died when she was two, in childbirth; her father had remarried — badly, to a wicked stepmother — and she may have left in a pique or on a dare. She never saw any of them again.

The circumstances on Ellis Island when she arrived would have been much the same as when James toured it later. *The American Scene*, the book he wrote about his visit to the United States after an absence of twenty years, is the best contemporary response we have to the immigration, "that loud primary stage of alienism," by a "native American." (By that designation James seemed to mean not simply a Yankee but anyone who had lived here long enough to have no tie to another language; he hardly mentions, for instance, the Irish as part of the immigrant life of the time, perhaps because his family, two generations before, had come from Ireland. At any rate, the "natives" in his book are "established Americans" — and of course white Protestants. They are the New Yorkers who lived in the city before the skyscraper, before Ellis Island, before Castle Garden, the earlier immigration point.)

The casual (native) visitor to Ellis Island, James wrote, "comes back from his visit not at all the same person that he went. He has eaten of the tree of knowledge, and the taste will be for ever in his mouth." The knowledge, the betrayal, the sad truth (but of course for James it was also the *interesting* truth) was change: New York had changed, was changing, would continue to metamorphose under the strange rule of the "aliens." The city, the country, were, he sensed, no longer *his,* but now by sheer force of numbers and the bursting forth of those numbers, *theirs.*

"He had thought he knew before," James writes, putting his own experience in the third person of the native, "thought he had the sense of the degree in which it is his American fate to share the sanctity of his American consciousness, the intimacy of his American patriotism, with the inconceivable alien; but the truth had never come home to him with any such force . . . Let not the unwary, therefore, visit Ellis Island."

Nor did the experience fade with time. "This affirmed claim of the alien, however immeasurably alien, to share in one's supreme relation was everywhere the fixed element, the reminder not to be dodged. One's supreme relation, as one had always put it, was one's relation to one's country — a conception made up so largely of one's countrymen and one's countrywomen."

Now that "supreme relation" must "suffer the indignity of change." Not only change, but loss (but then, change is always loss to those who sustain its jarring blow). What was lost, James said, was "the luxury of some such close and sweet and *whole* national consciousness" like that of "the Switzer and the Scot."

He could not make anything of it all. Maybe that was his most rueful admission, the defeat of the analyst of society by this giant cultural surprise that jumped out at him on his return from England. He confessed he could not hazard a guess as to what it all meant, what it might come to. He felt, in the face of this usurpation by the aliens, "flat fatigue," and wanted to avail "himself of the liberty of waiting to see."

But what he could say was that they — the Slavs, the Italians, the Armenians and Jews, the hordes — "were *at home*" (it is his emphasis). And he, James, the native son, was not. It was not his twenty-year absence that caused his unease; it was their presence that had changed the meaning of home.

The faces that crowded the Bowery Elevated testified, he said, "without exception, to alienism unmistakable, alienism undisguised and unashamed." There were so many of them, they were such a crowd, that "they tended to make the observer gasp with the sense of isolation." The aliens bring, as their offering, alienation.

It wasn't simply that they weren't American — he rather thought that America *would*, eventually, be them. That was the point. He was also alarmed — maybe even more so — by the fact that they didn't seem to be Italians or Slavs or Armenians anymore. He could only discern a single repeated identity in them. "Face after face, unmistakably, was 'low,'" he said, using the word self-consciously, with quotation marks. The working-class Italians he met on the job in America were not the Italian workmen he had been delighted by in Italy. All the nationalities, once across the Atlantic, partook of the same impoverished identity. The "low" faces had a single pride — "that of consciously not being what they *had* been."

The aliens were neither fish nor fowl, but creatures of some indeterminate stage, "no longer being for you — for any complacency of the romantic, or even verily of the fraternizing, sense in you — the foreigner of the quality, of the kind, that he might have been *chez lui*. Whatever he might see himself becoming, he was never to see himself that again, any more than you were ever to see him. He became then . . . a creature promptly despoiled of those 'manners' which were the grace . . . by which one had best known and, on opportunity, best liked him. He presents himself thus, most of all, to be plain — and not only in New York, but throughout the country — as wonderingly conscious that his manners of the other world, that everything you have there known and praised him for, have been a huge mistake."

This is the alarm that rings when a horde of people, enough to fill a continent, decide not to be peasants anymore. James was afraid he wasn't going to lose only America, but Europe as well. My grandmother who in fact did lose Europe — and who knows if she felt she'd gained America? — would have waved it all away, directed him to the table where the coffee and poppy-seed kolatchy were, and said, "Come eat."

James has been accused, on the basis of *The American Scene*, of being anti-Semitic. In his introduction, Leon Edel quotes F. O. Matthiessen who felt that James "drifted dangerously close to a doctrine of racism" in the portions of the book that contain his walks and visits to the Italian and Jewish neighborhoods of New York. At the very least James can be taken for a snob in these passages, one who notes the smell in the Yiddish Theater and whose alarm at the presence of the "aliens" is clear.

But the fact remains for me: when I first read that sentence — "Face after face, unmistakably, was 'low' " — I felt a strange relief, the sort of relaxation of breath that comes when the truth has been spoken. Children usually perform this service, embarrassing and unwanted, but lightening. James as a child: an absurd idea, as if that writer of two-ton sentences could be anything less than the most sophisticated creature who ever lived. But I knew when I read that sentence that I had found my man, my witness to the contemporary truth. Yes, I thought, she was low. My grandmother, one of his aliens. And undeniably mine. My own "native" self always recoiled from her, and then rushed forward to her, with love, with curiosity.

James speaks without the reservoir of self-consciousness, the product of diffused guilt, which has become almost predictable luggage among social analysts of our own time. He has not yet become a resident of a world that knows that, in its time, it has committed atrocities. And he is only beginning to touch the strange contours of a shape both fascinating and new: the idea that for him — for his kind — to exist might mean that these others cannot exist. That, after all, is the core of racism: these others, because they are discernibly unlike us, *must not* live. Or, in relatively tolerant times, *need not* live. Or most typically, in liberal societies, need not live as we do.

We have become more touchy about language; obviously, this is essential. James could speak as he did because he harbored no terror of his own power, his own lurking genocidal tendencies. We do. We are terrified of too much attention to differences among us for fear that our very acuity in matters of racial characteristics will unmask our essential racism. As a result, people with good intentions will actually talk about "a person of the Jewish persuasion," or, sometimes in the Midwest, will say, "Are you from New York?" which, given the context, means, "Are you Jewish?" In Minnesota, Polish jokes are changed from being about Polish characters (which would be "unkind") to being about Swedes or Norwegians (that is, the largest national groups in the state). The idea here is to erase — as a courtesy to the other person! — any racial identity. Yet the jokes are told, endlessly. And they seem to require an ethnic character (not a black — oh no). It is the hinge between the wacky stupidity of the character and his "nationality" that flavors the joke. These characters are not Polacks, not bohunks or wops. They are green-horns — "the loud primary stage of alienism." They are the left-over mixed shame and pride of immigration.

It is as if we are so afraid of what *has* happened (the concentration camp that is in the middle of every "decent person's" mind as the worst thing) that we are determined to make the evil impossible by masking the victim. We cannot, after all, enchain the villain: our very trouble is that we sense, obscurely, that he is us.

In this way, matters of ethnicity have become entangled with those of racism. And the bitterness that whites feel — often *low* whites — about blacks and American Indians, is the bitterness of their own cultural, even racial, renunciation. Why should *they* get to say Black Is Beautiful — *we* didn't, way back when (in 1904, in 1894), get to say Bohemian Is Beautiful. We had to melt, to assimilate. It's nonsense and it's ahistorical, and nobody *says* it anyway, but it's there at the heart of white society: the grudge against the past. Against those low grandmothers who thought (but they didn't think) their past and the national beauty (that is, culture) wouldn't be needed.

The speculations James makes and his alarm about the aliens suggest something we tend to forget: it was not clear what would come of the fabulous mixture of nations and languages that was so apparent at the turn of the century. There they all were: so obviously different. It was a scene absolutely made for speculation, for *thinking*. (When I asked an English friend what he felt distinguished Americans from the British I expected him to say — maybe because I'd read James's novels — "Your naiveté." But he said, "Oh, you're all so *analytical*, you analyze *everything*.") James gave up in "flat fatigue," but he was trying. Now we know what happened — on the surface. The colors faded, the differences became less distinct, and we are left with our ethnic "cuisines" as the dominant cultural legacy of our diverse past, and a murderous distinction between black and white.

James is left saying, "It has taken ages of history, in the other world, to produce them ["the various positive properties of the installed tribes"] and you ask yourself, with independent curiosity, if they may really be thus extinguished in an hour."

It does not seem so strange, at the end of this century, to think of things being "extinguished in an hour." But James is at the beginning of the century and he is full of questions as he leaves the subject. "Do they burrow underground, to await their day again? — or in what strange secret places are they held in deposit and in trust," these "various positive properties of the installed tribes"?

In the children, of course, and the children's children, we who arrive, hardly knowing it, with our hearts born aggrieved.

5 ❦

*W*HEN I THINK of the past, I have the impression that a door closed just behind me, practically grazing my shoulder as I passed, throwing a rush of air and then silence around me. It wasn't slammed, it just clicked shut; it probably wasn't even much of a door. It is the sound of the screen door shutting, the door of the little screen house in my grandmother's back yard where my brother and I were put to bed on hot nights. A screen door — the least absolute of doors, letting in much, shutting out little.

The house was a square box of a room with screen windows that let in air but no light because of the sweeping eaves. In winter it was used only as a storage place, but in spring my grandmother gave it a furious cleaning that began with its being emptied for the day of boxes, beds, and screens, and ended in a hosing-down and scrubbing that left the room smelling even more emphatically of old clothes and cigars and of the mustiness of the men in cotton-ribbed undershirts who had smoked those cigars several decades before. The cleaning seemed more a method of releasing the essential oils of the place than of actually washing them clean and away.

My brother and I slept lightly there, as if in a tent. It was better than a tent; it was a miniature house, a private domicile away from everyone else in the adult house, closer to the garden, which smelled sharply of dill and less precise things, and near the old mattresses whose smell was partly ours, partly the scent of earlier, perhaps now dead but definitely grown-up, ancestors, an odor which lingered like a ghost that was not finished with that cool dark place. We slept surrounded by stacks of storm windows and snow shovels, boxes of salt and sand, wooden sleds, tire chains — all the equipment of Minnesota winter had been crammed into the tiny room, which was called, as if in defiance, the summerhouse.

One night, the summer I was six, I lay there, saying at intervals to my brother on the other side of the storm windows, "You asleep?" And he kept saying yes. Finally the patient, noncommittal replies stopped; no more *yes* hissed across the heavy windows, and the night was mine.

Just above me, sagging from a wire strung from the front to back walls of the room, hung heavy coats and jackets, canvas hunting pants, union suits, old sweaters, the chimera of winter man above me as I laid on top of the sheets in my seersucker pajamas. I stared at the dreary winter clothes, and I decided to stay up all night. I'd never done it before.

For a while the sound of my brother's regular breathing was enough to keep me alert, to preserve the thrill of solitary life. I listened to the throaty crickets whose sound had been explained to me by my father as being no voice at all, but a kind of leg-rubbing. I raised my arms and stuck out my elbows, rubbing diligently, in silent, dreamy fraternity.

But it was fear that finally caused me to give up the watch. I wasn't afraid of the dark, or not exactly of the dark. I was afraid of the *Communists* who lurked in the dark. What they were, the Communists, I did not know. Whether to watch for man or beast, goblin or reptile, malicious intent or natural disaster, something large and looming or a thing so insidiously small that no degree of vigilance could assure safety: I didn't know, I didn't know.

Strange terror, so formless it positively cried out for a body of some kind. It remained, maddeningly, terrifyingly, without shape, merely a word. Later, I came to think of the Communists as a kind of mouse and, by degrees, I began to be afraid of mice, and forgot for a long time that the real fear was of something else altogether, something never sufficiently defined.

My parents could not have instilled in me this horror of the Communists. Although they were civic-minded, they weren't political, and in any case, anti-Communism would not have been their style. Certainly they weren't Communists themselves — a straight Democratic ticket and a yes vote on all bond issues took care of politics nicely. Although as Catholics, my mother pointed out, we didn't actually *use* the public schools, we had to vote yes, always yes. She also told us, as a kind of civics morality tale, of her high school American history teacher who had announced to her classes that she voted the Socialist ticket, "even though," my mother said, "she knew she was throwing her vote away." My mother had been deeply impressed, and admired the lavish rectitude of such a gesture as if this teacher of American history demonstrated the real point of enfranchisement — not the winning or losing, but the pinpointing of individual conscience. Never mind who got *elected*.

I didn't get my terror of the Communists from my parents, or not directly. I'm convinced the word was, literally, in the air: my aunts had just bought their first televisions, and we sometimes went over to their houses at night to watch *I Love Lucy*. The living rooms were hushed, bluish from the little cube that looked very cold — its pictures were malignant and toneless — but was warm to the touch like any working machine. We all clustered around the cube, silent, intent, solitary — unlike ourselves. We usually stayed for the news. I don't remember any conversations about the Communists, I don't even remember seeing McCarthy on television. But the silent religiosity that accompanied that early television watching ("refreshments" were served afterward, giving a post-Mass quality to the affair) was deep and definite. Lucy went deep, the news went deep.

At night in bed when I chanced on the thought of the Communists, I was lost. At home this meant that if I woke in the night — and *they* were always there at such times — I could not get out of bed to go to the bathroom, where they would certainly be waiting in force, because I couldn't reach the light switch. I had to lie in the dark and humiliatingly wet the bed, losing for another week the possibility that my mother would remove from my bed the rubber sheet that held me back from adulthood.

In the summerhouse at my grandmother's, the thought of the Communists meant I could not stay awake all night after all. I had to give up the camaraderie of the crickets, the superiority I briefly felt over my older brother because he slept and I, awake, was thinking. I had to sleep because then I could not think, and not thinking, I could not concoct my Communists. For I sensed in some rudimentary, unhelpful way that they were of my own creation. Yet I never dreamed of them. They never gained form, never approached definition. They remained, simply, dread.

I slept. It was a night in the summer of 1952. I had been told that in September I would learn to read; I wanted to live. I slept to save myself. I slept also because I was tired and would have slept anyway, bored and lulled eventually by the night. But I thought my night awake had been stolen by the Communists, the formless terror I sensed came from within myself.

I woke early. Birds had become the sound, and my brother still slept. If I could not have the night, at least — better really — I could take the day. The real day of the first hours, before it had been touched by any other hand.

I didn't get dressed; my clothes were in my grandmother's house. My father, who had brought us there for the weekend, had carried me out to the summerhouse the night before in my pajamas so my feet wouldn't get wet running across the yard. I crept out of the noisy bed, the springs clanging like bells. I stared at the dead face of my sleeping brother, and left him behind as I went out the screen door, free of the night.

I crouched down and swept my hands across the grass and washed my face, like a good savage, with the dew. I strolled around the yard and wandered down the narrow grassy driveway to the street, Webster Street, which was one block from the railroad tracks on one side, and a little over a block from the

Schmidt Brewery in the other direction. I saw nobody — nobody was awake in the neighborhood. I looked, I suppose, as if I were asleep myself, in a soft dream that had drawn me guilelessly out of my bed. I stood on the edge of the grassy, curbless boulevard in my pink seersucker pajamas and stretched, trying to reach the sky, as my mother said.

I must have closed my eyes briefly as I stretched. I don't remember any warning at all, not even the sound — which must have been there — of the horse's hoofs on the tarred street. There was no sound, no prelude. I opened my eyes after my stretch. A large wooden wagon stood in the street before me, a gray buckboard drawn by a huge sad horse. The wagon was filled with tin cans, some bicycle tires, heaps of old clothes. An old man, ancient and bearded like nothing I had seen on earth, held the reins, sitting on a flat board which was slightly raised to form the driver's seat. His beard was long, yellowish, the grass of a life. I wanted to sit next to him up there. I wanted to hold the reins of the hardly moving horse. I wanted to go with him to the end of the block, the end of the earth.

This was the rag sheeny and his horse. I had heard my grandmother talk about him. "Oh, just put that junk out back of the shed for the rag sheeny," she said to my grandfather, pointing to a pile of tarpaper scraps left over from a roofing job he had done on their house. Who was the rag sheeny, I had asked. "He picks up all the junk," she said, "with his horse and wagon." "Not a truck?" I asked because a horse was too fabulous. "He's too poor for a truck."

The man did not look at me, nor did the horse. Maybe they didn't see me, but I was the only bright, pink thing on the street. I waved, I expected to be smiled at, I expected the offer of a ride. Nothing happened.

They were exactly in front of me now, moving slowly. I looked up and spoke out distinctly, politely, "Rag sheeny, may I please have a ride?"

They kept going, without a look to left or right, the sad horse, the baleful beard, the cargo of drab junk going down the short street in the direction of the brewery. The pace was slow, like a cortege, as rhythmic and yet unmusical as a drum. I waved harder, repeated my request more loudly. No sign, just the unreadable beard directing the gloomy horse. They were past me now, past me who had been so near and so delighted, and there had been no answer, no response.

They were drifting down the block, near Jefferson Street beyond which I could not follow them. I began running. "Hey, rag sheeny, wait. I want a ride. Rag sheeny, rag sheeny," I hollered into the empty street, the fresh morning.

The horse clopped across the intersection, my boundary, and I stood on the far side, peeved, knowing, as adored children do, the rights of indulgence that were my due and that had been trampled on by the aloof rag sheeny and his dolorous horse.

I went back to my grandmother's house. She and my mother, who had arrived to take her grocery shopping, were in the kitchen, fixing breakfast. I had seen the rag sheeny, I told them. I had asked him for a ride, but he hadn't paid any attention.

"You got into that dirty wagon!" my grandmother cried, wheeling her small plump body around from the stove. "You got up there with all that *dirt?*" She was wild with the passion of hygiene, one of the profoundest in her heart.

I explained that he hadn't paid any attention, he hadn't let me up.

"Stay away, just stay away from the rag sheeny," she said. "There's germs there."

"The rag sheeny has a horse," I said.

"Don't say rag sheeny," my mother said from the table, which she was setting in the dining room. "Say rag man."

"Why?"

"Rag man is nicer. And he can't help it."

But I held with my grandmother, I held with the lustrous sound which, onomatopoetic animal that I was, I responded to in the magical, meaningless word. He was the *sheeny,* the glossy, shining name whose attention I could not get, the glow that eluded me, the golden word. He was the first person to ignore me, to purposely deny me something I wanted.

I saw him many times that summer, not always in the morning, and I ran after him every time, crying out his glittery name, as my race-conscious grandmother did, begging to be taken up beside him until, sometime in August, I saw it was useless.

6 🦋

MY MOTHER'S "people," as family was referred to, had arrived a full generation, almost two, before my father's. Both of her parents were American-born, even a grandparent or two. Not "lace curtain," but still, "natives." A great-grandfather had owned — or operated — a hotel in Galena, Illinois, a great-aunt had been born in a covered wagon on the way to worthless land in Oregon which sent the whole crew back again in the wagon, pioneers twice over, forward and backward. "Pioneering" was their mythology. They were Irish, Catholic, Midwestern to the marrow, so much so that my mother, after a trip west once, returned very ho-hum about the mountains. "Oh, the mountains are all right," she said. "But they do get in the way of the scenery."

This other half of mine was somehow older (and they really were older, a family of great-aunts, not children), more fragile, than my father's family. Even their skin was lighter, Irish, not meant for the sun, burnt pioneer skin that belongs under a sunbonnet, staring with those wounded light blue eyes across a flat field. Not like "us" (the choice had been made, maybe on St. Luke's playground: I had my "nationality," and it wasn't Irish). *We* were brown-eyed, we turned brown as berries in summer.

But my grandmother's ignorance — her lowness — was a problem to the berry-happy heritage. Why was this, why did it matter? Why was I such a snob? More to the point, what *was* it, this ignorance I met with a cold heart? "She knew what she was," my Aunt Sylvia said simply, with natural pride, when I asked her. Not *who* she was — that wasn't her kind of question. But what she was, the racial instinct. And, as my aunt and I understood implicitly, it was a complete and final statement: *she knew what she was.* It cannot be followed with the brutal question, "Well, what *was* it?" Such a pure and refined description of personality can have no explanation.

This is the way we talked about people in my family. The empty glass of conversation filled not with wit, not with the telling detail, but with the thing itself. We were not American — not according to the definition my English friend gave me later: we did not analyze. We savored. This way: "Oh, she was something. Grandma was something, wasn't she?" And we said, "Yeah, she was something." And she was there again, briefly, flickering, but there.

She was something — I don't know what. But *she was something.* And *she knew what she was.* And it included the ignorance that drove me, uncertain of myself, fretful that I was nothing, to an ugly shame in her that it is wrong to feel — I knew it — for someone who loves you simply because you are of her.

As I got older, I asked her a lot of questions. But she said she didn't know the name of the village where she had been born. She had some question, I think, about the year of her birth — 1882 or 1883. But her birthday was definite, the appropriate one for an immigrant: October 12, Columbus Day. She was not sure which war her favorite brother, Rudi, had been killed in. ("No, not the First War, some war.") Though she had wept impressively over the pictures of Prague, apparently she had never even been there, except perhaps (perhaps!) briefly on her way to Hamburg (or Bremen?) and the trip to America. So why did she weep, and what was she missing? Something, something. Just as she was, for us, something.

She was iffy about this, confused about that. It wasn't senility, it was disregard. It infuriated me, even as a child. She was just living, moving through her life easily, as if everyone's childhood were spent in the feudal world (her brother shot for poaching on the noble's estate, the way she said "noble" as if she knew what it meant), and then progressed by degrees naturally to adulthood and the atomic age when everything could be blown to smithereens. She didn't bother to have a store of anecdotes, a makeshift biography, something to hold up alongside history. She set no significance to things that touched her, and would not have pondered, as Teta did, the possible applications of her surname.

I found it possibly thrilling that she had come from so far away. Possibly — if she would deliver the goods, and deliver them in usable form, not in her wordless, elemental manner. Her life, to me, might have represented something, but she didn't know or didn't care. "What are you talking about?" she would say, when I kept up my interrogation: "Do you remember your mother?" "What did your father do for a living?" "Did he own the farm or rent it?" "Did you go to school?" "What did it look like over there?" On and on with my off-the-mark questions.

Sometimes she came to me with questions. I was the modern world and, as I got older and older and kept staying in school, she became both a little alarmed and mightily impressed. She had seen me coming, the family intellectual, and in her way had tried to nip it in the bud. Books were something she had suspicions about. The book was somehow an insult to the supremacy of human conversation and busy activity of any kind — cooking, gardening, home-permanenting of all female children, canning, preserving, cleaning, cleaning, cleaning. Reading was boring, it was annoying to others (herself), it was unhealthy and unnatural for a child (myself) to be curled up on the plush sofa under the picture of a voluptuous girl strumming a lute, to be reading the day away, reading when I could have been messing around outside, preferring Maud Hart Lovelace, then Louisa May Alcott, finally Charlotte Brönte, to Life.

She wasn't personally threatened by my immersion in books; it was as if she, who read nothing but the St. Paul Pioneer Press (she could read English, but she didn't write it) and her lodge magazine in Czech, sensed the danger of this kind of travel, the velocity of the mind, how it flies to other worlds and lives quickly, without care for any safety, as if that flight were not a little death. She knew better: the curled body on the sofa was an empty husk. "That child has been dead to the world all afternoon," she said fretfully when my father came to get me, as if reporting a mounting fever. She sensed my absence, not just from her, but from the life of the living. She paced in and out of the room where I read, offered hot chocolate (declined), watered the plants ("excuse me, honey"), noisily vacuumed the rug ("I'm afraid you'll have to move for a minute"). She came in, nervously flipped the switch of the radio to the station that played only Whoopee John polkas and began softly humming and dancing around the room by herself as I shrank further into my book, trying to withdraw from the dancing and dipping till finally she grabbed *Jane Eyre* out of my hands ("It's bad for your eyes") and pulled me back to life as we danced our ungainly polka around that room, she lightly in the lead.

Maybe she thought all my novel reading had led to my endless education. In spite of how I badgered her, she seemed to trust me. With her I felt an authority. My subject was the modern world. When she was very old (she lived to be ninety and I was at last out of school), she stroked my cheek gently and said, with a sadness that scared me, "You're nice, a nice girl. You're kind." She said it as if I were a foreigner, as if nothing could be expected from this alien place, full of cruel "natives," not even love from one's own family. As if it just happened that I was kind. A greenhorn's piece of luck, merely.

When my older brother went to the university, she asked me what he was studying there. The university was a new aspect of life, introduced by my brother and me.

"Science," I said.

"What is science?" she asked. We were in the back yard behind our house where she had come to live, in a small attached apartment, a few years after my grandfather died. I turned away from her, and broke off a piece of chive from the window box and chewed on the peppery stalk. That ugly shame, the fury, was on me.

"Science," I said angrily. "Science, you know, *science*." Brutal, cutthroat voice.

"Who do you think you are," she said, turning back to her apartment, "somebody smart?"

Later I felt guilty. Actually, I felt guilty instantly, almost before I felt anything else. I went to her little neat apartment and asked if I could have dinner with her. I knew what to say. "You're a much better cook than Mother," I said.

She put her cheek out for me to kiss. Her skin was perfect. I have never seen skin like it, flawless, more refined and beautiful than a girl's because the color, steady and delicate, was not as alert and harsh. "I wish I had a complexion like yours," I said truthfully. She liked that. Food and beauty, those were her subjects. Sometimes I didn't mind the lovely old subjects of women. I wasn't always fighting her.

We sat down at her table, by the window overlooking the back yard, which was nicer than the bare grass of the front yard which our dining room looked out on. She had a whole row of roses in summer to look at, my mother's roses. We ate roast pork and noodles, which she'd made, chopping in her manic, virtuoso way, a woman who knew her business. We ate, I sighed, she said, "Your Mama doesn't like me. Why doesn't she like me?"

Later, when I went into our part of the house, just a few steps away from the vestibule that divided the two parts of the house, my mother was fixing dinner. I ate a second time, not mentioning I'd already eaten.

When we washed dishes together, my mother liked to talk. I could never tell what she would bring up. If we had fought during the day, it was anguish to dry dishes with her washing silently, bitterly. But mostly we talked and were very close over the dishwater. That night she said, "You know, your grandmother is driving me crazy. She follows after me, turning off the lights. She waits up at night and asks us why we stay out so late — and we came home at eleven o'clock! This afternoon, I went down in the basement. Of course I turned the light on. Five minutes later, off it goes, and I'm down there in the dark. I yell and yell, but she's gone. So I have to come up, turn on the light, go down again. I tell her, I tell her . . ."

I kept drying the dishes. I had two dinners inside me; I was full of duplicity. Every day I perched like this on the family fence. A fence that seemed to be set down on the boundary between the crazy past and the sensible future. I felt significant in a twisted, private way, in some inversion of my grandmother who seemed to feel insignificant in an untwisted way. Things depended on me, depended on which way I went, which side of the fence I chose.

I fell softly on the far side of the fence where my mother was waiting. I was there with my mother, holding my dishpan of spite, looking across at my grandmother on the other, unkempt, side of the fence where the past — the real past, not of history but of mythic, granite secrecy which is ignorance — refused to lie down and play dead.

I fell on my mother's side, a pioneer, and hit the ground running. There was something scary, shameful, about not knowing the word *science*. It was medieval, like the plague. I didn't want that much past; I didn't want to grasp history that deeply.

7

MY GRANDMOTHER, when she first came to St. Paul, got a job on the hill. To work "on the hill" was St. Paul lingo, meaning you were a maid or some kind of domestic help in one of the mansions along Summit Avenue or in the Crocus Hill area nearby. The hill was not just a geographical area; it was a designation of caste. It was also really a hill because St. Paul, like all romantic cities, draws its quality of personality, of identity, from its geography. Its topography mirrors its economy, its history, its image of itself.

There is a feeling of inevitability about the terraced, hierarchical topography of the place, as if St. Paul was bound to be a Catholic city, an "old city" as Minneapolis is not, as if F. Scott Fitzgerald, born here, was predestined by this working replica of capitalism — the wealthy above, the poor below — to be obsessed by the rich.

I always took Fitzgerald's side in the exchange he and Hemingway are supposed to have had about wealth. He was the hometown boy. But beyond my loyalty, I felt his romantic cry that "the rich are different from you and me" — a pure St. Paul cry — was more to the point than the answer Hemingway gave himself. *Of course* "the rich have money" — but it doesn't end there. Romantics are rarely given credit for anything beyond the flourish, brilliant, like spread plumage, of their style. But how often behind the indefensible rhapsody of a romantic statement

— Fitzgerald's "The rich are different from you and me" — there is the hard fact of how people actually feel.

The rich get to live differently. They are therefore different. Fitzgerald's line is less chumpy than Hemingway has made us think. It speaks the case for many people and explains in part why there is such a thing as a celebrity in our culture. His unguarded cry is true, even if he was "romantic about the rich," as people say. His statement speaks more truly than Hemingway who merely got the last word in a conversation. Fitzgerald wrote the book on the subject and made it stick: *The Great Gatsby* is romantic and it says the harsh truth: that the rich are different because we — the rest of us and they themselves — cannot help making them so.

In St. Paul, the metaphoric significance of the hill was further emphasized by the fact that the grandest of the mansions on Summit Avenue, the one with a view only rivaled by the cathedral across the street, had been built by the city's chief resident, whose name was Hill: James J. Hill, the Empire Builder. Which is exactly how he was invoked in my family: the name, followed by the title. He had connected east and west with his railroad, the Great Northern; he had made St. Paul a railroad town, shifting its first allegiance, as a river town, away from the Mississippi so that even today the city turns its back on the river, as if it weren't the Father of Waters but a wet inconvenience.

This disregard for feature and advantage — the back turned on beauty — strikes me as American, but even more so as Midwestern. It is compounded of the usual pioneer arrogance and also, strangely, of diffidence: the swagger of saying we don't *need* beauty is coupled with the pouty lack of confidence of a wallflower who thinks of nothing else but beauty, but charm, what she lacks.

And so I became a snob . . . again. This time as a Midwesterner: the provincial anguish. My grandmother, I feared, had immigrated to Nowheresville. My family would have thought this nonsense. They loved Minnesota, preferred "a small city" like St. Paul, and, without my knowing it, caused me to love it eventually too. But I spent my moody girlhood aloof from my town, saving myself for the World. A Midwesterner to my toes.

My mother always sighed seriously, "God's country," when we crossed back from Wisconsin or the Dakotas after a trip. "Thank God," she said, "we have scenery." "This is paradise," my father told us every year as we went into the dark of the woods to fish at one of Minnesota's "10,000 lakes" and batted at mosquitoes. "Mosquitoes? What mosquitoes?" my father said, glaring at the child-traitor who spoke against paradise. "Look around you," he cried, gesturing with a casting rod, "this is heaven." He fished and my mother read her two-inch-thick historical novels.

We were not really the Midwest, my father explained; that would be Iowa or Nebraska, Kansas — hopeless places. We were the Upper Midwest, as the weatherman said, elevating us above the dreary mean. My father pointed with derision at the cars with Iowa license plates, hauling boats on trailers behind them, as we passed them on Highway 200 going north. "Will you look at that," he said. "Those Iowa people have to lug that boat all the way up here." My brother and I looked at the dummies in the Iowa car as we passed. "They're crazy to get to the water, they'll even fish in the middle of the day," he said, as if the Iowa Bedouins were so water mad that a school of walleye could toy with them in the noon heat, while my father coolly appeared at dawn and twilight to make the easy Minnesota-savvy kill. He pointed out to us, over and over, the folly of the Iowans and their pathetic pursuit of standing water.

Our supremacy came from our weather, and the history of our weather: the glacier had given us these beautiful clear lakes, my father explained. The glacier receded and — Paradise, with lakes. And as if the single great historical event, the glacier, had been enshrined as a symbol, in my family we were not to speak against the winter. Our cold was our pride. We watched the *Today Show* weather report and a shiver — not of cold but entirely of civic pride — ran through us as, week after week, some aching Minnesota town came in with the lowest temperature in the country. We did not delight in the admittance of Alaska, our icy rival, into the Union. We said nothing against it, but it was understood that it didn't really count, it had an unfair advantage which caused us to ignore it. "Didn't Alaska belong to Russia?" my mother said. "I mean, isn't it strictly speaking part of Siberia?"

Much better to think of International Falls, the Minnesota border town known on the *Today Show* and elsewhere as "the Nation's Ice Box." We took pride in our wretched weather ("St. Paul–Minneapolis is the coldest metropolitan area *in the world*," my mother read to us from the paper) the way a small nation does in its national art, as if the ice cube, our symbol, were the supreme artifact of civilization. And like a small nation, we hardly cared among ourselves that the myths and legends, the peculiar rites of the land, were unknown and undervalued elsewhere, as long as we could edify ourselves again and again with the stunning statistics that constituted our sense of ourselves: the weather, the god-awful winters, which were our civic, practically our cultural, identity. I didn't personally hate the winter; I hated that there didn't seem to be anything *but* the winter.

The cold was our pride, the snow was our beauty. It fell and fell, lacing day and night together in a milky haze, making everything quieter as it fell, so that winter seemed to partake of religion in a way no other season did, hushed, solemn. It was snowing and it was silent. Good-bye, good-bye, we are leaving you forever: this was the farewell we sent to the nation on the *Today Show* weather report. Or perhaps we were the ones being left behind, sealed up in our ice cube for winter as the rest of the world's cities had their more tasteful dabs of cold, and then went on to spring. "Even Moscow! Even Leningrad!" my mother read to us from the newspaper, "can't begin to touch us."

"If you stepped outside right now without any clothes on," my brother said one day when we had not been allowed to go skating because the temperature was 25° below zero, "you'd be dead in three minutes." He sounded happy, the Minnesota pride in the abysmal statistic — which, for all I knew, he had made up on the spot. We looked out the dining room window to the forbidden world. The brilliant, mean glare from the mounds of snow had no mercy on the eye and was a mockery of the meaning of sun. "You'd be *stiff*. Like frozen hamburger," he said. "Or a frozen plucked chicken," regarding me and finding a better simile. "And when you thawed out, you'd turn green." The pleasure of being horrified, standing there by the hot radiator with my ghoulish brother.

We shared the pride of isolation, the curious glamour of hermits. More than any other thing I can name, the winter made me want to write. The inwardness of the season (winter is *quiet*) and its austerity were abiding climatic analogues of the solitude I automatically associated with creativity. "Minneapolis — a great book town," I once overheard a book salesman say with relish. And what else was there to do in the winter? Stay inside and read. Or write. Stay inside and dream. Stay inside and look, safely, outside. The Muse might as well be invited — who else would venture out?

The withdrawn aloofness of what had been, recently, leafy and harmless, now had a lunar beauty that was so strange and minimal it had to be foreign. But it was ours, our measure of danger and therefore our bit of glamour and importance. Or perhaps the relation between the winter and writing, which I felt was a negative one: maybe I hated the season and wanted to cover up the whiteness; a blank page was the only winter I could transform. That's how little I understand winter, how it can bewitch its inhabitants (for it is more like a country than a season, a thing to which one belongs), so they cannot say and don't know whether they love the winter or hate it. And we always said "*the* winter," not simply "winter," as if for us the season had a presence that amounted to a permanent residence among us.

Spring didn't exist. I read about it in books that I read curled up on my grandmother's horsehair sofa, the English springs of the Bröntes, full of brave early flowers and all that English reawakening of life:

Spring drew on, she was indeed already come; the frosts of winter had ceased; its snows were melted, its cutting winds ameliorated . . . a greenness grew over those brown beds, which, freshening daily, suggested the thought that Hope traversed them at night, and left each morning brighter traces of her steps. Flowers peeped out amongst the leaves; snow-drops, crocuses, purple auriculas, the golden-eye pansies.

Jane Eyre's April. Sometimes in St. Paul it snowed in May, once, definitely, in June. We skipped spring and plunged right into summer, maybe to get warmed up. "Don't plant until after the fifteenth of May," my father warned his customers at the greenhouse. They didn't always listen. "I told her," he would say at the dinner table, giving us the news of Mrs. Beauchamp's punishment by the season, as if her folly in planting her geraniums and petunias before May 15 and the result ("she lost a couple of hundred dollars there") were a working lesson in the effects of hubris in daily life. "I told her not before May fifteenth. I said, the twentieth would be better — in fact, why not just wait till June. What's the rush?" My father allied himself with winter and therefore could always feel righteous.

By April my brother and I were charmed no longer, but my mother and father were loyal. April 10, snowing a blizzard, and my mother, looking out the window, said mildly, "Well, at least we get a change of the seasons." She and my father shook their heads over the appalling uniformity of the weather in places like Florida and California.

The winter and the conundrum of wealth (the hill) became attached in my mind, became related in an unapproachable coldness. This may be because of the story I read by F. Scott Fitzgerald titled "Winter Dreams," which affected me strongly. The story is set in St. Paul. It is about wanting what the rich have — specifically, it is about Dexter Green wanting Judy Jones, the daughter of a rich man, with all her golden, buffaloing beauty. To begin with, I was overpowered by living — for the first time

— in the setting of a story, of fiction, a state of mind and life I sought and expected to find only on English moors and in other inaccessible places like New England. But here, as I walked home from school, was "the avenue" where "the dwellings of the rich loomed up . . . somnolent, gorgeous, drenched with the splendor of the damp moonlight." Summit Avenue, the hill, nearby.

The story hardly takes place in winter. Winter happens, for the most part, off-stage. The romance, the action, the betrayal — are all part of the summer and the long days at the lake. But the story's title is apt. For it is the dream of Dexter Green, with his self-mocking springish name, whose mother, we're told, "was a Bohemian of the peasant class" who had "talked broken English to the end of her days," this dream of beauty and possession is the winter thing, the longing, the vast desiring for the world and for the light that comes only from long winter and its deep burial in a provincial city where, because there is wealth and winter, there are dreams — of beauty and beyond.

I realized and I believed that winter light was, precisely, dream light. The gauzy winter light of a snowy day is the light of dreams because it is easy on the eye, and allows the sleeper to watch the dream's action, to look long and relaxed, without the eye being transfixed by darts of brightness. You wake from such dreams with no desire to analyze or understand the dream's meaning — the dream itself is enough, to have dreamed it. Winter dreams of this sort grow and grow, the eye steady, dilating, creating its tableaux and then succumbing to them, perhaps dangerously, as Dexter Green succumbs to Judy Jones, the beautiful rich girl. Judy Jones betrays Dexter not simply by dumping him but, many years later when he no longer lives in "the Midwestern city" and has lost track of her, she betrays him again, more devastatingly. He hears, from a business acquaintance (he has become rich, a New Yorker, himself), that gorgeous Judy Jones has faded, is a drab figure, a wife who stays home with the kids: her husband runs around. She betrays Dexter then by ceasing finally to be reckless and unusual — beautiful, in a word — as the dream of loveliness must always be. The dream, not the woman, causes his real sorrow. He could sustain the loss of her, but not of the dream she was: that was himself. The dream of this kind happens in the light of winter, the silent, private season. These are the dreams of "the beauty that must die." And then dies.

❧

My grandmother, knowing *what she was*, knew also what the rich were: her employers. Like Fitzgerald, she found them different; unlike him, she didn't care. They, also, were *what they were*. She worked as a maid or kitchen help in various places, before and after she married, but her longest employment was in the house of Pierce Butler, a justice of the United States Supreme Court. She learned English in the classic way, by serving. Asked to bring a broom, she appeared with an iron; she cleaned the kitchen floor instead of the hallway stairs: till she learned the language. An odd, completely unsnobbish, result of this method of learning was that she picked up several expressions and pronunciations that went strangely with her Czech accent and grammar. She always said tom*ah*to (though a potato was a potato), and when reprimanding me, she said, like some first son of an English lord, a dandy at the end of the last century, that I "dasn't do that." She spoke Czech, much of the time, to my grandfather, a man I remember mostly as an icon of silence, stirring his tan coffee, adding endless spoonfuls of sugar that should have sent him bouncing hyperactively off the kitchen walls but instead left him meditative and austere as if he'd been sucking on a lemon. He played the concertina, but like many amateur musicians, this did not make him sociable, but gave him an excuse not to talk. He was more presence than person to me, and I can't remember his ever speaking directly to me, which is strange. He often went out on the back porch where he kept a parakeet and I clearly remember his voice as he talked sensibly and softly to the bird, sometimes chuckling, as if he and the parakeet were recounting old times. My grandmother banged around behind him in the kitchen and sometimes called him

The Crab. Maybe he was. Apparently my grandmother had driven him mad during their long family years when he gave her two dollars a day (or a week? I am lost again in the history of inflation) from his wages as a packing clerk at a stationery supply store downtown to run the household: she was one of those housewives who could not resist the wares of the Fuller Brush man, the coffee man, the matched-set-of-sharp-knives salesman, the merchants with their stores in their suitcases. She bought and bought, and finally, in anguish, had to pay, had to ask for more than the two dollars. There were scenes, my father said, which caused him to become the kind of man who endorsed his paycheck and put it on the table for my mother to take care of — perhaps to make it go away.

My mother said my grandfather was a gentleman, "A wonderful dry sense of humor," she said, approving. "Very *Celtic*," trying to claim him for the Irish though he too was a Czech immigrant. On their fiftieth wedding anniversary he gave my grandmother a diamond ring (which she lost somehow in the washing machine) and a card that he signed The Old Crab. They were deeply married: opposites. And although I don't remember him speaking to me, he must have understood things about me. As a Christmas gift he once gave me a small desk, carpentered and varnished entirely by himself. He died when I was still small. I imagine he too knew *what he was*. In his case, patience. When he was dying he said no, he didn't want the priest, priests were crooks. The Church had the last word, however; he was refused a burial Mass, which the family had requested. So we hung around the funeral parlor saying the rosary, and, my mother, her loyalties badly at odds, kept whispering to me, "He went to heaven, of course he went to heaven."

My grandfather's stern face. Perhaps it wasn't stern, but what else is silence to a chatterbox child? Therefore: my grandfather's stern face, the face of a working man. And then the city's great stern grandfather, James J. Hill with his monster house, his

Great Northern, the lordly power of a frontier magnate. Fitzgerald put him, name unchanged, in his story "Absolution": he is compared to God, the simple obvious simile. Sinclair Lewis was also attracted to Hill as a character. He lived for a time in St. Paul in the twenties, near the hill, writing a novel based on the personality of James J. Hill. He never finished it, and abandoned the project. Hill was probably a man better memorialized in architecture, not literature, in any case. What a piece of granite that face is in the formal photographs one sees now and again in St. Paul, and in the dark bust at the entrance of the James J. Hill Reference Library — his gift — downtown. The eyes are those of a just slightly toned-down Gurdjieff. The Empire Builder: naturally, architecture was his art form.

His mansion is kitty-corner from the cathedral, as if Fitzgerald was right: he and God were squaring off. The Hill house is a fortress, very dark, of rude dimension, with a black iron fence and a stone gatekeeper's lodge near the street. Inside, he had an art gallery, a pipe organ, and, to my surprise when I visited there in college when the building was used by the archdiocese for offices, a tiny cave of a study on the main floor, practically a secret room, it seemed to me.

There was nothing disappointing about the mansion of James J. Hill. It knew what it was: money, the bubble of being on top, being not only on the hill but the Hill itself, wrapped around by mortar and stone, endlessly hidden. That small, hidden room — where decisions were made, I thought solemnly as I stood there with somebody pointing out the wood carving — was the moist kernel, the serious business, from which the rest of the outlandish tree had grown. It was devious and dark, and I loved it.

Next door was the son. Louis Hill, son of the Empire Builder, had constructed his own mansion. It was light, classical, with cool doric columns like pillars of fondant in front of the rosy brick structure. It was the rational mind, elegant, a little superficial, closer to the avenue than James J.'s pile, a denial of nightmare, antigothic. Not a fortress but a manor. In the early sixties it had become a retreat house and was named Maryhill. Our class was sent there for "the senior retreat" over a weekend, not long after President Kennedy was shot. We weren't supposed to talk all weekend, and, for the most part, we didn't. We went to Mass in the ballroom on the second floor, the parquet floor smooth and intricate, fascinating to follow with the eye. Queen Marie of Rumania, the one who later advertised cosmetics for a while, had been a guest here in the twenties. The Louis Hills were elegant and gave elegant parties. I felt effortlessly religious the whole weekend I was there for our retreat. It was winter (of course). I looked out the east window of the glowing yellow sunroom toward the James J. Hill house, and not really seeing it and yet looking at it, contemplated the happy paradox of losing one's soul in order to gain it. I thought of St. Maria Goretti, as the retreat master had told us to: had she been just a prude? he had asked, throwing out the rhetorical question in a tough, thinking-man way as if he had himself just come away from considering this very explanation of her martyrdom at the hands of a "sex fiend" (who was also a "poor soul"). By degrees I arrived at the moving scene in which I astonished my parents (and she was always such a *talker*, my mother would say) by announcing my intention of entering the convent: I would enter this very one, I thought, staring out the lovely mullioned window to the other mansion. I would help run retreats, treading the parquet floors in sweet silence. I wanted, badly, to live in that house.

The St. Paul Cathedral — that is, God — has a better piece of real estate than the Empire Builder. It is poised on the crest of Summit Avenue, in a perfect angle to see and be seen. Archbishop John J. Ireland, a man with a country for a name, had seen to God's supremacy. The cathedral, modeled on St. Peter's (and my mother told me early that St. Paul "like Rome" is built on seven hills), was erected as a monument of faith on the part of immigrants, mainly Irish, but all the nationalities were represented. Almost all. In the circlet of chapels running behind the main altar and dome, there are altars commemorating the patron saints of various groups including "the Slavic peoples." The one intended for the Scandinavians was eventually dedicated to St. Thérèse of Lisieux because the Scandinavians turned out to be Lutherans. The first church in St. Paul had been dedicated by the missionary Lucien Galtier in 1841. "I blessed the new basilica," he wrote of the old church which no longer stands and which was not a basilica, "and dedicated it to St. Paul, the apostle of nations." It was given to the immigrants in advance.

My parents were married in the cathedral; it was my mother's parish. They used to say that the cathedral was not finished, it would *never* be finished: that was in the nature of the thing. It was constantly being added to, changed, its details amplified, refined, deepened. In this way, I grew up with the cathedral as an immense example of the creative act. The product was itself the atelier. The eternal was the progress of the fragment, of what was inevitably incomplete, unfinished. Its essence was longing and movement, not permanence and wholeness at all.

But it is untrue to say it this way because my notion of all this was cloudy, unconcerned, a matter of unsorted sensation. Only now, as I remember what my mother and father said as we drove by (and it was said with pride) — *the cathedral will never be finished* — do I see why I remember that casual statement at all. I remember because it contained what I was later to try to understand. The cathedral will never be finished. Nor life, nor longing, the endless *reaching* we do. Therefore the metaphoric power of art.

Our cathedral had its lore and legends, as the medieval cathedrals of Europe had their gargoyles: images in which the whole of life — not just the spiritual, not just the good, but the base as well — could be contained. My favorite story from the building of the cathedral: one day the masons were bricking up a part of a wall. It was summer, hot, parched. It was midafternoon, the worst time of thirst. They decided to send for a pail of beer (to the Schmidt Brewery? I don't know, I don't expect things to be that neat). They sat, high above the city on their scaffolding, drinking cold beer from the pail. At which point

Archbishop Ireland happened to come across the street — they could see him coming in the distance — to check, as he often did in an idle moment, on the progress of the cathedral. The masons, drinking beer on the job, got instantly to work: they grabbed the pail of beer, wedged it into the unfinished wall and slapped brick and mortar as fast as they could. "And so," my father said, "there's a pail of beer bricked into that church to this day." Religion and the spirit of beer, Apollo and Dionysus, saints and gargoyles, empire builders and bishops, our endless story of opposites.

Even today now that the cathedral *is* finished, my parents do not talk of it that way. It remains unfinished and they see its maintenance as part of its eternal emergence, not as a janitorial matter. They grew up with it high above them, visibly incomplete. They knew that the Depression or the War caused the abandonment of this chapel or that statue. And a window envisioned but not executed is still a window, a window, for them, unfinished and therefore eternal.

8 🦋

In St. Paul, F. Scott Fitzgerald was our author. We tinkered
with his byline, casting away the official F., and spoke of him
always in the familiar: Scott Fitzgerald, or just Scott, as if we
had known him. And some people had. His mother had gone
to my school, his daughter had been baptized in the little white
powder puff of the school chapel.

"Did you ever meet Scott Fitzgerald?" someone asked one of
the older nuns who taught us English. "I danced with him at
the cotillion," she said. This made me shiver with pleasure.

One very old nun said that they had all sat in the visitors'
parlor, behind the grille, listening while Scott read from his composition — "The History of the English Empire" — when as a
child he came with his mother to visit the sisters. Their very
disinterest thrilled me; it made their intimacy more real. Yes,
they had known Scott. So what?

Proximity to literature. There it was around me: the single
rising bubble in the pan of water, the transparent nothingness
I sulkingly felt around me. Scott, Scott, I was practically praying:
you lived here too. That soft, on-target blow to the head had
happened to Scott Fitzgerald here, not more than six blocks
from home. At school the reality was even more definite: Sister
had danced with Scott at the cotillion, his mother had been a
student, his daughter baptized . . . Literature was a lightning
that had struck close to home, splitting the tree in half, sending
the burnt singe of wood into the neighborhood, the tree itself

perhaps dead now (St. Paul and the Midwest were dead wood — I knew that) but a monument at last. St. Paul had not been passed by. Scott Fitzgerald had run down Summit Avenue, they said, to stop the cars when he got his letter from Scribner's accepting *This Side of Paradise.*

Neither the naiveté of such a need for a model nor the depth of the worthlessness of the Midwest was less real than this. Behind every shred of boosterism, lurking in the pressed leaves of regionalism, of the local statistics and lore, was the sour hopelessness of the provincial capital. But even those phrases — "the provinces," "the provincial city" — are too limpid and carry the charm of Chekhov's touching bores and pedants. The European grace of irony, of something amusing, touches the bitter denials of geography and makes the Russian Podunks glow and tremble in their reflected light.

St. Paul had — has — the streetlights for a Chekhov story. They throw their buttery rounds on the heaped snowbanks and seem to promise not light but warmth. Their frail yellow always reminded me of snow, even in summer, for the little blobs of light seemed to need the greater radiance of the mounded snow to *be* streetlights at all. Their charm was their ineffectual streetlighting, their inability to do the job. They led, in their evenly spaced formations down Summit and the other smaller streets, from darkness to darkness, sentinels of the night, not its illumination.

But streetlights alone do not make a city. And I wanted a city. Not a town, not even the capital of Minnesota, but a city. It was the Midwestern desire that, in part, creates or sustains the empire quality of New York, of Gotham. New York, left to its own devices, without Podunk dreams and ambitions flying to it generation after generation, would hardly be a city, but a collection of steamy, squabbly neighborhoods where everybody is selling sandwiches to each other, the ethnic diversity forever unmelted. New York looked old-fashioned to me when I first saw it: doormen and elevator operators (with gloves), whole lives devoted to service — shoe shining, the squeezing of fresh orange juice, endless detailing of tasks, my grandmother's life repeated by each wave of immigration. The Midwest did away with that long ago. We go up in our elevators alone, pushing the numbered squares ourselves, while in New York they still rise to the sound of a man clattering his castanets.

St. Paul, because it refused to be — couldn't be — a city, was a constant irritant. It was too personal, too Catholic, familial, but not really kindly for all that. These are the things I sense in all of Fitzgerald's work, and which are satisfactorily explained by an evening walk down Summit Avenue, his street.

"As they turned into Crest Avenue," one of Fitzgerald's sketches from *The Crack-Up* begins, "the new cathedral, immense and unfinished in imitation of a cathedral left unfinished by accident in some little Flemish town, squatted just across the way like a plump white bulldog on its haunches . . . The cathedral inaugurated Crest Avenue. After it came the great brownstone mass built by R. R. Commerford, the flour king, followed by a half mile of pretentious stone houses built in the gloomy 90's. These were adorned with monstrous driveways and porte-cocheres which had once echoed to the hoofs of good horses and with high circular windows that corseted the second stories."

After the long ride from the cathedral to the Mississippi River where the avenue ends at another bluff, the girl in the sketch who is driving the roadster turns to her companion and says, "This is the end of Crest Avenue. This is our show street."

The visitor, a man, replies, "A museum of American architectural failures."

The strange thing is that today it is not a collection of architectural failures. Victorian taste is popular now perhaps because it is deeply bourgeois, but also because it is crammed with detail, with ornament. The traditional modern aesthetic is one of mordant line, form conceived of as minimal, unadorned structure, as if beauty were a matter of the skeleton, not the flesh. The static statement of a perfectly smooth, finely finished, unornamented block of wood is the highest rendition of "table" in such an aesthetic. Lines and geometric rectitude — where even curves do not suggest excess — are what we have come to recognize as contemporary or modern. The stereotype is by now an old one, almost as old as the century.

Even the words — *modern, contemporary* — suggest an unattached, almost hostile quality, emptiness. It is the design of aliens for aliens. Such design is functional, and we are meant to appreciate, even enjoy the duct work.

Contemporary design is cool (even cold), sleek, elegant, severe. Color is often monochromatic and muted or bluntly primary. It is perfect in the literal sense in which death is perfect; it is final. It is simple, it is stark. It is intensely sad. That is, we are aware of melancholy in entering such an environment, such perfection. We are not touched by this form of depression — melancholia — when, today, we consider Victorian architecture. How strange that we do not, for theirs was the era of languors, of great (particularly female) melancholia. We are amused or feel cozy in such environments. We even acknowledge some kind of whimsy in Victorian stuffed, overstuffed, plush. The crammed interior, the thirty-year-old fern spinning itself out like a spider in "the parlor" — all of it suits our sense of ourselves as essentially harmless, as nice people. The contemporary design of stripped surfaces and emphasis on line and thin color is frightening because it is without ornament. For most of us flourishes disguise fear. Fear of what? Of the naked soul. Life, we sense, ought not to be too bare. *Anything* might happen on an entirely empty surface.

Summit Avenue avoids, up on its bluff, this abyss. And now it is not a "museum of American architectural failures," but "the best-preserved American example of the Victorian monumental residential boulevard," according to Ernest R. Sandeen's recent book *St. Paul's Historic Summit Avenue*.

The Avenue has acquired this distinction recently, this sense of itself as *something*. Even Fitzgerald, whose life in a sense was staked on the very values and conflicts that the puffed-up mansions of the street represent, could not like the Avenue, could not claim it for himself. He had to prove his superiority by *naming* it. The hodgepodge and loony fantasy of the buildings amounted to a failure — even a museum of failure. By saying this Fitzgerald was able to make his escape. He got New York.

This avenue, where my grandmother first came to work, was in my girlhood putting in its most precarious years: the years after the frankness of its power (Fitzgerald's years, Hill's, and my grandmother's) and before its serenity as history (the current period). A descendant of the Empire Builder still lived on the Avenue, but she was old, feeble, fading; rooming houses and ruins seemed to be its future. In some helpless way, pioneer cities that had been based on the idea of progress found it difficult to believe they had any control, any recourse as "progress" razed the past.

Then, just in time, the Avenue became historic and, no matter what happens now, its identity is assured. When I see the tour buses passing along the Avenue, or a walking tour with a guide gesturing with a microphone, who announces that the James J. Hill house, no longer the archdiocese's but the Historical Society's, is being restored, I don't feel the glimmer of something old, but of an entirely new thing, a recently recognized passion: the fact of history. For there they are at last, the earnest citizens, ready now to bow their heads, to appreciate. To appreciate themselves, in a sense, to acknowledge that something happened and that it was not a failure, but simply history. Perhaps these shy, proud groups walking down Summit with a guide mean that in the future it will not be necessary to go to New York, to France, to wherever *it* is. Regionalists have said so for generations, rhapsodically or sourly. I sometimes think that my generation is the last to "have to go to Europe" and, at the same time, the first to turn in such numbers in the other direction, toward Asia, for its spiritual and cultural direction.

My grandmother was a maid on the Avenue. All her life she referred to "the hill" as she did to the earlier, European caste, "the nobles." Her avenue was Fitzgerald's.

Mine was different. Every May Day, during the fifties and early sixties, the Catholics of the city marched down Summit, divided into contingents by parishes, in a giant procession, saying the Rosary. We walked in the direction of the cathedral where Mary, Queen of May, Queen of the Rosary, was crowned. The rosary was led by the archbishop from the steps of the cathedral, his voice echoing down the length of the Avenue from loud-speakers that were hoisted onto the just-budding trees. After each rosary we said a special prayer for "the conversion of Russia and the overthrow of atheistic Communism."

This procession is still held, I think. Last year, in early May, I saw a group of men putting loudspeakers in the trees, and the last blocks of the Avenue approaching the cathedral were posted against parking. I was living on the Avenue. I had rented a car-riage house behind the old Lindeke mansion (wholesale gro-ceries), less than a block from the Louis Hill house, directly across the street from the Weyerhaeuser mansion (lumber). The rent for the place was ridiculous, the quarters cramped, and heating fuel in the winter, because of the poor insulation, was impossible. My landlords were the Society of Friends, who had bought the mansion for their meetinghouse at a time when the big houses were not yet being restored and could be had cheaply. The Quakers were solicitous, but along with the price they asked and I was foolish enough to pay for the place, they had the defect, as landlords, of finding it painful to do anything about the squirrels who had chewed their way into the attic and nested noisily above me.

The winter was full of phone calls and meetings, confronta-tions and discussions about the squirrel situation. The negotia-tions were depressing because I was cast in the role of a person who *seemed* to be at one with the Quakers on matters of politics, the Vietnam War, civil rights, nuclear power, but who in fact wanted some exterminating done fast. I began by pointing out that squirrels are, after all, rodents. The Quakers murmured that, as the squirrels were *nesting*, care must be taken that "the young" not be endangered. I mentioned that I couldn't sleep at night.

"Because of the scurrying around?" one of the Quakers said, sympathetically.

"Because of the orgasmic cries of the squirrels," I said, feeling brutal, for some reason, in mentioning sex to a Quaker, even squirrel sex. Thus emboldened, I went right on, brought up the idea of poison and used the word *kill*. The Quakers employed passive resistance, as they do.

The squirrels came and went, chewed holes for easy access into various places in the eaves, perhaps chewed their way into the elderly electrical system. Finally, toward the end of winter, an arrangement was worked out whereby a high school boy, in the pay of the Quakers, appeared once in the morning and again at night to place and check and replace a contraption in the attic. The contraption had a name like Animal-Saf or Kind-a-Pet. It was a cage in which the high school boy placed wilted lettuce with peanut butter smeared on it. Squirrels liked lettuce and peanut butter, he told me the first time he came into the apartment with it. Every day he returned to check the contraption and, if an animal had gone for the bait, he took the cage out, past me in the kitchen where I sat eating my dinner. He explained to me that caged squirrels might make a little noise in the contraption before he returned to check them. But none ever did. They were silent, depressed perhaps by having been caught. They were not squirrelly, but just looked at me steadily from their contraption as the boy took them out. Later he was supposed to drive them somewhere across the river in West St. Paul and liberate them in a park. "But you know," he told me with admiration for the race, "those squirrels can find their way back to their nests from miles and miles."

I decided to move. I had wanted to live on the Avenue: I'd lived on the Avenue. It was a mean little apartment on top of a smelly garage, I decided, for which I paid a sum that made my friends laugh and pity me. The windows were set very high, too high to see out of, giving enough light but no view except for the tops of trees and chimneys. On dark winter days, I'd forlornly hoisted myself onto the kitchen counter, and sat there drinking my morning coffee, getting a view from my cell. In the hallway I'd noticed a telephone, some sort of ancient intercom system. There was no way to dial out, just a little black box attached to the wall with a place to speak into and a small round receiver to be placed near the ear. I kept my books on shelves near this little telephone and sometimes, idly, I picked up the receiver, held it to my ear and, as I scanned the shelves for the book I wanted, said, "Yes, yes, anybody there?" There was something attractive about a telephone that didn't work.

"Oh," said the Quaker lady who came to inspect the place for damage when I was moving out, "that isn't a telephone. It was used to summon the servants." And it struck me, what I'd known all along; I hadn't moved onto the Avenue at all. I had put my money down to live in the small airless rooms, the viewless back alley of a former mansion. I was paying big money to live in the servants' quarters, my grandmother's place.

9 ❦

FOOD WAS the potent center of my grandmother's life. Maybe the immense amount of time it took to prepare meals during most of her life accounted for her passion. Or it may have been her years of work in various kitchens on the hill and later, in the house of Justice Butler: after all, she was a professional. Much later, when she was dead and I went to Prague, I came to feel the motto I knew her by best — *Come eat* — was not, after all, a personal statement, but a racial one, the *cri de coeur* of Middle Europe.

Often, on Sundays, the entire family gathered for dinner at her house. Dinner was at 1 P.M. My grandmother would have preferred the meal to be at the old time of noon, but her children had moved their own Sunday dinner hour to the more fashionable (it was felt) 4 o'clock, so she compromised. Sunday breakfast was something my mother liked to do in a big way, so we arrived at my grandmother's hardly out of the reverie of waffles and orange rolls, before we were propped like rag dolls in front of a pork roast and sauerkraut, dumplings, hot buttered carrots, rye bread and rollikey, pickles and olives, apple pie and ice cream. And coffee.

Coffee was a food in that house, not a drink. I always begged for some because the magical man on the Hills Brothers can with his turban and long robe scattered with stars and his gold slippers with pointed toes, looked deeply happy as he drank from his bowl. The bowl itself reminded me of soup, Campbell's chicken noodle soup, my favorite food. The distinct adultness of coffee and the robed man with his deep-drinking pleasure made it clear why the grownups lingered so long at the table. The uncles smoked cigars then, and the aunts said, "Oh, those cigars."

My grandmother, when she served dinner, was a virtuoso hanging on the edge of her own ecstatic performance. She seemed dissatisfied, almost querulous until she had corralled everybody into their chairs around the table, which she tried to do the minute they got into the house. No cocktails, no hors d'oeuvres (pronounced, by some of the family, "horse's ovaries"), just business. She was a little power crazed: she had us and, by God, we were going to eat. She went about it like a goose breeder forcing pellets down the gullets of those dumb birds.

She flew between her chair and the kitchen, always finding more this, extra that. She'd given you the *wrong* chicken breast the first time around; now she'd found the *right* one: eat it too, eat it fast, because after the chicken comes the rhubarb pie. Rhubarb pie with a thick slice of cheddar cheese that it was imperative every single person eat.

We had to eat fast because something was always out there in the kitchen panting and charging the gate, champing at the bit, some mound of rice or a Jell-O fruit salad or vegetable casserole or pie was out there, waiting to be let loose into the dining room.

She had the usual trite routines: the wheedlings, the silent pout ("What! You don't like my brussels sprouts? I thought you liked *my* brussels sprouts," versus your wife's/sister's/mother's. "I made that pie just for you," etc., etc.) But it was the way she tossed around the old cliches and the overused routines, mixing them up and dealing them out shamelessly, without irony, that made her a pro. She tended to peck at her own dinner. Her plate, piled with food, was a kind of stage prop, a mere bending to convention. She liked to eat, she was even a greedy little stuffer, but not on these occasions. She was a woman possessed by an idea, given over wholly to some phantasmagoria of food, a mirage of stuffing, a world where the endless chicken and the infinite lemon pie were united at last at the shore of the oceanic soup plate that her children and her children's children alone could drain . . . if only they would try.

She was there to bolster morale, to lead the troops, to give the sharp command should we falter on the way. The futility of saying no was supreme, and no one ever tried it. How could a son-in-law, already weakened near the point of imbecility by the once, twice, thrice charge to the barricades of pork and mashed potato, be expected to gather his feeble wit long enough to ignore the final call of his old commander when she sounded the alarm: "Pie, Fred?"

Just when it seemed as if the food-crazed world she had created was going to burst, that she had whipped and frothed us like a sack of boiled potatoes under her masher, just then she pulled it all together in one easeful stroke like the pro she was.

She stood in the kitchen doorway, her little round Napoleonic self sheathed in a cotton flowered pinafore apron, the table draped in its white lace cloth but spotted now with gravy and beet juice, the troops mumbling indistinctly as they waited at their posts for they knew not what. We looked up at her stupidly, weakly. She said nonchalantly, "Anyone want another piece of pie?" No, no more pie, somebody said. The rest of the rabble grunted along with him. She stood there with the coffeepot and laughed and said, "Good! Because there *isn't* any more pie."

No more pie. We'd eaten it all, we'd put away everything in that kitchen. We were exhausted and she, gambler hostess that she was (but it was her house she was playing), knew she could offer what didn't exist, knew us, knew what she'd wrought. There was a sense of her having won, won something. There were no divisions among us now, no adults, no children. Power left the second and third generations and returned to the source, the grandmother who reduced us to mutters by her art.

That wasn't the end of it. At 5 P.M. there was "lunch" — sandwiches and beer; the sandwiches were made from the left-overs (mysteriously renewable resources, those roasts). And at about 8 P.M. we were at the table again for coffee cake and coffee, the little man in his turban and his coffee ecstasy and his pointed shoes set on the kitchen table as my grandmother scooped out the coffee and dumped it into a big enamel pot with a crushed eggshell. By then everyone was alive and laughing again, the torpor gone. My grandfather had been inviting the men, one by one, into the kitchen during the afternoon where he silently (the austere version of memory — but he must have talked, must have said *something*) handed them jiggers of whiskey, and watched them put the shot down in one swallow. Then he handed them a beer, which they took out in the living room. I gathered that the *little* drink in the tiny glass shaped like a beer mug was some sort of antidote for the *big* drink of beer. He sat on the chair in the kitchen with a bottle of beer on the floor next to him and played his concertina, allowing society to form itself around him — while he lived he was the center — but not seeking it, not going into the living room. And not talking. He held to his music and the kindly, medicinal administration of whiskey.

By evening, it seemed we could eat endlessly, as if we'd had some successful inoculation at dinner and could handle anything. I stayed in the kitchen after they all reformed in the dining room at the table for coffee cake. I could hear them, but the little man in his starry yellow robe was on the table in the kitchen and I put my head down on the oil cloth very near the curled and delighted tips of his pointed shoes, and I slept. Whatever laughter there was, there was. But something sweet and starry was in the kitchen and I lay down beside it, my stomach full, warm, so safe I'll live the rest of my life off the fat of that vast family security.

Sometimes, after dinner, I went out in the garden. My grandmother's garden had flowers that only grandmothers seem to grow. Snapdragons whose mouths she parted so I could see the thin stamens where the smoke would come from; delphinium and double daisies; floury white peonies with the faint begin-

nings of pink at the center that made them more beautiful than
gardenias, and red ones the plush color of a horsehair sofa;
bleeding hearts with the scary aptness of their names, an actual,
fascinating droplet dangling from the red and white heart-shaped
blossom: all those ancient perennials that put out their blossoms
every spring on time like cuckoos from a well-oiled clock.

It seems there were hydrangeas too, both pink and the stranger,
more lovely blue whose color is only suggested by the thought of
rain blurring ink on a tissue-paper letter. But maybe the hydrangeas were gift plants that she kept inside and I remember
them from there. She always had a menagerie of Christmas and
Easter and birthday plants — azaleas, poinsettias, lilies, chrysanthemums — which she kept alive long after they should have
been dead. Sometimes she would plunge one of these, clay pot
and all, into the garden for the summer, leaving the bright
ribbon it had come with tied to one stalk, where it wilted in the
rain and got muddy.

There were certainly lilacs in that garden and also puffballs,
big bushes of them that came out early in May with their
greeny-white clusters that bleached and opened a cream white
by Decoration Day (as it was always called in that house), and
in the fall became dust-colored dried flowers that my grandmother put with a bunch of yarrow or cornflowers. She had
tulips too — but first, crocuses that sometimes lived and other
years came up too soon and were killed by a late frost — tulips
and crocuses and any bulb she had planted in the fall like a
strange squirrel who hoards for spring, not winter.

She planted annuals too, pansies and petunias and blue lobelia
(for borders) and starry lantana that she planted from cartons
my father brought her from the greenhouse. There were dahlias
and zinnias; stunted carnations that smelled like ground cloves;
tiger lilies that didn't look like tigers although she would say,
"Look at the spots!" She had all the old-fashioned flowers that
seem always to have been old-fashioned, even to her: sweet
william and phlox, alyssum and pinks (which were not pink: no
explanation). There were gladiolas that looked like monstrous

flowering asparagus stalks; yellow chrysanthemums; and the white day lily with its crumbly pollen and explicit center. Sometimes there was a giant rangy weed that she didn't know was a weed until my father told her. Then she pulled it out regretfully because, after all, it didn't belong there; once, at least I know, she left it because it too had a beautiful wheellike flower and why should it go?

She managed to generate several microseasons in that garden out of the single rushed one Minnesota makes of spring and summer. Each of her seasons had its crop of flowers that gave way to another, different breed and then to another — from tulips to lilies to asters and petunias, through roses and more roses (which always required a scissors for cutting, though in general her hands were the instrument in that garden) until only things as sturdy as the mums and the dry red flames of the salvia were left in the shadowy corners by the shed. Finally even those were cut back or taken indoors, and she was back again on her knees burying the bulbs that would start it all over again next year.

In front of the house, which had hardly any yard, and along the fence leading to the large back yard were the hedges of bridal wreath. The blossoms were full and round like half-globes made of tiny stars, but they soon wilted and shed the little stars onto the table like flakes of rust off an old wheel rim. I wasn't supposed to pick them — whether because my grandmother knew they wouldn't last long or because she didn't want to puncture the white perfection of a bridal wreath hedge in bloom, I didn't know. But I dasn't pick them.

There weren't many rules in that garden, though, and none that carried harsh penalties. My grandmother had a dulled curiosity about the activities and safety of children that I'd never met with in any other grownup. I could run up the block without telling her and stand by the tracks waiting for the train to go by and wave at the conductor and at the hobos who sometimes waved back and smiled like kings in progress. Once — this was a mystery — a hobo frantically motioned me to quit waving.

I could wander around the block, and go up to the big green wooden fence that enclosed the old farmyard of the Bremer family. I put my ear to the high boards and listened to the cackling of the chickens that were still kept there, and, by lining up an eye with a crack between two boards or by jumping as high as I could, I tried to *see* those chickens strutting around in there; one of them was supposed to be entirely red, according to a boy who claimed to have seen it — though not everyone believed this story. Sometimes I thought there might be a cow or even pigs back there too. But there were only the chickens: everybody said so. Although Aunt Therese had said definitely: at one time goats and sheep had been kept there and the fence had only been a wire one; you passed the animals on your way to the streetcar, she said, as naturally as if they were people.

I could disappear for whole hours in the basement, puttering around among the Ball jar lids and wooden-handled tools; I could practically dematerialize and my grandmother wouldn't seem to notice or care. She had the blessed carelessness of a woman who has had a lot of children.

❧

Her real garden wasn't flowers. She loved the vegetables most of all. With five children and a husband who brought home twelve dollars a week, a vegetable garden was essential. Even when I knew her, which was past the time when the garden was a financial necessity, she spent a lot of time in the vegetable plot, which was always much bigger than the flower garden anyway. No weed, no matter how strange and wheellike, was allowed to remain long there.

Rhubarb, which was planted in a long row on one side of the big square garden, always came up first. The celerylike stems turned pinkish under the huge cabbage-leaf greenery before the peas or beans had even begun to flower. She took one of her murderous-looking carbon steel knives with a bleached wood handle and slit the rhubarb off near the ground and carried it, with the giant leaf dangling, to the hose, washed it and gave it to me. Then she went back and cut more, a big leafy pile for sauce or pies. Some years I asked too early and the rhubarb was green and sour and puckered my mouth. I learned to wait until the veins of the stalk had filled with sweeter juice and the stem was pinkish beneath the apple-green. I sat on the slant cellar door and munched the first raw rhubarb of the season and thought reverently, as if it were an idea, *it's summer, it's summer*.

The big vegetable plot was a minuscule southeast quadrant divided into grids by narrow paths, as the whole of the Midwest farmland is divided tidily into sections, as precisely square as if the earth were flat. The garden seemed dark but probably it wasn't, or not most of it. I must be thinking of the shadow cast by the two or three fruit trees, a shadow that only covered the front of the garden and was broken by its own open leafiness. They were small trees, an apple and a plum that produced large fruit with wine-colored skins whose flesh was yellow-orange inside, bright as a cantaloupe but with a wetter, less meaty texture. Maybe there was another plum tree too because it seemed that, in summer, the kitchen table always had a bowl heaped with smaller midnight-blue plums, their skins befogged as if they'd caught the first frost but hadn't begun to wither yet.

What grew in that garden, was eaten fresh, or, in later years, given away. The fruits and vegetables for canning were bought by my grandfather in bushel loads at the farmers' market downtown and brought home in a red coaster wagon. He walked all the way back home.

My grandmother, during the prime of her housekeeping years when canned goods were a new thing, had a vicious scorn for families who, as she put it, ate out of cans. Not to provide for your family *wholesome* food in your own kitchen by your own hand was barbaric. Once she pointed to a neighbor's trash bin and, seeing the telltale heap of cans, said significantly to my father, "The Kosaks eat out of cans." Nothing else was left to say about them.

By winter the dark cavelike fruit cellar, which was lined with sagging grayish wood shelves, was packed with jars of tom*ah*toes;

peaches and plums and apple sauce; jams and the jewels of clear jelly; and the two kinds of pickles that were always served as a Sunday dinner relish in the cut-glass divided dish, sweet disc-cut pickles that were sugary and vinegary in one taste and the softened garlic dills that were cut in narrow strips and packed with a russet-colored pepper that clung to the side of the pale-green jar like a red leech.

My grandfather stored his homemade dandelion wine there too. I never tasted it, but "dandelion wine," which was served, like the whiskey, in that intimate one-to-one portioning (only, for this, the women were included in the communion rite), suggested to me something marvelous, improbable, as if someone had said butter could be churned from tiger lily pollen. Like the chickens in the Bremer yard, the hobo with his balletic admonition to silence, the billowing brewery, that neighborhood with kitchen gardens and mashed languages, dandelion wine was alien, fantastical. Why everyday things glowed there, before I ever heard the word *nostalgia,* is unclear: a happy child should not be nostalgic. And I was happy. More than an adjective — in the way of my family, as an adored child I was happiness, the noun itself. I do not know how I had come upon the tainted sense of things being too good to be true. I suppose I was already one of James's natives, and I looked at that neighborhood, my dandelion wine–drinking family, and was alarmed — the observing native — wondering where had all this foreignness come from and where, as they threw the future deftly to me and my brother with their heedless love, they expected it to land. As if — the cold acknowledgment — our lives had anything to do with theirs.

❦

My nose remembers that garden, not my eyes. The eyes close at the moment of deepest sensation, and we are thrown on the precision of the more private, less communal, senses. Maybe the vegetable garden on Webster Street wasn't dark at all, even the fruit trees may not have shaded it. It may be dark because it has *become* dark. Or it was dark in its essential quality, the black earth and stern rows of its miniature farmishness. It is dark, anyway; it must be presented as dark.

The important growing was underground and hidden. As if that garden were given over to roots and bulbs, things that grew, as I thought, upside down, their fruits buried in the dirt like the dead. The food of that house was full of dark, fermenting things: sauerkraut in the cellar tub; beets from the garden that were maroon and whose leaves had maroon veins; bread that wasn't a uniform white (this was the beginning of the child-consumer: I walked away from the television into the kitchen and told my mother to get Wonder Bread because it made strong bodies grow eight ways), but a bread with flecks of caraway in its pale brown. The loaf was round, heavy and my grandmother held it to her bosom like a member of the family as she hacked off what was not a slice, but a hunk. There was something dark about that garden, as if those bulbous beets and all the other vaguely non-American vegetables were as forbidding, as wrong as the tulip bulbs my father, a florist who I figured knew, said that the Dutch people had ground up into flour and made into bread during the War.

I ate dirt there. This is the first taste I remember, besides the rhubarb — but even the rhubarb had crumbs of dirt on it. Al Radesky who owned the sweet shop on the corner by our house had once said, when I'd dropped a jawbreaker on the floor and picked it up and put it back into my mouth, "Well, you have to eat a peck of dirt before you die."

I said nothing, but it was one of those chance comments that divides a life, and for a time I was worried about how I would ever have the stomach to ingest my quota. I was haunted by a vivid picture of an old woman (myself), a bushel basket filled with dirt before her, spooning teaspoonful after vile spoonful into her mouth, crunching it down — all because I had not taken care of my allotment during the easy days of my youth, and they wouldn't let you die until you'd eaten it all up (death was that unreal). So I ate dirt. I also ate it out of curiosity, putting it on my tongue like brown sugar and waiting hopelessly for it to melt.

❧

I would like to take a bean, a yellow wax one from the white trellis at the back of the garden covered all over with sprawling bean vines, and snap it under your nose (the eyes are closed) and wait for the smile, the nod, that says I have written the perfect description. Or, with your eyes closed and your mouth open, I might pop the four green peas from a split pod right in a row into your mouth. And wait to hear how sweet they are, how you never tasted such grainless sugar, and can you have more, raw, right now, out of the garden, out of my hand.

But vegetables cannot be described. They are as essential as the dirt they grow from, the dirt I ate conscientiously in the garden, preparing for death. Her garden was huge and dark. It remains dark, unseen, undescribed. Her love of it, what she thought there, who she was (not that she thought or cared about being a *who*, being an individual; her allegiance was with the racial *what she was*), and what she knew and in which language she thought — it all remains dark and not mine. When you are poor, something that saves you money year in and year out is beloved; and, when that thing is alive and needs care, more so. And I don't see it entirely as coincidence that my father, the only son left her after Frank, has always been a florist, doing the essential work of the Northland: keeping the plants alive.

My grandmother left her garden undescribed, intact, untouched. Then suddenly (it seemed sudden), she was an old woman living in the apartment of our house, her own house was sold, and she was asking if she could plant a clump of chives in the window box; fresh chives for cottage cheese. She sneaked in a tomato plant at the end of my mother's rosebushes. She was a busybody about the roses themselves, hanging around and telling my mother how to cultivate them. She took to watering the roses with a whoosh of the hose early in the morning before anybody else was up, sending all the petals gushing into a sodden heap of pastel on the ground under their bald centers. "That one," she said to my frowning mother, "should have been picked yesterday." Tom*ah*toes in the daughter-in-law's roses, chives among the son's begonias. She got on everyone's nerves, the vegetable urge sprouting its persistent peasantry among the flowers of forward-looking children. It was her final garden.

The other garden, the real one, remains dark in its undescribed, curtained, memory. Dillweed, like a sensation, fills the air of the whole square plot with a scent that gets heavier and heavier as summer goes deeper. Dillweed and a clump of parsley that smells like finely ground pepper; dillweed with its pickle future lurking over the cucumbers. A fringed curtain of dillweed obscures that place sheerly with the pungency of its remembered scent: the eyes close. I can't get beyond it. I don't want to, just as we never really want to see the future, but just to glimpse its light and know that, like the past, it is securely there.

II

Beauty 🌿

1 ❦

OVER THE maroon horsehair sofa in my grandmother's
house where I took my afternoon nap, there was a picture
of a girl with black hair. She wore the kind of garment that is
not so much dress as drapery. It folded in dozens of deep creases,
and was a dark, hypnotic green. In her arms she held a lute. One
hand was draped over the strings near the sounding board's hole;
the other hardly seemed to exert any pressure on the frets. Her
hair was rich and heavy, like the dress; it was curled and tangled
beautifully, alluringly. She was an art nouveau figure, relaxed
in what looked to me like extra flesh, the arms just round
enough to suggest sausages and in that association to attach her
and her beauty to the plain earth, in spite of the fantasy of her
hair. She looked, except for the upholstery fabric of her dress,
like my grandmother in the wedding picture I had seen.

The girl's mouth was parted slightly. She might have been
meant to be singing, but I always thought the song had just
ended. Her gaze was not directed at me as I lay on the sofa,
looking up at her in the midafternoon half-light of the parlor.
Her gaze was higher, above me, pure and direct, undeflected.
I thought she was beautiful. It is to her I would like to tell these
things. Because she was beautiful. Beauty, like the past, was
what I sensed was missing. I must begin, as women do, with the
body.

Beauty, for my grandmother and my aunts, was divided like
a territory into estates, each part governed by a different seignior.

There were no alliances among the fiefdoms. A woman was not "beautiful," not even "pretty." It was more complicated than that. She had perfect skin, but her hands were bad; she had lovely brown eyes, but she was fat; her legs were good, but what are legs if your teeth are crooked? The body was a collection of unfederated states, constantly at odds with each other, recognizing no sovereign to sort out the endless clan feuds.

Only one kind of woman lived outside this feudal world. "Gertrude is a plain woman," one of my aunts would say musingly. And no discussion of parts took place. They stirred their tan coffee-and-cream, and fell silent for a moment in the grip of the ineffable. Gertrude's slate was wiped clean. Homeliness was a ticket to freedom, to a no-nonsense world where you walked around in a sober suit of sad flesh — the less said the better. You were out of the running in some absolute way, but you were free. The way a child feels when sent to bed with a cold: away from the bustle of the house, hardly human in the usual way.

My grandmother worked at her prettiness even as a very old woman. Sunday was the day of great dinners; it was also the day for beauty, when she went to church. I often walked with her up Webster Street the two blocks to West Seventh Street, where we turned right and went past the shops with their Czech and German family names closed blankly against business for one day. She usually wore a print dress of definite, not subtle, color. She always wore a hat. A serious one, too formidable for her small round self. It was often a dark two-layer cake of a hat with a net veil which she turned up over the crown like a pouf of meringue, the inevitable return of the food motif. The veil gave an incongruous dash of airiness to the solid helmet which she wore dead center, pulled down carefully over a forehead which, she said as she pulled on the hat, was too high and had to be "lowered," as if the body were a problem for an architect to resolve.

She walked proudly, her short legs perilously bowed; she'd had rickets as a child. Rickets — a disease I didn't think of anybody getting anymore, at least not in St. Paul; children in India maybe and other remote places, but not here. I knew nothing of real poverty any more than I did of the past. Those rickets-bowed legs were another sliver of her foreignness and it did not occur to me that such things existed near to home.

Her face, with the exquisite skin that was made more perfect rather than ruined by its map of wrinkles, had been rouged and powdered with a dusty puff before we left the house. Her mouth looked like two mouths, superimposed. One was the larger, thin-lipped, undermouth of mauve flesh, the other was a surprised little red mouth of lipstick set on the first like a cartoon kiss. This red mouth never stayed long, faded gradually, but it was always bright and fresh as we began our walk. It was flirtatious like the mouth of a girl in a silent movie. It must have been her version of beauty, the lifelong belief that each generation has in its own idea of loveliness. For her, it was the surprised — but only half-surprised — innocence of the pursed mouth on the silent screen sometime before the Great War. She kept it all her life.

From her faithfulness to the ritual, I gathered very early on that beauty might fade, but never a woman's allegiance to beauty. No one in our family spoke about sex, but beauty was discussed endlessly. The body was an endless topic and, as far as you could tell from our conversations, the body's purpose was beauty, not sex. I became fascinated very early by style, the road to beauty.

Children must be natural stylists, small but discriminating aesthetes. How often is the adored bachelor uncle, the passionately admired girlfriend of one's mother, any visitor to the house that a child hangs on a person with some kind of elegance, no matter how tattered. Sometimes it is only the nonchalance, the carelessness of the self-absorbed that wins children; this may account for the seemingly perverse habit children have of adoring those who neglect them: the beautiful, thoughtless mother, the roué father. It is as if a child, even a child who has suffered neglect in this way, understands that man does not live by kindness or love alone, that hell is paved with the good intentions of better people, maybe even with their good deeds, and that the brutality of beauty bespeaks a higher, more mysterious, calling. To be called to beauty, as if to a vocation, is a turning aside from the triviality of daily life, to go up the steeper gradient of perfection and the abstract.

My Aunt Lillian was such a heroine for me — except that she wasn't cruel and didn't neglect me. She was Uncle Frank's twin sister, the remaining, female, half of that élan everybody loved.

I did not like to call my aunt by her nickname — Lill. I wanted her to have the whole name, to luxuriate as God intended her to in languorous, pillowlike syllables. Lillian, Aunt Lillian. A name I found it impossible not to linger over, a name that seemed to beg for a French accent — and got one, from me at least. "Aunt Lill-i-*an*," I said, even at nine sliding into the lazy lu-lu tones of a cosmopolitan. "Ye-es," she replied, in two perfectly unrushed syllables. And that was all. Just her *ye-es* to my *Lill-i-an*. All the time in the world — that seemed to be what she, for her part, was cooing with her *ye-es*, a practically Southern drawl. She never said, bluntly, as adults did, "What do you *want?*" Just that languorous, patient affirmation to which I needn't reply in words. Style.

I was under the impression that she and her husband, Uncle Bill, were phenomenally, unspeakably rich. Rich to the point of hush, stupefied by money and transformed by a blow of silver into purely ethereal creatures. They had died to the old man, to mere economy, and had been born again, angels, spenders.

I don't know why I thought this, where in the modest indulgences of their life I found the idea of wealth. Maybe I thought *somebody* had to have money. When I was very young they lived in the tiny apartment on Webster Street that had originally been a kind of lean-to attached to my grandparents' house. The two households were connected by the bathroom they shared. My aunt worked as a secretary downtown. Uncle Bill, at this time, had only been out of the army and home from the War for a few years. He was a salesman for a small firm that sold big machines to the railroads — cranes, I think, or things like cranes. His work involved taking people to lunch. He didn't talk anybody into buying anything. He just went to lunch and waited for them to call. Then he sent them their crane. Maybe it was the going to lunch in restaurants that caused me to decide he and my aunt were rich.

Uncle Bill loved trains. We sat in the dark, I on the steps, he watering the lawn as the bright moss roses closed tightly against the dew, and he recited to me the names of the trains, their runs, their schedules, where the train that *used to* be called the Chief or the Ram had once run. "Ah," he would say, "*that* was the line — through Mankato and out to Worthington by sunrise. You could get fresh squeezed orange juice and watch the sun come up over the turkey sheds. You'd sit in the dining car and think they were on fire. But," he said, as if it still amazed him and was improbable, "they weren't on fire."

His Minnesota was a complex system of ingeniously laid tracks, arriving at strange destinations ("that used to be a thriving community, *thriving*"), in cool revenge bypassing a farming town that "hadn't treated the railroad right," a town now cast aside and left in its folly he said, sloshing the hose over the closed moss roses, to *wither away*.

Uncle Bill fit into our family beautifully; he was crazy about the past too. And maybe because he and Aunt Lillian had no children, they did not look into the future with much real interest. They held to the past and recited their youths to each other. They loved the past as if they owned it. And I loved that. I often stayed overnight at their house on weekends.

While I was still in grade school they bought a house in a newer, solidly middle-class neighborhood, not on the hill, but rather past or beyond it, in a newer area that did not hold to the severe hierarchical topography of old St. Paul. There was a large, grassy yard (no vegetable garden), an apple tree, moss roses, tidiness. The exercise of good taste was practiced here as if it was the pursuit of happiness.

Maybe it is this that explains my belief in their phenomenal wealth: their taste. That, and the fact that my uncle had a pair of brown-and-white "spectator" shoes. The white upper of the shoe made a sort of lattice, as if a tiny rose trellis had been laid on each foot. He wore his spectator shoes only "during the summer months," never past Labor Day. The extravagant, spotless white and the careful observation of the season were indications to me of the style to which he and Aunt Lillian devoted themselves. Or maybe my devotion was inspired by the shoetrees made of golden wood that rested their smooth fists in the leather of the spectator shoes through the long nonsummer months, deep in Uncle Bill's "wardrobe." I was dazzled by these unnecessary details, but I think the shoes, even the shoetrees, were only emblems of the marvel, not the marvel itself. Style was the marvel, slicing the world into fine wedges, unnecessarily delicate but pleasant to the taste. My aunt and uncle were aesthetes. The art of living was their form. They made much of — of nothing, I suppose, if I look at things steadily.

They drove into the country on Saturday mornings, myself in the back seat of the Buick (another sign of their wealth). They drove many miles, trying to remember all the words to "Glow, little glowworm, glimmer, glimmer"; they went to a place called Ghostley's Egg Farm, the Ghostley family with their apt name tending the spooky chickens and the hosts of the never-to-be-born. They drove all that way not just to buy their eggs, but to *choose* them. Mrs. Ghostley displayed the dozens in their spongy cardboard boxes and my aunt said, "Oh not these, I don't know . . . How about *those*, Mrs. Ghostley?" And my uncle, who loved my aunt to distraction, I think, only truly relaxed when she had found her perfect, pale but not white — never white — ovals. On the drive back, he sang "The shrimp boats are acomin', there'll be a party tonight" all the way through and my aunt hummed, holding her cartons on her lap.

My father said it was nonsense, driving so far for eggs. "They're no fresher than store eggs," he said. "Everybody knows that. Those chickens are drugged just like the rest of them," he told my uncle, as if he were satisfied to announce the ubiquity of poison in our lives.

My uncle was ashamed, I think, before my father, the un-yielding male intellect. "They are fresher," he said belligerently, sheepishly. "We find them fresher."

"We like the ride," Lillian said airily, not stooping to any male practicalities about groceries.

On and on they went, my aunt and uncle, making much of little, grooming the savage day, reclaiming it from its rush to oblivion, slowing it, relaxing it under the delicate massage of their careful fingers. Breakfast was "served" and those two always "dined." Snacks were taken from china plates, my humdrum drink of milk got its own heavy lead-glass tumbler. Linen napkins — of course. And napkin rings. It was an exhausting attention to detail which, amazingly, seemed to invigorate them.

Picky, picky, picky, my mother said. She kept to her plain ways, and blessed the fate that had made her a housewife, as she put it, "in the frozen food age." But I was all admiration: the Ghostley eggs, pale beige shells almost pink with life *were* fresher. I noted, as my uncle directed me to, how the yolk *stood up* from the doily of the basted white. I untwirled my linen napkin from its silver holder in passionate imitation of a style which I sensed this minor gesture only began to intimate. A life, I felt, was beyond.

I was cast down briefly in high school when I learned in English class that this life had a name: aestheticism. And an age: late Victorian. Even a dismissive adjective: decadent. So the art of living exquisitely was not, after all, a good thing. Part of my fascination with the art of living probably was the illusion all the busyness unconsciously created of there being no end, no death, just the eternal procession along the avenue of small rituals.

I wasn't after domesticity. Very early I adopted a bohemian (certainly not Bohemian) contempt for the household, choosing crystal, choosing husbands. And in those I admired — Aunt Lillian, Uncle Bill — I did not see the fiercely domestic passion, the timidity of two loving housekeepers adrift in a careless universe. I concentrated instead on their exercise of taste and saw it as the exercise of freedom. To live for beauty — in beauty —

was to live in liberty, one choice after another. This was more appealing and more comprehensible than the Loyolan idea of losing one's life in order to gain it. There was religion in my secular creed — and of course I had no idea of it as a creed. I just shopped.

Window-shopped, for the most part, in neighborhood second-hand shops, or shoppes. At twelve or fourteen, I wandered into these dusty rooms, fingering the pale china painted with flowers in some Dutch or Italian pottery factory. I seriously inquired about prices, with a quarter in my uniform pocket. The elderly female clerks were kind and nervous, wandering a few steps behind me but saying nothing, perhaps unable to decide if I brought trouble in the form of theft or breakage. But I never broke anything and stealing was out of the question. Once I bought a little china inkwell, rose-colored with a sprig of violets. It cost fifty cents. But I was not allowed to keep it in my desk at school because, my teacher told me, it was an antique and belonged at home.

The glamour that I sensed touched my Aunt Lillian's life and which I pursued in imitation was somehow related to a sense of the past. Not simply that the past itself was glamorous; nostalgia was only the surface, hardly the deep parallelism I acknowledged, the twinnishness I saw in the faces of beauty and history. I responded to Aunt Lillian's glamour as I did to any indication of history that came my way from the stories my father and the rest of the family told about the Depression, the gangsters, the low prices of yesteryear: here, in my aunt's pursuit of style was something which, although apparently made of the immediate stuff of this world (eggs and napkin rings, shoetrees and summer shoes), was in fact slightly out of this world, an emblem for the vibrating aura of things. I did not, of course, see this at the time. Beauty and history were not so much related in my mind, as they were the same thing, the thing I wanted and had at the time no name for. They were metaphor. I had to have beauty, I had to have history: they transformed. Later I had to have poetry for the same reason. The hunger for metaphor is surprisingly ferocious. Language, which is a warehouse that displays our desires without guile, proves that it is so. "What was it *like?*" we say when we really want to know the truth of something. We don't say, "What *is* it?" What it *is* is nothing, is hardly the point. What it is like — that is the metaphoric reality, the ripple of seemingly discrete things into each other, the field theory of life, of transformation. And that, we sense — language senses — is *it*.

I wandered through department stores behind my dreamy, yet purposeful aunt, stalking with her the expanding rudiments of style, hunting down what gorgeousness we could, stopping only for lunch in the Sky Room of Dayton's Department Store. There, on the twelfth floor, high above the pile of merchandise, nearer to heaven, we would take our time over lunch because, Aunt Lillian said, we had been working hard.

We sat at a table, a rounded banquette holding us and our purchases. The bags and boxes always had their own segment of the upholstered seat, as if they constituted a third person. Aunt Lillian encouraged me to order from the full luncheon menu, citing again the morning's hard work.

"Do I have to eat my creamed onions?" I once asked sullenly.

There was the brief, puzzled pause of the childless woman, far enough removed from riding herd over a ten-year-old that she found the question unanswerable at first, the kind of abstruse problem only mathematicians or Eastern religions bothered with. When she recognized it as a child's challenge to authority, she still could not quite play the game. She gave what, at the time, I considered the most eccentric possible answer. "You musn't eat," she said, "what you don't like." Mustn't. Not the aristocratic spirit of my grandmother's dasn't. Mustn't. Another duty style demanded. Fantastic. "But," my aunt added, "creamed onions are an elegant vegetable."

This was the first appearance on my horizon of what I later learned were critical standards. I looked down at my plate, at the despised onions pooled next to the acceptable Salisbury steak and the luminous round of mashed potato with its volcanic depression glowing with melted butter. The onions were different, just slightly different now. It wasn't just me and the creamed onions anymore in our wordless stand-off. Now it was me, the creamed onions, and the creamed onions' reputation. I did not eat them; I did not give in so easily. But it was something new — how I, because I did not *like* creamed onions, must not eat them . . . and yet they were elegant. Beauty was not, after all, in the eye of the beholder, not just any beholder. The way of style, of beauty, was not an easy road, not just a matter of opinion. There were givens. Here was authority greater than the parental one I had known. Aunt Lillian might not care about my relation to creamed onions qua creamed onions (unlike my mother who propped me up in front of congealing breakfasts in a test of wills), but, about the place of creamed onions in the world, my aunt was firm. They ceased to be domestic and began to be cultural.

In the afternoon we continued our shopping. I was logy and listless, sated from lunch, and I drooped against posts or curled up in chairs in the fitting rooms or in the model living rooms Aunt Lillian always visited, drifting by the mock-ups like a spy taking her notes. On the rare occasions my brother came with us, the afternoons were torture. He was worn out by then, listless from the heavy lunch — his only reason for coming along — and he lacked my passion for style. Once, when his whining had gotten him nowhere and Aunt Lillian stepped up her pace, adding Bedding and Towels to his troubles, he sat down on a chair in Better Dresses and simply wept, the tears of boredom gushing down his cheeks.

But I was happy and followed my aunt wherever she went. The whole enterprise suggests entombment, I suppose: we arrived at 9 A.M. when the store opened, checked our coats in a locker in the ladies' lounge, and methodically covered every inch of the largest department store in Minneapolis until, at 5:30 P.M., we retrieved our coats, and departed to the sound of some loudly clanging clear-out bell, from a door already locked to incoming customers, which was opened by a custodian leaning on a large broom, smoking a cigarette, waiting to begin his sweep. Uncle Bill waited outside at the curb in his Buick, ready to hear of our day.

Aunt Lillian always shopped in Minneapolis, another essential facet of her otherness, her glamour. Another indication of her wealth certainly, for in some strange algebra of my own, I felt that Minneapolis, being bigger than St. Paul, must cost more. In my own family shopping in Minneapolis was frowned upon: "You make your money in St. Paul, you spend it here; why go to Minneapolis?" But this only heightened the charm of our shopping trips, of Aunt Lillian, of any affectation at all. Even then, I had become a firm believer in the greater greenness of faraway grasses.

2 ❧

T HE POWER OF beauty, the authority of loveliness. I must
have sensed that, like music, physical beauty has an overpowering command. It asserts itself without any apparent effort,
without conscious thought. In the way that music is more absolute than literature, beauty has more authority than intelligence.
Beauty is ineffable, a gift, a grace. It is a rule-breaker.

All of which makes fashion particularly comical, but also
deeply touching: it is in this striving that we are human.
Through it we expose our avidity and powerlessness as women.
Beauty itself is somehow inhuman and masterful, and its essential quality is aloofness. For a woman, in the world of fashion
there are no masters, only slaves. On one of my shopping trips
with my aunt I remember seeing a stout woman, about forty,
before a mirror in the ladies' lounge. She ran the red grease
roller of her lipstick swiftly across her lips, blotted them neatly
with a square of toilet paper, and then stood for a brief, frank
moment before the mirror. She smiled slightly. An amused
smile — there was no possibility of a satisfied smile. Amused at
the relentless, pointless striving behind it all. She wanted — or
she had probably started out wanting — to be beautiful. Like my
grandmother, she had come to know *what she was*, although
her method was different. My grandmother knew *what she was*
as an immigrant, this woman before the mirror in the ladies'
lounge knew, had learned, as an unbeautiful woman.

Once a salesclerk at a cosmetic counter told me, "I know

I'm not beautiful, but I think we all should *try*, don't you?"
She wanted to show me how to make up my eyes, she said. And
I wanted, suddenly, passionately, to learn.

"You wouldn't believe," she said as she sketched and patted
and buffed, looking at me as no one ever has — as if I were
impersonal clay — "how many women think they're *nothing*
because they aren't beautiful. They come here, they pick up
something. They don't *say* it, but you can tell. I try to show
them something else. I give them this eye cream — it's made out
of good ingredients. I say, try it. Or the facial mask. Or the false
eyelashes. I wear them myself. Maybe they'll feel better. They're
somebody. They've made an effort. I see myself as helping other
women. I'm a women's libber, put it that way. They should feel
better about themselves. But," she said severely, standing back,
assessing me and my new, startled, eyes, "you have to try."

But trying is exactly what beauty is not. Beauty is the absence of effort. It is the casualness that announces: this person
is special, was *born* special. And deserves — deserves what? Why
does beauty elicit the desire to pay homage? The Trojan War
was fought not simply because a woman was stolen: a beautiful
woman was stolen. Something beautiful was taken from the
nation and could not be lived without. The Greeks didn't fight
only over a woman, certainly not over a rape, but over the possession by the nation of supreme beauty, the nonpareil.

Physical beauty is priceless, perhaps because it states emphatically, without the machinery of language or even of
thought, the divinity we feel within us. Beauty is the evidence
of the divine possibility that is real but hidden, obscured and
reduced most of the time in most lives.

The striving for personal beauty, which women have, traditionally, seen as their work is really, like all regimens of excel-
lence, a striving for perfection, for a triumph over death. The
irony, of course, is that death is itself perfection. It is the
stillness of unwavering form, the finish, the completion. Perfection is the subject of all women's magazines and, although
the confines may widen or narrow according to fashion (it is

now possible, I recently read, to have "furry, sexy legs" *or* "sleek, smooth legs": the former vaguely feminist, the latter "the traditional feminine look"), there it is always before us: the goal of perfection and of control.

The striving for beauty is a way to feel powerful, to control the world. It is completely engrossing; it breaks the world up, as my grandmother and aunts and I did, into morsels that can be attended to one at a time: fingers, nails, toes, eyebrows, eyelids (eyelid creme: I have a tiny jar, yellowing like rancid mayonnaise, from the day at the cosmetic counter), on and on, tirelessly, over the vast steppes and plains of the body, through its tangled hair, over the distressing angles and bulges of elbows and stomach. It is a sweet slavery, beauty itself rising beyond like the gorgeous mirage cities pioneers used to see quivering on the horizon of their desolate homesteads. It is a frontier that is never broken, where one is always, everlastingly, riding one's starving horses over the same endless prairie, the huge task still beyond.

I have never met a woman who felt she was beautiful — and I know beautiful women. Or if a woman admitted she was "attractive" (never "beautiful"), who took pleasure in it. ("I'm pretty, all right, I am. But people aren't interested in me for *myself*," etc., etc.) I suppose this means that it is not possible to be masterful and beautiful, only enslaved and beautiful. Beautiful women who are said — usually by other women — to "use" their beauty and who seem, as a result, powerful, often are genuinely guileless, unconscious, displaying an insouciance that enrages other women; the beautiful woman emerges not simply victorious but clean, while her helpless rival comes out covered with spite — most unattractive. Such women — who often seem, oddly enough, beautiful after the fact, beautiful after the misery they have caused (before, they were merely "nice looking," "pretty": friendly, disinterested words) — are something like scientists who certainly don't feel they *possess* electricity and don't even know what it *is*, but find to their surprise that the thing *works*. Women who use their beauty *are* quite innocent —

which accounts for their success, their fragility, their bewilderment in the face of direct confrontation. I am talking of course about the kind of using one's beauty that *is* unconscious, that involves friendships and affairs, triangles and betrayal and despair. A woman who makes $200 an hour as a model is another matter.

The pursuit of beauty, and beauty itself, hold a ghostly power over most women (even youth — "a younger woman" is usually translated to mean a more beautiful one). The rituals of beauty are confused rituals of self-love and purification. The shaving of one's legs is an example of this double-edged ritual: one must rid oneself of hair, of that coarse, unruly *growth;* this is purification. But one is also paying the greatest attention to the intimate body, to the care of detail, the sensuous, stroking touch; this is self-love.

But above it all is the sense of striving for perfection, a world that is static and yet not dead. Like the family pictures from the past where history allows us to live and yet be fixed in something beyond mortal flesh, beyond self, the pursuit of beauty attempts to turn self-absorption itself into an impersonal form.

Radical feminism, with its attentive, acute, sometimes dogmatic, interpretation of acts, encounters, moments, according to a sexual theory, is perhaps deeply grasped as a theory meant to break the bonds of the ritual of personal beauty. It is particularly judgmental on just this issue. The fact that fashion magazines are now writing in their manic way about the possibility of having "furry, sexy legs" is what is known as co-option of a movement. Put another way, it is evidence of the inevitable filtering of a large idea which occurs in a mass society.

I am putting aside, here, the attempt to create theory. I want to dwell on the idea of beauty as I have on the idea of the past. It cannot mean nothing that the primary identity for women has been related to beauty. What *are* you? The peerless singing beauty that hung over the horsehair sofa where I took my naps, where later I read my endless novels that put me to sleep in a

· 99 ·

different way, that girl in my grandmother's house rises up not only in her beauty but in her slow, vacant serenity, the inarticulate woman asleep in beauty.

The strange adjective of the fashionable woman: *smart*. As in, "Smart women never wear mink before five." (I first heard this statement, incredibly, from a nun.) Sometimes, in newspaper society pages, the adjective slips off the woman and adheres not to her but to her proxy, her clothes: "Mrs. Eldredge wore a smart black moiré gown last night at the . . ." It is an adjective which suggests that fashion, not sex, is the fulfillment of the female body, the act that gives it coherence, integrity, purpose, even intelligence. There is something hard and predatory about the aggressively well-dressed woman.

The "smart woman" who is "making a statement": it might be the cutline beneath the portrait of a new feminist. But of course the relation is wholly ironic. A woman who is wearing an absurdly expensive fur coat and $250 boots into which she has tucked her designer jeans, is not necessarily smart. She may not even be rich; the flashy extravagance of shop girls and secretaries is legendary, stereotypical, and therefore sometimes quite true.

I was such a one, wandering like a dreamer through Dayton's (without my aunt this time, in the St. Paul store) on my lunch hour from my first job. I worked on the night copy desk of the *St. Paul Pioneer Press*. It was 1968; by coincidence, my scant year as a journalist was packed with news, events, disasters. Martin Luther King was assassinated, then Robert Kennedy (the St. Paul late edition got it, the *Minneapolis Tribune* didn't: someone on our desk got a bonus); President Johnson announced he would not seek reelection; Andy Warhol was shot. And then one night in August, when I was sent into the clattery wire-machine room to get the latest report from the weather bureau for the rural edition, I stopped by the Associated Press wire and held the gray paper that came out of the machine like a scroll, and read that Warsaw Pact troops were crossing the border of Czechoslovakia. It felt like a personal telegram;

standing there, watching the words form — from where, written by whom? — on the sheet, I had the absurd sensation that I was the first person in the world to know, as if there were no television, no radio, and I held the European message in my hand, as unpublished as the weather forecast for north-central Minnesota.

My job at the paper was to mark paragraphs, correct grammar, write headlines, and sometimes put together a News Briefs column from the wire services. But for the most part, it was headlines. My best headline, which had the technical charm of being "a perfect count" — that is, the letters filled the available column width exactly on each line — was written after Pope Paul VI made a particularly strong statement — an encyclical — against birth control. It read

POPE WON'T
SWALLOW PILL

It was rejected, of course.

The work was easy, tedious, and I liked everyone who worked on "the desk"; they were men, older than I. (*"Everybody's older than you,"* one of them said; I was almost twenty-two.) They were kind, the fathers of large families. They laughed at my prize headline, but they were craftsmen and they would not have thought me clever if the count had not been perfect. They were decent, humble but sardonic, and were in the not upwardly mobile position of having the grammar of the English language as the passion of their hearts. They loved looking up words in the dictionary, and patiently explained to me over and over, as my eyes glazed and I became stupid, the rules governing the use of the subjunctive. When the copy boy came around to take dinner orders, the men with the largest families pulled out brown bags packed at home or metal lunch pails with thermos bottles like workers; the rest of us, rich and single, bought the damp, steamy "hot dagos" from DiGidio's Bar and Bowling

Alley and threw our dimes away heedlessly on the coffee from the vending machines on the floor below us where the printing plant was located.

We ate "on the desk," marking the copy and leaving our greasy fingerprints on the porous paper. But the lunch hour itself we each spent as we wanted, not eating, but on break. Some people read; others, caught in the tireless embrace of words, quietly worked the crossword puzzle. One man prepared his weekly column on stamp collecting for the Sunday paper. Another plugged in his blender which he'd brought from home and he whirred up health drinks that were cottony with bran flakes. I, however, shopped. At least on the two nights of the week, Monday and Thursday, that the downtown stores were open at night.

I seemed to be the only one in the stores, the merchandise and the bored clerks with their arms propped on the showcases positioned there for me alone, the solitary shopper of the night. I lost paycheck after paycheck to the soft fantasy of fashion on those nights, while my comrades stayed safely on the desk, reading their spy novels, working their crosswords, checking the box scores, arguing politics (Eugene McCarthy was running for the Democratic nomination, and on my days off I went clean for Gene — I was clean anyway — and knocked on doors in Wisconsin towns where a primary was held.) They stayed on the desk, saving their money. But I threaded my way through the maze of boutiques that cleverly, phonily, evoked the color and brio of a street bazaar, although every cash register was wired to the single credit department above. I knew and didn't care. I spent and spent.

I bought homely, mismatched things; sometimes, they were breathtakingly expensive and my mother gasped when I came home and modeled them for her. "You went *there?*" she said, gesturing to the black bag of a deadly elegant little shop, appalled at my audacity. Sometimes I almost cackled with greed at how cheap I'd gotten a rumpled wool skirt at the bottom of a basement clearance table. I seemed to have no taste or common sense, no ruling principle. I bought absurd things I never wore or wore only as a kind of penance (you bought it, now you wear it). It occurred to me that I didn't have Aunt Lillian's knack and was devoid of taste.

But the whole enterprise was too dreamlike and compulsive to have anything to do with taste. I see the vacant, ungrasping faces of the evening clerks of Dayton's, not eager, not even interested, in my money. And there I am, rushing and crazed, careening through the aisles in my forty-five minutes, frantic to make a purchase. I scrambled in and out of my clothes three or four times a night in different fitting rooms, exhausted and steamy by the time I got back to the newspaper.

All I knew was that some gnawing hunger abated briefly when I left Better Blouses clutching the smooth beige bag lit from within by a silk shirt that was possibly perfect. I've sometimes thought it was the bag alone I was after: the evidence of purchasing power, the badge of the consumer. Maybe it was, partly. The bags of great department stores and, even more, those of elegant small shops seem to me the seizable emblems of those aloof, intractable places. Like Dexter Green in Fitzgerald's "Winter Dreams," maybe I "wanted not association with glittering things and glittering people," but, as he did, "the glittering things themselves."

But it was more than the crisp bag, and more than the object within it. It was the elevated sphere of the perfect that I sought, away from the grimy newsroom and what had turned out, to my snobbish sorrow, not to be a glamorous occupation after all, but a disspirited tending of wire-service machines and the tedious grammar work that wasn't much different from the sentence diagramming I'd done in third grade. I bought stupidly, things that either didn't fit or didn't suit me, and depleted my salary so that at the end of six months I had nothing at all, because I wasn't buying clothes. I was after the abstract.

I was always the last person back at the desk after the lunch hour, the next wad of copy already laid at my place where I left my welter of soft copy pencils. Nobody ever complained.

I was the mascot. Or maybe, after all their years and all their economies, they understood. "Well," one of them would say as I rushed in, "and what did you get tonight?" They all paused briefly, and smiled, and said it was pretty, whatever bright rag I pulled out of my smooth bag.

3 🦋

THE DIFFERENT kinds of beauty got mixed up in my mind, confused. There was first the beauty of the female face and body which was a cruelty that neither I nor any woman (especially girls) troubled by its elusiveness can believe is lodged democratically in the eye of the beholder. Then there was the sheer beauty of the natural world, and the made beauty of art, and the comforting, familiar beauty of one's own culture — if you could find it, if it existed. Finally, there was the beauty that was method, that wasn't actually beauty at all but the deep craving caused by the lack of the other kinds, the willingness to be enslaved by sensibility: the life sentence of the bourgeois woman.

The confusion of these different sorts of beauty, which I tried (unsuccessfully, largely unconsciously) to unsort, I now see as the point of my obsession rather than a mess to be cleared up. How *do* such things get confused? How has female physical beauty, the metaphor women have been required to embody, been confused by me (in me) with art, or even with the traditional American greed and the recent acknowledgment of our ruin of the natural beauty of the continent, and with the American insecurity over culture? My sources are odd, sometimes trivial, but they embody the obsession, the confusion. They are *what they are*.

I have even made lists, rudimentary charts, looking for the relation among these different strands, reasons for the confusion, for the root of the obsession that has connected these things in my mind. Did it begin with Sister Mary Patricia, who taught us Modern European History (which was not modern: the textbook stopped with the end of the Hapsburg Empire, and was itself bound in green watery moiré, a book not only about but from a former time). Sister told us one day that Hans Christian Andersen, the fairytale man, was supposed to have driven through the streets of Prague, hanging lovesick out his carriage window, smitten with the beautiful Czech girls, crying, "Pretty maiden, pretty maiden, let me kiss you!" In passing, Sister mentioned that Bohemian women were considered the most beautiful in Europe. She was a history teacher who could be counted on for this kind of satisfyingly useless remark.

I raised my hand.

"Yes, Patricia," she said.

I stood up — we had to rise to recite, giving our classrooms a churchy up-and-down quality — and I said, as if in a dream, fatally unconscious, "I'm Bohemian."

Everyone hooted. Even Sister, kindly poker face, smiled and said, "Well, is that so." As I sat down, almost before the room filled with laughter, I came to myself out of that momentary ethnic trance. I couldn't believe I'd actually stood up — braces, pointy glasses, pimples — and said what I'd said.

As a rule, I thought of myself as monumentally ugly. Was I in fact as homely as I thought? Impossible. But the mere thought of my looks inflamed my imagination and caused me to see myself as a freak — for no particular reason, simply because I had a physical existence. Like many people obsessed by their appearance, I had no idea what I actually looked like. I was afraid of photographs as if they were evidence brought forward by the prosecution. I studied the mirror solemnly and then, minutes later away from its image, was dismayed to realize I could not remember what the girl in the glass looked like. It was a typical adolescent self-consciousness, but it seemed to last forever. In fact, can I truly say it is finished? Writing about it as an adolescent preoccupation only seems to place it in the past.

I was probably — to use my mother's sane phrase — nice enough looking. My mother was not obsessed by beauty and thought a woman had done her level best if she "put on her face," kept her hair decently combed, and manicured her nails once a week. Perfume, lipstick, nail polish were not, for her, rituals of self-love; they were the spit-and-polish discipline of a good soldier who kept to the forms. She spent no time worrying about the face and body fate had dealt her: they were "nice enough." Beauty was another realm, something that, like inherited wealth, struck rarely — and to other, stranger, beings. Unlike my grandmother and aunts, my mother did not ponder the elusive qualities of beauty, did not ache to be gorgeous — at least, not as far as I knew. Why bother — she looked nice enough. Those who *were* beautiful were, in my mother's cosmology, a joy for the rest of us to behold, not our competition. And in our family it was my father who, everyone agreed, was the beauty. "Handsome as a movie star," my mother's friends would sigh. For a while in first grade I was under the impression that he was president of the United States (he was president of the church Men's Altar Guild that year, I believe). It seemed natural that someone so handsome should run the country.

My father was not only handsome. As a florist he was, to me, somehow in charge of beauty. A man "handsome as a movie star" whose business was beauty. In second grade, when we were given an assignment to find out how our fathers' work "helped the community," I went home with foreboding, sensing that my father's work did not help the community in any way, that in fact it was superfluous to the community. As I saw it, children whose fathers were doctors or house painters, for instance, were home free. But my father's occupation struck me as iffy, lightweight, positively extraneous and therefore (to my Catholic puritan logic) not useful to the community.

I felt this foreboding in spite of the fact that I loved the greenhouse and often played in the palmhouse (which was Africa). I once saw a rabbit give birth to her babies in the root cellar, and in the summer I trailed my finger teasingly across the low pool in the back lot where the goldfish — some of them alarmingly large — and the water plants were kept. In winter I wandered through the moist houses, as each glassy room was called, watching the exotic trick my father played on the Minnesota weather. I read the labels on the huge, ancient rose trees and great geranium plants in expensive pots, which wealthy matrons had left in the greenhouse to be cared for while they went to Florida or Arizona, or, the really ethereal ones, to Italy.

The odor of crushed evergreen, the intense little purple berries of juniper, the fans of cedar and the killing hard work of the Christmas rush *were* Christmas to me. I preferred this marketplace Christmas, full of overworked employees and cross tempers and the endless parade of "gift plants" and boxed cut flowers, to our own family Christmas with its ordinary tree and turkey like everybody else's.

But was any of this of use to the community? Did it do any good? I did not want to put my father on the spot. Still, I had the assignment and I asked my question, beginning first with the innocuous part: what, exactly, was his job? He answered at great and technical length; he loved his work.

Then the real question: "Is your job of any use to the community?" I had decided to word it this way, rather than asking *how* it was useful, sensing as I did that it was of no use whatever. I thought that he could simply say, as painlessly as possible, no. And then we'd just drop the subject. My handsome father, who had been enjoying the interrogation, the opportunity to explain his place in the world, frowned. "What do you mean — is it of any use to the community?" he asked sharply.

"I mean, does it do any good — to the community?" I was flustered and was losing hold of what community meant. I was only eight and the whole thing was beginning to unravel as I saw my movie star father frowning at me.

"Who asked you to ask that?"

"Sister. Sister said," I practically cried, falling back on the Catholic school child's great authority.

"Sister," my father said. He was angry. It was as I had thought: he served no use to the community. He was silent for some time, not weighing his words, but apparently deciding whether to speak at all.

"You tell Sister," he finally said, coldly, as if he were talking to an adult, "I do the most important thing for the community. Do you think people can live without beauty? Flowers — do they kill anybody? Do they hurt anyone? Flowers are beautiful — that's all. That's enough. So they're sending you home to find out what's the *use!* You tell her they're beautiful. Tell her I bring beauty to the community." He said the final word with regal contempt, as if he only used the grimy jargon of Sister and her band of philistines for purposes of argument.

It was less than ten years after the Second World War; the Korean "conflict" was just ended. My father wasn't talking to me, not to an eight-year-old, and probably not to a nun with a "unit on work" in her social studies class. He spoke, I think, to himself, in a cry for values, dismayed that the use of a red rose had to be explained, as if my question were proof that the world had been more brutalized than he had known.

The confusion I had about the types of beauty might have come a little later, in 1966, when I wrote my first published book review, for the university newspaper. The book was *Ariel* by Sylvia Plath. I didn't know that this was not just a book, but a legacy that I — and practically every woman writer of my generation — was about to claim, disclaim, "relate to," and "deny." A few years later, in Women's Literature classes, people were saying, "If only feminism had happened sooner . . ." This meant in effect: Sylvia Plath would not have killed herself. Whether or not this was believed, it was said and mused over at least during the coffee breaks of these — at the time informal, noncredit — classes. Plath's suicide didn't interest me much, not deeply. Maybe because suicide itself did not fascinate me, as it does some people. I was untouched by what A. Alvarez calls the savage god. To me, suicide was, simply and bluntly, hurting oneself — something I went to lengths not to do. I did not respond to the spiritual and metaphoric implications of such an act.

But suicidal or not, women identified with Sylvia Plath. Women poets especially, but not only poets: Plath was a figure for the mass of educated American women and, beyond that, a figure for all women touched by feminism as an idea. The greatest dynamism of feminism, in fact, has had to do with its cultural vitality. The economic and political implications of the movement are important, of course. But in a country where even people who consider themselves not only educated but literary don't read poetry and have said to me cheerily, as if I will appreciate their candor, that they "just don't understand poetry" and therefore "just don't read it," when a group bands together to discuss the work of a poet like Plath who is undeniably obscure at times and definitely difficult, they are acknowledging, against the grain of the culture, that her work contains essential information they *must* have and that it can be had only by cracking the rind of poetic difficulty. And this, in our country, is revolutionary and is eloquent of a ravenous cultural appetite. Sylvia Plath's work, coming at the time it did, created this focus. People — women — who did not read poetry, read poetry. And they understood it; they bothered to.

Beyond Plath's poems there was a novel, letters, more poems, memoirs by those who had known her, critical studies. In a word, fascination. The allure included the works, but went beyond it into biography. For me, the most poignant of these biographical lures was not, as it was for others, the suicide, nor even the brilliance of her mind or the pluckiness of her ambition. It was the period of her life that is the major background of her autobiographical novel, *The Bell Jar*: her time as a guest editor at *Mademoiselle* magazine.

The summer internships of college seniors on a fashion/ beauty/general interest magazine (which publishes poetry and fiction) aimed at college women is an odd American literary institution. It is a distinctly female tradition, in spite of the fact that there are a few men in the program each year. The women are the focus, the would-be writers, the winners of fiction or poetry contests, women with talent, with some sort of accomplishment behind them and, probably, some ambition ahead of them. They are brought to New York to get experience working on a national magazine; they live for a few weeks in the city, hanging out at least on the fringes of publishing. And they get a make-over: haircuts, make-up consultations, fashion tips, wardrobe counseling. They are reminded of their primary allegiance: to beauty. In the midst of work, they are reminded of self, of their sexual self.

It may seem a small thing, but it glares at me, out of the biography of Sylvia Plath. The absurdity of it, the hopelessness of the mixture of beauties — the female body's old rituals in honor of the ideal form and the duty any artist assumes toward beauty in art are brutally tossed together for a woman in a way they are not for a man. The first compliment that women began to turn over and over, wondering at its insidiousness, was, "You think like a man, you write like a man." The statement meant vaguely, imprecisely, that one wrote without frills, without sentimentality. More precisely, the statement "You think like a man" probably means simply "You think." Perhaps it *is* easier to think ("like a man") if the apparatus of thinking is not split, deflected, even as it goes about what everyone agrees is business.

Sylvia Plath had gone to Smith College. I wrote my book review for the student newspaper of a land-grant institution. Plath came from New England, and I was in the Midwest. She was a figure of success, of accomplishment for me (the suicide was beyond me, or maybe in a romantic way, even her suicide seemed grander than any gesture I could command). Her ambition soothed me somehow, and made ambition seem less wrong. I read the rules for the *Mademoiselle* fiction and poetry contests. I think I entered once or twice; at least, I intended to enter. But in 1966, by the time I wrote my review and heard for the first time my own opinions (for that was the puzzling relationship I discovered I had with writing: I wrote to find out what I thought), I realized that I was ashamed that Sylvia Plath had been a guest editor on the magazine. I recoiled and I didn't know why — I hadn't read *The Bell Jar* yet, didn't even know of it. I was humiliated (if I had recognized my confused feelings) by this mixture of fashion and art. I felt, obscurely, that *Mademoiselle* guest editors were, like the Miss Americas are to other young women, representatives for me. The contest was *my* contest. It didn't matter that I didn't win or perhaps even wasn't a contestant: that was my world. And I was humiliated in absentia that even here — in art, poetry, thinking and doing, "the world of the mind," I'd thought — here too, everything still rested on the premise that women must pursue beauty, that we must be made over.

The desire to cut the bond with beauty has been intense. It is one of the cultural currents of feminism, the reason everybody was suddenly dressing in overalls, wearing combat boots (this was a war, this was work), and didn't own lipstick. The best, most astonishingly powerful motto of the times was Black Is Beautiful. And suddenly they *were* beautiful, knocking the country over with raw superiority, genuine style, not only with a cause that was just. But our motto, if we were to find a cry to express the freedom we wanted, would have to have been something ungainly and negative like We Aren't Beautiful, Lovely Is Lousy, Female Is Ugly. But we didn't mean that either. We meant . . . but that is the suicidal part: it is hard to sever the cords that tie us to our slavery and leave intact those that bind us to ourselves.

I could not think of beauty in a usefully diagrammatic way, each type in its slot. In front of me now I have a picture of Keats, given to me by a friend; it has printed beneath it, deadpan, "A poet who considered beauty the most important thing in the world."

He knew what it was:

> *"Beauty is truth, truth beauty,"* — *that is all*
> *Ye know on earth, and all ye need to know.*

It's because of those lines that the inscription on the picture strikes me as so funny: the donkeyish prose parses, solemnly, the famous last lines of the grand ode.

Keats, to my mind, is the model of the modern lyric poet, the first of a line that continues. In the "Ode to Psyche" he initiates what has become a modern assumption of the poet's use of the mind, of the self:

> *Yes, I will be thy priest, and build a fane*
> *In some untrodden region of my mind,*
> *Where branched thoughts, new grown with pleasant pain,*
> *Instead of pines shall murmur in the wind.*

In this poem the old mythic structure collapses: no more Psyche — now we must inhabit the psyche. The myth is real: Keats is "psychological." His poetry has a purity and exhilaration of quest that is not just the result of his youth, but is born of the newness of the exploration itself. More even than Wordsworth (whose *Prelude* is subtitled "The Growth of a Poet's Mind") and in a more achingly lyrical way, Keats's poems and letters state the subject that has dominated poetry since then: consciousness itself; not Psyche, but the psyche.

But it is the blunt sentimentality of a copywriter below the (arty, not authentic) picture that I find myself brooding about. I believe it: beauty for Keats was the most important thing in the world. And for me. But it is not the same thing. Anyway, I do not think that I mean truth. And it will take me a long time to extend my sympathies and unify my sense of what beauty is to feel that the equation between truth and beauty is all I need to know. My sense of beauty is troubled, clouded, confused. Like my sense of the past, it is splintered, part of the longing I feel and which is placated and deflected from the real search by my willingness (society's willingness) to live in a consumer culture with its array of consolation prizes for the middle class. Keats wasn't a consumer. Beauty, I suppose, was not an equivocal word to him. And it is *him*. The history of women is the history of beauty. Our bodies have been the metaphor for an entire aspect of life, a deep layer of consciousness: the beautiful woman, even to women, is the image of beauty itself. It is the word made flesh.

I would like beauty, like the past, to be something that can be traced, a theme, as my English-major self would have it. The word, unfortunately, is a touchstone for too many things: *beauty* has become a switchboard through which I route and connect the various desires and disappointments of my own life and also what I sense more confusedly are those of the culture. I persist in believing that the perception of beauty, the hunger for it, is somehow (but how?) all of a piece, or at least related, no matter how different the meanings are behind the uses of the word itself. It's an old trust in language and I can't shake it: if we use the same word for vastly different subjects, I believe in their relation before I can prove it, even before I entirely sense it. My desire to *be* beautiful (a woman's desire), to create beauty (as an artist), to live surrounded by beauty (a citizen's sense, which is both aesthetic and, in the entirely public sense, cultural) are connected only by the word. They are in themselves quite different things. I sought the agility of mind that could find their relation. For I sensed that if I could find a relation to beauty in which beauty is truth, I might also discover a relation to history that is generative. It is the old American quest, perhaps the first heritage of white people in the New World: to stand on the new, beautiful continent and decide where to put the first mark. This is the work of history and of creation.

Technicians speak of making a beautiful bomb. And I suppose that has meaning. We are most outraged morally not at the absence of beauty in life but at its ironic presence: Mozart quartets in Terezin, the "model" concentration camp, for example. Beauty misplaced in this way is obscene. During the Vietnam War my friends and I, young poets, shuddered to learn that McNamara read poetry — or was it religious philosophy — on those long nights at the Pentagon. Rilke or Teilhard de Chardin — someone like that. Whoever it was — and whether or not the story was true — we found it eloquently horrible and its power came from our sense of the dislocation of beauty.

To be a woman of taste and sensibility is the accepted way (for those in the middle class) to bind the self together, to make the fragmented, frustrated parts a working whole. Aunt Lillian had been my first instructor. And later, when I had the money from my newspaper job in my hand, I embarked on my career as a consumer (the word itself was just beginning to be used; Ralph Nader was just being mentioned here and there as a possible presidential candidate.) We had become a consumer nation, but it is strange that this sad, greedy noun we chose for ourselves did not instantly make clear that beauty is our problem, our lack, even in an introverted sense, our obsession.

There are other figures of the romantic quest in my life. Orna Tews was one. She was an artist (I never saw any of her paintings — maybe she was a sculptor). She was invited by the nuns every year to give one of the weekly "assembly speeches" at our school. To most of the girls she was a plain woman wearing aggressively homely clothes, shod in sensible shoes like our own uniform Girl Scout oxfords. How lucky we were to be wearing them, too, we were always told. How happy we would be years later when our metatarsal bones were straight and true, unlike the deformed and painful feet of foolish public school girls who wore penny loafers or — worse — moccasins.

Here in this holding-pool for ugly ducklings who, one fine day, would give geeselike cackles when they turned into the swans that were Catholic wives-and-mothers, Orna Tews, spinster artist, was invited by the Sisters to address us. To me Orna Tews with her odd and faintly elderly name and her aggressive disregard for fashion (a far cry from Aunt Lillian), was the epitome of a spinsterishness that was postively glamorous. I hung on her every assembly hall word (I believe she had an accent) as if she were a missionary only briefly returned to the tepid homeland before rejoining, drab herself, the world of macaws and jaguars and savage religion to which she belonged. An artist, speaking of art.

She said to observe everything. Actually, she said *Observe perpetually.* I went around for a week with my head on a swivel, eyes popping, looking so diligently for "the significant detail" that I was in a state of chronic peevishness. I could hardly fall asleep at night because of my earnest attention. I was an exhausted, querulous wreck. But I was observing — perpetually.

Fifteen years later when I found that Orna Tews's dictum was the final entry in Virginia Woolf's *Writer's Diary,* a line itself quoted from Henry James, I didn't feel deceived. In fact, I was often drawn to people who lived only the shell of life in our measly present, in St. Paul where God had absent-mindedly dropped them, speaking in their own inauthentic, timorous voices. They lived, actually, in literature. The first boy who kissed me, a French horn player who soon after explained that he had to be careful of his lip, held me in a long embrace and said, "My God, you're fun to kiss!" Scott Fitzgerald, *Tender Is the Night,* book II, chapter 9, spoken by Dick Diver to Nicole: *their* first kiss. My French horn player didn't care if I found out his magic line was not his own; it was he, soon after, who loaned me the novel and said I ought to read it. The language of the art crazed is rarely our own, almost never in youth. Orna Tews quoting from Virginia Woolf's diary, the boy of my first kiss copping an exclamation from Fitzgerald — we spoke the same language though it wasn't ours. It was the alluringly aged, dusty voice of an author. It was prose. We bowed our heads and spoke in quotation, excising the citations for the sake of the moment.

Miss Tews talked about art in life, the beauty of dailiness. I was all agog. She was a sort of arty Aunt Lillian, the next step; an intellectual providing theory where my aunt had been all wonderful praxis. Her message seemed to be that art was made of nothing. Or perhaps that nothing — that is, everything — was art. She dwelt at length on the art that went into baking a *truly beautiful* cake, the care in sifting, the delicate folding of egg whites into batter, the attention to preheated ovens and well-creamed butter and sugar mixtures. Details, details, the art of the tiny could fill a lifetime. Our mothers were artists! Our fathers, oiling a creaking hinge on a door, were artists! Our grandmothers were artists ("the fine old American art of darning — how many of you girls have ever thought of darning as an art?"). The well-driven bus, the carefully plowed street in winter, the beautifully set dinner table, the diligently written history theme: art, art, all art!

I wanted to sign up for the whole package: the lifetime of oxfords, the doughy resilience of a belief in the beauty that resided in all things, the fanatic's ecstasy as she toiled her way through the art of cakes and pastries, the itty-bitty harmlessnesses that, translated into what Miss Tews called at the end of her speech "formal art," were the business of perpetual observation. And perpetual observation was the first tool of any questor. Which is what, though she stayed at home to practice her formal and informal arts in her manic way, Orna Tews was.

Though deeply unbeautiful, she had further involved me in this pursuit of beauty. I didn't know it, I only knew what attracted me. But now I see her, and Aunt Lillian (who was beautiful) and my grandmother (who also was) as the triumvirate they were: my figures for the pursuit of what I felt I did not possess myself but which, I sensed, the world might provide: beauty, the loveliness I was willing to seek, to make, if I could not *be* it, as I understood was woman's way.

There were kindred spirits my own age too. A girl in our parish fascinated me, and although I didn't know her well — she was two or three years older — I was always aware of her. Her name was Helen. I can remember with unusual clarity our few conversations, Helen looking directly at me as we talked, curious, so curious to hear what I would say next. She was genuinely interested in other people. She was the ugliest girl I had ever seen, ugly beyond her years, with an elderly witchlike angularity that thrilled me and made me shy as if it was love I was feeling. It was pity, though, and it made my heart move toward her. She loved to read and was very intelligent; this somehow consolidated her homeliness. She was a heroine, I thought, in the best mode: brilliant, original mind, hopelessly unbeautiful, like Jane Eyre, my great favorite.

The last time I saw Helen, the summer before she began the university, she told me, "I tested out of freshman English. I can go straight ahead and take literature courses." We had met by chance on the St. Clair bus, she coming home from the University of Minnesota, I from the St. Paul library downtown. I was deeply impressed. I resolved, when the time came, to test out of freshman English myself, a thing I hadn't known was possible.

We sat in the darkened St. Clair bus, the forest-green upholstery worn smooth and almost gray, the two narrow bands of yellowish light running along both sides of the interior above the windows. Romantic, gauzy light, even then. The light of our town with its buttery streetlights, the softened light of memory and dream. Helen's face that night is one of the clearest pictures I have of any human being. She sat in the shadowy glow, all the angularity of her strange face and attenuated body throwing their own shadows. "Hey, that's great," I said. It was somehow only fair that such homeliness should at least test out of freshman English. The thing about her that took my breath away was the poise of her ugliness. She was smiling, a perfectly natural and yet somehow alarming smile. It dawned on me: she doesn't know she's ugly.

How this had occurred — the vast deception of a brilliant mind, a mind that could test out of freshman English at the university — I couldn't begin to understand. She was not troubled, she was not downcast, she was not even self-conscious. She didn't care that she wasn't pretty. Apparently, she didn't think about it. Beyond the ugliness, which she hadn't registered, she was simply a very eager girl. Eager to live. Testing out of freshman English was just another stroke that cleared away the intervening dross, a little leap that brought her nearer to experience. Like me, she was literary and she "wanted to experience life." I wanted to ask her . . . so many things. But mainly, how had she received this inoculation against beauty? Like the women of my grandmother and aunts' coffee conversations on the subject, she was plain: she was free. She had tested out of freshman English, she had tested out of the rougher course, the college of good looks from which the rest of us sensed we would never graduate.

But who asks questions, who even knows, staring fascinated at another person and absorbing her mystery, that these things are *questions* that beat their wings on just the other side of consciousness? I asked nothing. Yet I felt our kinship was complete. I'd always felt the sisterhood of gawky homeliness was ours and that, just as she was smarter than I, she was homelier. Not essentially different, just *more* ugly, *more* undesirable. But twins, all the same. Two homely girls who liked to read long novels about English governesses.

She left the bus before I did, getting off at Victoria Street, queenly and unaffected herself, stunning me again with her mystery which I finally understood was grace. She waved gaily from the curb as I, a lit face in a darkened rectangle, passed down St. Clair Avenue toward home.

A couple of years later, when I was at the university (where I had not tested out of freshman English and had gotten an F on my first theme: "didn't follow directions," the notation said), I heard Helen had gone to Paris to study. She got married there. She's settled down in Paris, my mother said, who liked Helen's mother and liked Helen and likes life, I sometimes think, because she likes fiction. She is always trailing after somebody's dénouement, keeping track of her old friends, my old friends, the deaths of other people's relatives, reading to the end of everybody's book to see how things turn out. It's because of my mother that I know what happened to Helen.

I was living in a different state when my mother sent me a clipping from the *Pioneer Press,* which she reads every morning with her X-acto knife in hand. It was an article from the Women's Page, as it used to be called and as my mother still calls it, though the title now is Trends.

The article was about Helen who had come home to visit her family. Home from Paris. The picture was huge, a three-column portrait of a beautiful woman, her elegant head looking from atop the languid frame, looking not at the camera, not at anything in particular, absorbed apparently in her thought: selfless, *thinking.* The expressive hands were held out slightly in some gesture of thought, grasping her idea.

What was she explaining, this enigma of my girlhood, this proof of the mystery and transformative power of time? It didn't matter. She had become gorgeous, utterly, utterly beautiful.

Helen had become a fashion model in Paris after she married. You're just right for my clothes, Coco Chanel had told her. She was on the cover of *Elle, Vogue,* whatever the rest of them are called. She only worked part-time, here and there. It wasn't a career so much as a lark. "Clothes are toys," she said in the article. She explained it wasn't a matter of beauty. She said she saw girls all the time, everywhere, to whom she wanted to say, "You could be a model if you want to." It wasn't beauty, she said. All you needed was to have high cheekbones and be skinny.

The reporter wrote that Helen seemed *unable* to gain weight, that she ate what she wanted — according to the reporter, a whole bag of Tom Thumb donuts just that morning — yet kept her bony beauty, throwing her stylish shadows from the planes of her high cheekbones.

She had taken a professional name. She had chosen the name of our bus line: to Coco Chanel, to the editors of *Vogue* and *Elle,* she was Helen St. Clair. Helen of St. Clair, of the shabby and romantic St. Clair bus, poised on the hills of our town, as Helen, that night, had been poised on the curb, waving, our emissary to the light, to the City of Light.

4 ❧

THE GHOST OF a lost, smudged Europe and its culture, and the ghost of the undefiled American continent: these, to me, are the two spooks of our immigrant heritage. The most troubling American relation to beauty rests in our perception of our geographical body. It is this: we are aware that our presence on the continent has made it less beautiful. Our history presents us with emphatic before and after images of our land. Before us, after us. Before is beautiful.

We know the land used to be beautiful . . . and then we came. It is interesting that white American artists find it easier to acknowledge, to appropriate Indian culture than black culture (except jazz). I can't think of any white poets writing today who genuinely try to use black mythology or culture in their work. But many poets use and study — sometimes in fake and unconvincing ways — American Indian mythology and religion; it is even fashionable to do so. They seem to want to bury themselves in the rich significance with which every object, season, animal and color is drenched in the Indian cosmology. The American Indians, at least, knew how to live here. We feel, with troubled mind, often obscurely, that we do not.

We have not been able to use our past, more specifically our folk heritage, as other cultures have. The whole matter of folk culture and its uses by artists in America is complicated and confused because the "folk" have often not been an indigenous peasantry, but an oppressed minority (and have not been "us," but have been black or Indian). Oppressed minority — the refrigerated phrase of the social sciences is the right one because the very thing that is missing between artists and the oppressed minority (what in other cultures would be the peasantry) is some kind of authentic *relation*. My grandmother spoke blandly, easily, of "the nobles": she was a peasant. All the "little Father" business of czarist Russia and the overpowering soul bond that characters like Levin in *Anna Karenina* feel toward the native peasantry are part of the romantic cobwebbery that, apparently, caused people to feel related one to another beyond their castes, minorities, interest groups. It is all too attractive — that is, too dismissive — to say that this was "just" romantic; what about the fact that it worked emotionally and spiritually? Worked for Levin, worked for my grandmother. Our own methods and answers, resolutely unromantic (the welfare state bureaucracy) or sometimes just kooky (the exotic religions and airy cults of individual "conversions") are lonely and don't work. That is, they don't create or sustain culture and therefore do not draw the population together, but create isolated enclaves. We create yet more pockets, interest groups, fanatics, more fragmentation, more chance of being disaffected. And this in turn tends to make people romantic about the peasantry and about the past. It may be why Americans are suddenly, after generations of doing the opposite, digging up their roots (if they can be found) to look at them. And then to . . . but that's part of the problem. What *do* you do with your roots? Aren't they supposed to be buried, isn't that where they belong?

In 1892, a wealthy and apparently thoughtful woman, Mrs. Jeannette M. Thurber, invited the Czech composer Antonín Dvořák to come to the United States. Her idea was to bring a composer who was established as a national artist in his own country to train a nation of American composers, in an attempt to create a national music. She had considered inviting Sibelius, but Dvořák was her final choice. Clearly, we are dealing with a desire for and recognition of culture as necessarily belonging to a *people,* not to a country: Dvořák was a Czech composer, a composer of his nation at a time when the nation existed only in its culture. There was no "country"; the land was and had been for centuries a province of the ruling Austro-Hungarian Empire. In the nineteenth century the Czech nation was in a sense created by the writers and artists of its romantic period who fashioned the *idea* of the nation and by so doing managed to save the language itself from extinction.

Dvořák came to America. Yet he influenced less than he was influenced. He used American Indian songs in his music; he noted the songs of the native birds — including the scarlet tanager — and used them as motifs. He wrote in the *Atlantic Monthly* that he wanted American composers to make use of Negro spirituals, Indian music, the natural sounds of their country. He spoke as a European whose folk melodies gave him more music than a lifetime could transcribe. He was not ambivalent about the peasantry: he was the flower of that root, not only personally but in his music.

But American composers who have done this — I am thinking of Ives, MacDowell, Copland — don't seem to *use* folk elements. They remain a kind of undigested morsel, sometimes even a showpiece, within the work, as Dvořák's folk and natural elements are not. Perhaps Dvořák could *use* them because it never occurred to him they might not be his.

It is harder for American artists to be nourished as Dvořák was. It is seen (usually rightly, inevitably) as sheer arrogance for a white person to write "from" the culture of American blacks and Indians; more recently women have used the same criticism against male writers' depiction of female characters. Recently, when I went back to re-read *Anna Karenina,* I was astonished to find that I couldn't: I didn't believe in the formation of this woman, not as I once had. Levin, the landlord dreamer, on the other hand, was authentic; I believed in him. Anna seemed contrived. Specifically, her final despair seemed inaccurate, not residing within her personality, as real tragedy must, from her glistening start in her beautiful black dress. I began to suspect authorial motives. I even considered that Tolstoy was giving his heroine not Tragedy but Punishment. And Anna Karenina, who had lived for me, finally did die, crushed by something other than a train engine.

It is hard, maybe impossible, if we come from the bland middle of the country (geographically or psychically or both), to get our bearings as artists. Perhaps as citizens. I look at the Ku Klux Klanners on the TV news with their long white nighties and their dunce hats: there they are, My People, crying wa-wa (and not even knowing it or knowing it so strangely and obliquely that it is like not knowing) because they don't have a culture. The great white sulk: *they* got rhythm . . . and we don't. We want to sway and dance to the music more than we ever thought.

This is the longing for culture that I feel has informed my life — not only as a person who became a poet, but simply and plainly as a citizen, a resident of this place. A poet is usually nothing beyond that: a citizen who keeps detailed notes. This longing for culture — how dead the phrase seems — has to do with a nation's possession of some gladly held source to which The People remain firmly attached, and which both gladdens and consoles them. *We are The People and this is Our Way:* this should be the peaceable message of every nation's culture. But there on the TV, the cold little instrument of our culture, are the confused mourners, dressed in drag, in white like brides, who, in their messed up way, acknowledge our truth: we don't seem to *have* A Way, and we are The People routinely only when we are an empire, arranging to maintain ourselves as consumers. For all our bombs and death machines, our greatest evil (because it is daily, pervasive, and killing) is our cultural one, the zero we expect to sustain ourselves with.

In his book *A Backward Look,* published in 1979, the American journalist Daniel Lang has written about returning to Germany and the border country of Belgium where he had been a war correspondent during the Second World War. He went as a journalist on this return trip, but of course he had his own more personal quest: he had been young then, he had seen friends and others die. He wasn't looking for history — he probably had more than enough of that for a lifetime; he was looking for history's effect: how do Germans, young and old, East and West, perceive the history of the Third Reich. Inevitably, he also came upon his own frustration with "looking backward": the terrible self-righteous illusion "that contemplating the sins of the past was an absolving force for the living." It was worse than that, worse than any lesson that history could teach: "One had to earn the right to mourn," he says. In a sad and oblique way his own destination, just as history's, had to be his encounter with the present moment, the galling implacability of time, moving always forward, senseless, unfeeling — glad, simply, of the sun on its face.

The book itself, until this moving (and not at all "triumphant") finish, is about the pursuit of attitudes toward the past. A terrible past. Here, in the visits he has with Germans who had been young men — boys really, about seventeen years old — pressed into service toward the end of the War, Lang presents startling testimony about the connection between history and beauty.

He is talking to Rolf Lantin, a schoolteacher in an Aachen *Gymnasium*. He is by far the most attractive of all Lang's subjects. A gentle man, about fifty, a man haunted (the look was in his eyes, Lang said) by the German past and by his own observation, in January 1945 while on guard duty at the Weimar railroad station, of a work detail of *skeletons* from Buchenwald. "They ran!" he said. "It wasn't necessary, but they were being forced to run to their forced labor, and they were all skeletons, hundreds of them — unburied skeletons shrouded in striped uniforms."

Later, Rolf Lantin and his three young guard comrades agreed that if they ever saw inmates trying to escape, they would do nothing to stop them. They were probably about seventeen years old when they saw this, guards at the railroad station. "Nothing had come of the pact," Lang says, but Lantin told him that "the image of the running cadavers had chased him down through the years, never letting him forget that he had seen with his own eyes that inmates of concentration camps did indeed exist, enslaved and degraded."

He had had nightmares about it, Lantin admitted when asked. But he volunteered stranger, more startling, information as a consequence: "His sense of beauty," he said, "had been damaged." Lang paraphrases him: "That might sound to some like a precious punishment, he said, but it was important to him, and he didn't see how he could fail to mention it. He quoted a line from a book by Theodor Adorno, an Austrian musicologist and thinker: 'To write poetry after Auschwitz is barbaric.' "

Lantin's statement clanged in my mind: *his sense of beauty had been damaged* (and, the sentence had gone on, *his enjoyment of art numbed*). But the impaired enjoyment of art was the result of the greater, more essential wound.

In our own country we are so often unbeautiful. We almost take it for granted, tearing down fine old buildings and then racing off to Europe to gaze at old fountains, old villas, old this, old that. It may be our worst hurt — one which we inflict on ourselves and on other nations. It is a source of whatever actual devastation we have wrought and comes from our impoverished sense of beauty, our grudge against loveliness.

5 ❧

"You've got the beauty disease," a friend of mine said a few years ago, exasperated with me — the flowers, the attention to detail, the domestic fussing with myself and the materials at hand, the stark neediness and extravagance of wanting to be beautiful or, failing that, wanting beauty around me. We were living, five of us, in a farmhouse in the middle of the Minnesota nowhere, near the South Dakota border, in a vaguely communal arrangement. We were supposed to be living cheaply (the rent was $10 a month per person) and writing (that was more iffy, especially when one of the group came up with the idea that writing was implicitly sexist because discipline was macho; I cannot begin, now, to explain this reasoning or why it made a kind of sense at the time). We were also considering the idea (pretty abstractly, in our case) of nonexclusive relationships. We were casting about after university years of protesting the Vietnam War, seeing how far we could push our new idea, feminism.

It didn't last. We spent most of our time being appalled by each other. One of my insupportable traits as a roommate turned out to be the beauty disease, my infuriating habit of plunging a bouquet of wildflowers not into a milk bottle but into the Waterford decanter I'd hauled with me like the willowware a pioneer wife wrapped in cotton wool and put defiantly into a barrel, even if the tallow had to be left behind. My too-suave hand with a Mornay sauce got on everybody's nerves. When we woke one morning to find that the mice, whose home the place really was, had eaten a rounded bite out of the Linzertorte I'd made from scratch the day before, I don't think anybody really felt sorry for me. I was their embarrassing revisionist. "You remind me," my fellow communard said, trying to get a handle on the beauty disease, pausing for the worst, "of . . . of my *mother*."

Woman as aesthete; the "civilizing sex," as we have always been honored, burdened, as if the true female heritage were a handing down of certain obsessive-compulsive genes that are not simply housekeeperly traits but the very essence of the sex. The beauty disease as a way of feminine life. The phrase has stayed with me because, except for the brief, easily forgotten introduction to decadence and Dorian Gray in high school, this was the first time it had occurred to me that there was anything odd — pathological, even — about wanting to be beautiful. Feminism had made me feel vaguely uncomfortable (everybody was starting to wear combat boots and overalls . . . but it was still fashion), but the ideas of the women's movement were so many and so grand that in contemplating them during those first years I flitted around from one to another, so free in my mind that I hardly considered my habits.

But here it was, harshly spoken: I had the beauty disease. And I felt shame, a female shame — because I had registered my identity most deeply as an aesthetic, not as a sexual, being. Many women do. Beauty is women's work. Male homosexuals, for example, are stereotyped most nastily as "not men" when they are seen as beings obsessed with appearance, interior decorators, hairdressers. And they are held in greatest contempt for just that quality, perhaps because beauty is designated, in the unexamined part of the mind, as peculiarly female, and therefore *queer*. Erma Bombeck, whose columns my mother slashes out for me with her X-acto knife (my mother thinks I have the beauty disease too), is the renegade philosopher of sloth and disregard in this matter. But she must adopt a silly tone; she must always make fun of herself, the slob. Like the Polack jokes we as a nation of unconscious greenhorns keep telling on our-selves, her humor is based on a sophisticated problem whose roots are so essentially unfunny that she has material for a life-time of columns.

Beginning with *Seventeen* magazine, the popular women's magazines have plotted out a woman's life in progressive publica-tions whose single theme is beauty. From *Seventeen* on to *Mademoiselle* (college) and *Glamour* (first job) and then, some-where in the late twenties, into the pure ether of *Vogue* where beauty leaves prettiness and the beginner thrills of "looking your best" far behind with their good intentions (that vapid theme is carried forward, as an occasional motif, in magazines for house-wives, such as *Redbook*, just as the overt sexual uses of beauty are relegated to *Cosmopolitan*). In *Vogue*, beauty becomes ab-stract, the way art did after the Second World War. Looking in *Vogue* at the spacy models and their minimal bodies, the aloof streaks of their facial features and sculpted heads, we see the inevitable destination of the *Seventeen* girl: the beautiful body is not a possibility — just as my grandmother and my aunts mused over their cream-and-sugar coffee. But they spoke of the body as fragmented, a series of endless patch jobs; the high-fashion model is a whole, she is the figure. Here, in the models of *Vogue*, we are given actual bodies whose extremity — of thinness, of mouth, of coiffure, of expression, of make-up — has rendered them in-divisible.

Never mind that we shiver at the obvious analogy of these figures: the model is reminiscent of the vacant, starved face of a just-liberated prisoner of Auschwitz. Never mind the blasphemy. Never mind the fascination. We have, unconsciously and hesitantly, claimed the beauty that must be ours, as if it were a historical, even an evolutionary inevitability. There in the swank fashion magazines is the sexless (or androgynous, as the word is carelessly used now, to mean either both sexes or none at all) figure, thin to the point of horror, looking out from the page with the bewildered vacuity of a refugee. Thin, thin beyond flesh. *All you need is high cheekbones and you have to be thin.* You must be thin beyond health or hope. There is no thinness, no disappearance of flesh extreme enough to satisfy our idea of beauty — for we call it beauty, this bruised sacrilege of the body. The human figure changed with the Second World War. The spontaneous image clouded and came back in that horrible way, the skeleton in its gruesome pajamas.

The femme fatale, which had been at the beginning of this century such a woman — the generous flesh and the insistent metaphor of all that glorious (or diabolical) hair in the portraiture of the pre-Raphaelites and of the art nouveau, in Burne-Jones and in Klimt and Mucha — became now as it had also after the slaughter of the Great War, masculine, the hair short, slicked back, cropped, the body just a backbone. The women who look out of the pages of *Vogue* in these extreme gestures of the figure are femmes fatales still, but their poison seems not for men, or not only. They are fatal now to themselves, not empowered as those earlier prewar (both wars: it started with the First) witches, but simply sick with their own malignancy. Another aspect of the beauty disease. The fashion model of this sort, the ultrasophisticated mannequin peering from the high-fashion magazine with her alarming cheekbones and professional concave body, is the dead risen to life, the ghost in our idea of beauty.

The beauty women perceive for themselves as the ideal — as opposed to that designed to appeal to men — is startlingly desexed. It is the beauty of the flat surface, the breastless, buttless set of bones upon which clothes are best hung. Two distinct models come to mind: Marilyn Monroe and Audrey Hepburn. Opposites, reigning figures at about the same time in the fifties and early sixties. Monroe, about whom so much has been written, her life having become as eloquent in its way as Sylvia Plath's in hers, is a body, a femme fatale of the old art nouveau school, a man's idea of a woman. She was not, for me or the girls I grew up with, an ideal. This was partly because adolescent prudery is ferocious and Monroe was too frank a sexual symbol. But why was everyone so crazy to look like Audrey Hepburn?

She played roles that involved a lot of costume changing: *Funny Face*, for instance, in which she is "discovered" (as a dowdy clerk in a bookstore, no less) and made into a top Paris fashion model, Fred Astaire snapping the camera; and, later, in *Breakfast at Tiffany's*, a movie that influenced schoolgirl style in much the same way as, more recently, Diane Keaton's Annie Hall has. The body we sought was the body for clothes, for fashion, for the remotely physical, not the sensual. The thinner the body, the better because to be thin was to be less — less woman. It is the simultaneous appearance of both these figures that suggests the significance of their differences. It doesn't matter that Monroe is a monumental figure and Hepburn minor. Perhaps she is minor because her power and allure remained within women's minds (and *young* women's, girls') and like much that influences women (and not men) she was simply not taken seriously. And of course there was no suicide. She was, really, a representative of the fashion magazine, not of movies. Her power was that of a *Vogue* model brought to movie life, given a story, given lines. But the allure remained that of the high-fashion mannequin. Therefore, beyond the typical adolescent prudery that made Monroe an ideal for only the rare ("fast"!) girls, Audrey Hepburn was given pride of place in our minds for other, more telling reasons. It was her aloofness from the female figure that we longed for.

Like modern architecture and Scandinavian design with its rectitude, this minimal female body (Twiggy, Penelope Tree, the other nameless ones) delivers its lean message beyond its fashion statement. The "boy look," the flat chest and curveless body, is not the result of feminism or any version of the women's movement. This stark body is the image of the slaughter of war in our century. The appearance of such figures as fashionable coincides eloquently with the end of the century's first European mass war. Women have been thin or fat, generous or lean, down through the ages: it is the *fashion* in body types that is indicative, a fashion for extreme thinness coming hard on the heels of the quite opposite image of the pre-Raphaelites and art nouveau. My grandmother with her little kiss of a mouth, was art nouveau and did not sigh to be skinny. One of the most striking aspects of the cheesecake pictures predating the First World War, especially the Belle Epoque photos of French music hall actresses (there's a wonderful one of Colette), is the relaxed flesh — not just big breasts, but a general plumpness. You can tell those thighs are *soft*.

The fashion for fashion (consumerism) that has recently been noted, principally by Christopher Lasch, as an indication of the narcissism of our culture is something different; it concerns the clothes. I am looking, for the moment, at the mannequin. The significance of the current craze, male and female, gay and straight, to "dress," to spend a lot of money on clothes, is probably not much different from the analysis Thorstein Veblen gave in *The Theory of the Leisure Class*. This phenomenon has everything to do with restlessness and insecurity, change and fear, greediness and high spirits. There is not an excessive emphasis in the current stylishness (which is part of consumerism) on the thin body. The clothes of Calvin Klein or of anyone else hang better on a not-fat person, but these styles are not geared for extremity. They are for, precisely, everybody. They are the middle range, and as part of the marketplace, they change endlessly, causing us to desire fitfully. That is consumerism, that is fashion, that is big business, that is the clothes. But how steady and unwavering the mannequin has remained. The haute couture figure has not changed, decade after decade since the Great War when, in our cruelly timed emancipation, she cropped her hair to bedevil the Edwardians: a gesture of freedom and life, all those bobbed heads after the First World War. Or perhaps more unconsciously, the ancient way women have always keened for their dead. The essence of fashion may be the feverish marketable *change* that not only creates an appetite for personal gratification but leaves no time for anything else. But the one steadfast image is the mannequin, the body that is the background for all the busyness. Strange and telling that there — and so unguardedly — we should meet the figure of our haunted history, the recently interred shapes of Europe: the camp prisoner with the bones that can be counted with the eye. This is our grotesque ideal. Like all metaphoric emblematic figures, there is no mistaking its historic resonance. There, a scant generation ago, are the concentration camp bodies and here, a world away, are the gaunt anorexic girls in American hospitals, starved and suicidal over the horrid blubber they imagine they are dragging repulsively through the world. Rich girls mostly, sick, truly, with the beauty disease, dreaming of perfection, wanting to disappear.

6 🦋

*A*ND MY GRANDMOTHER, the elderly art nouveau figure, finally disappeared. She ended up in a nursing home, in the modern way. We all hated it. My father cried and made a fist in his pocket. My mother, who got her household back after years of the ignorant lowness ruining her roses, ruining her role as chatelaine, was not happy and wanted her back, and did not root up the chive plant in the back yard but allowed it to take over so that even today there are chives everywhere, even in the chinks of the sidewalk. My aunts said, "What else can we do?" And what else could we.

I wasn't living at home anymore, but I got letters from my mother. The card parties and Czech lodge meetings with other old ladies who spoke some nineteenth-century version of Czech known only to themselves had come to an end. There weren't even any wakes or funerals for my grandmother to go to anymore; apparently everyone was dead, except for her. She had kept up her relentless cooking and the deep concern for her looks, a discipline held so long it had become a kind of honor. But slowly, steadily, as if they followed a plot, my mother's letters led to the nursing home: Grandma had burned herself one day when she didn't notice she'd left the gas flame on the stove. Her house-dresses, cotton flower-print dresses with rickrack trim (her uniform at home), were often not clean: unbelievable.

Then an account of how Grandma had gotten into the bath-tub and couldn't hoist herself out; she had sat there, her skin puckering in the water for three hours until my mother heard strange heave-ho noises in the apartment and came in to pull her out. Later, another report that Aunt Sylvia had decided to come every week to clean the apartment ("the kitchen is filthy"). Then Aunt Sylvia suggested that my grandmother should take a bath only when someone was with her. There was a follow-up report that Aunt Sylvia, cleaning the apartment, had been unable to pull Grandma out of the tub and had started to cry. My grandmother began to laugh. It was a stand-off, one of them too weak from crying, the other from laughing. Finally, my aunt called in my mother from next door, and the hoist was accomplished, their big elderly baby laughing because there was nothing else to do.

Then a letter came saying Grandma had fallen down the basement stairs. It might be a stroke. She would have to go to a nursing home: for a while, maybe for longer. She couldn't take care of herself. My mother and father both worked; no one was at home during the day.

A few days later I got a brief note from my mother saying my grandmother was in the nursing home (address included, suggestion that I send a card) and was confined to a wheelchair. She of the endless avidity and the boundless faith that work was life. My grandmother *sitting* — it was a contradiction in terms. Maybe it was an effect of the stroke, no one seemed sure. But she said she couldn't walk and sank into the wheelchair with no apparent intention of walking again.

For several months she was taken to physical therapy, but finally the head nurse told my father he might as well buy a wheelchair; the rented one was not economical for long-term cases. Then the therapy ended and she had a catheter as a permanent appendage, and showed it to her visitors, unasked, with a kind of wonder at its obvious functionalism. There was no more talk of her walking.

I think she went through some kind of nervous breakdown. It's strange to think of a dark night of the soul coming to someone eighty-seven or eighty-eight. By then it would seem that the husk of the personality has rigidified so that if it splits apart at all, it is only into the splinters of senility. I would not have thought of a very old person cracking the personality open and hurling out its pain and experience in sorrow and then, as if there were a future, turning upward in a huge cleansing wave, leaving the soul spent but free and wise at the last shore of its life. But something like that happened to my grandmother.

It took about two years. There are several indications that she went through the spiritual cleansing that saints and mystics describe. I was most struck when my father told me that she had said, apropos of nothing (not even of pain: there wasn't a lot of pain at the end), "Well, I think it's time to die tonight." And she did. Her body and soul were that finely meshed by the end. As my aunt said, she knew *what she was*. She knew she was about to be dead.

At first, in the nursing home, she fought like a tiger. She did not fight the good fight the physical therapy people wanted her to fight. She must have sensed that there was no future in being a goody-goody. She was out to break the joint. She fought her roommates who, each in turn, asked to be moved out. She fought the medication. She fought being put in bed and then snarled when she was taken out again and put in her wheelchair. She hated the food, but complained that she didn't get enough. She cried and demanded to go home; she sulked and then said casually that when she got home she intended to buy herself a new bed like the one she had in the nursing home — the best bed of her life, she said. She spoke authoritatively, as if acquisition implied mobility. And when no one, out of kindness, reminded her that she wouldn't be going back to her apartment, she reported to her next visitor that she was soon going home.

Her children or grandchildren and their children came every day to visit. Everyone talked to her, to each other, about what a nice place the nursing home was, how friendly the staff was, how clean the rooms were, how there were lots of people around to play cards with, and that the best part was that they could take her home anytime for dinners, picnics, holidays. And then they left, and hardly got out the front door before they burst into tears and cried aloud: why did their mother have to be there, in that nice, clean, friendly place?

This was not one of the miserable holes for the aged, gigantic and crowded, with loudspeakers blatting endless messages, not one of the sleazy places that is marginally in the news because of some legislative inquiry about mishandling of public funds. It was what we told her, told each other: a nice, clean, friendly place, modern and light with lots of windows, a yard too small and too near busy traffic perhaps, but the staff was competent, not cruelly overworked, often affectionate. The rooms were not large but were bigger than hospital rooms, and there were only two beds in each one, with a certain commitment to privacy. Large windows, a bath for each room, bright and tiled. I never saw or tasted the food, but my aunts said it was all right. My grandmother was diagnosed as a diabetic soon after arriving so her diet was restricted, probably bland. My family, always clannish, liked to visit her, liked to be with her, and it was generally agreed that even though the place was *very nice*, it didn't do any harm to make it clear that Mrs. Hampl in 106 had four children, innumerable other relatives, and that they came, one or another of them, every day to visit her. *If* the staff merely put on an act for visitors, our endless parade would keep them busily at it. This was the watchful thought.

In an effort to get her interested in the world around her, away from the apartment she kept refurnishing in her mind and conversation, her children and the staff tried to introduce her to other people. They got her to play cards, always her favorite pastime. But years of playing five hundred with indulgent children who let her cheat without much comment had blunted her technique, of playing and of cheating. She was hurt and angry, as chronic cheaters always are, when her new companions bluntly told her to cut it out. Besides, she said, some of them didn't talk right. This was the beginning of her acquaintance with those who, as she put it, were touched. Eventually, if she saw one of her visitors foolishly attempting conversation with someone woefully touched, she discreetly tapped her finger on her own forehead and shook her head, more savvy than her children about the signs around her.

Her wild-tiger time, when she fought the place, lasted less than a year, but it continued in occasional energetic jags for two years. It was a denial of the place and its purpose. She never talked about death or dying. Nor about illness or infirmity. She wanted to go home.

One of the last times I visited her, while I was home for a vacation, I noticed a change. It frightened me; I thought she was going to become one of the touched. She was sitting in her wheelchair moaning when I came in. This was something I hadn't seen her do before. She didn't stop or try to cover her tears. I thought she might be in physical pain, might need a nurse. But that wasn't it. She kept moaning and crying, rocking herself back and forth, not oblivious to my presence, but somewhere out of reach of the conventions of etiquette, the charm that had been one of her enduring principles, deep in her own anguish, not about to abandon her intimacy with it. She took my hand (any hand), stroked her own cheek with it, cried that she was lonely, lonely, looonely, hanging on to the *o* sound. She wanted to die. She made me promise I would come to her funeral. But mostly she did not talk. She moaned and rocked back and forth, like one of the anonymous touched. She wouldn't talk and acknowledged my inept affection (I held her hand, stroked her hair) only from a great distance. That is when she said, more greenhorn than grandmother, "You're good, you're kind."

When I left she didn't have me wheel her down to the big lounge picture window, as she had every other time, so that she could wave to me as I drove off — a procedure that always made me feel like a culprit and, really a culprit, made me glad to get away fast. This time she stayed where she was and continued to moan. I felt guilty, I still feel wrong, but I left her moaning there. Anything to get away from that mantra of sorrow, that awful moaning, toneless, impersonal, not *her*. It — if not she —

seemed prepared to go on moaning endlessly. That was the worst part: the eternity in that moan.

When I got home one of my aunts was visiting my mother; everybody was glad to see me: coffee, Christmas cookies, kisses around. I didn't want to tell them about the moaning. In some odd, callous way, I was already seeing it as less important than it had seemed at the time. And then my aunt said — mostly to my mother, for my mother — how good I was to take time during my vacation to visit my grandmother, and I began to focus, by degrees, on that aspect of the visit: my kindness. It had been my grandmother's comment too.

I thought this was the beginning of her descent into senility and mindlessness. And that the next time I went to visit her she would be babbling and incoherent, her mind woolly with bent memories. I thought her sadness had no bottom, or that there was no trap door to that moan, no escape but death. It occurred to me that she might arrive, in senility, back in Bohemia, the life and country she had had so little memory of, and that she would live there alone in her antiquated, mashed form of the language, mumbling, back in the embrace of the peasantry, lumpen. I didn't want to visit her again. I only saw her once or twice more.

But she wasn't senile and she didn't, ever again, moan that way. The curtain in her heart that split in half from top to bottom that day had mended — or hadn't been rent? I almost wondered if I had imagined it. She had become calm and humorous, patient, not the same as before — she had always been feisty — but not senile. After her death, my father wrote me about the end. There was a tone of wonder in his letter. The last six months of her life, he wrote, something strange had happened. He didn't know what to call it, he wrote. She just became, after her tiger period, very *kind*. It was she who talked sensibly and naturally to those who were touched in the worst, most unreachable ways; she who held a hand, wheeled herself over to someone sitting vacant and weird in a corner. She cheered the nurses (the nurses said; it was beyond a polite remark, my father wrote). She seemed to understand everybody's troubles, asked for nothing, gave amazing light. Everyone wanted to be around her. Teresa, they called her: her name, of course, but unusual to be called by one's most personal, authentic name in these end-of-the-line places where false affection makes everyone Grandma or, more courteously, more coolly, Mrs. this or that. She died Teresa, a person.

I didn't see any of this. I wasn't around during those last months. I know it from my father who was amazed, bemused by this turn of events. She had gone down and down, and, then, when everyone had every reason to expect her to go even more desperately down — into senility, into woeful bitterness — she made that strange, luminous turn. She glittered at the end not with charm, but with pure spirit, more than a brave salute. Our immigrant became a noble.

❧

I did not go home for her funeral. I was living in a tiny river town in Illinois, right on the river in fact, so close to the bank that in spring the channel flooded the narrow frontage road and almost reached the strand of houses facing the water. There was no getting away from St. Paul; we were still connected, in a direct line, by the river. In St. Paul the Mississippi is not the Father of Waters; it is narrow and threads its unromantic way past industrial plants. But in Illinois where it begins to become the river of Mark Twain and billows out in a wider, plainlike channel, it becomes aloof and serious.

After my mother called with the news of my grandmother's death — it hadn't been expected — I went outside by the river. I felt a satisfying finality, what I took to be acceptance. The river glided by, still, grand, metaphoric. I didn't go home for the funeral because a friend of mine had just had twin babies and I felt, solemnly and sincerely, that I was choosing life over death, staying near my friend who wanted me there. My grandmother, who had had twins herself, would have approved, I thought.

She would not have approved. But I was impervious to the

· 140 ·

last to her personality. I considered, philosophically, the misty middle ground between life and death that old people inhabit at the end. It was almost pleasant, this idea of fading. I thought I had probably already said my good-bye to her years before when she first began to get really old, or when she went to the nursing home. Or maybe the day in her room when she had moaned and moaned, as if she were no one in particular, just that grievous sound. She died a long time ago, I thought, as I stood by the wide river, and this recent death is just the expression of it. She had just made it into her tenth decade: she had been ninety on Columbus Day and she died in November. A long life, such a long life as hers, cannot end all of a sudden, I felt. She is at peace, I thought. And so am I.

Several weeks later I woke, jolted out of deep sleep in the middle of the night by nothing at all. I was drenched in sweat. I hadn't been dreaming, or hadn't remembered that I was. I was sobbing — I had no idea why at first. Then I focused: I had made a *terrible mistake* and should have gone to her funeral. This was the knowledge — not a dream — that had awakened me. And not having gone, there was no way to undo it.

I cried at sudden, unpredictable moments for two weeks after that, sobbing as I drove home, hunched over the steering wheel, unable to see through the tears, as if I were beating my way through a Minnesota blizzard. I moaned aloud in the public library stacks one day, again to my utter surprise. There was an elderly man on the other side of the stacks who peered through a chink in the wall of books to see what the matter was. He was wearing rimless glasses. Those are the cleanest glasses I've ever seen, I thought, and stared at them, fascinated, as if he were the apparition and not I.

I must have looked more astonished than miserable; my attacks (as I thought of them) were the advance guard of my emotions. I sobbed, I moaned stupidly, and only after the sound did I think, "Oh, it's Grandma. Because she's dead." The sobbing and moaning were acts dissociated from feeling. It was a weird sensation: to moan aloud in a supermarket check-out line, and then to look sheepishly at the bemused, unsobbing people around me. Yet I didn't miss her. And after a while the sobbing and my sudden public moans diminished and finally, left me entirely.

The picture of the luscious art nouveau girl with her lute went to my Aunt Therese. There was no will, nothing that self-conscious. Things just went, of their own accord, to the family members who wanted or needed them. My cousin ended up with the purple satin eiderdown, perhaps the most Bohemian of my grandmother's possessions: the great goose-down quilt of middle Europe. My father wrote in his letter that it seemed as if Grandma had everything beautifully timed: her savings left exactly enough for her burial and for checks of $500 to each of her four children and to Frank's daughter: she had left heirs. If she had lived a few more months, her money would have run out. Nothing would have changed, but welfare — or some version of it — would have paid her way. Ever the housekeeper, she had arranged to the end, tidily. She stopped on a dime.

I asked for the album of Prague views. My aunt wrote back that nobody could find it; somehow or other it was lost. She sent me instead my grandmother's ring, a Bohemian garnet set in white gold with an art nouveau design. I felt someone else should have had it, Frank's daughter perhaps, but this was the object that came to me, apparently it was what I was meant to have. I put it on my finger, the one on which the other women in the family wear their wedding rings; I was the only unmarried one among them.

Then, our personal Europe dead and buried, I decided I must go there.

III

Prague ❧ The Castle

1 ❦

IN MAY 1975, during the spring music festival that opens every year with a performance of Smetana's "Ma Vlast" ("My Homeland"), I went to Prague for the first time. The lilacs were in bloom everywhere: the various lavenders of the French and Persian lilac, and the more unusual — except in Prague — double white lilac. Huge flat red banners with yellow lettering were hoisted everywhere too, draped across homely suburban factories and from the subtle rose and mustard baroque buildings of Staré Město (the Old City).

The banners were in honor of the thirtieth anniversary of the liberation of Prague by the Soviet Army in May 1945. 30 *Let,* "30 years," it said everywhere, even on the visa stamp in my passport. Many offices and stores had photographs in their windows, blow-ups from 1945 showing Russian soldiers accepting spring bouquets from shy little girls, Russian soldiers waving from tanks to happy crowds. For the first time, I was in a city where the end of the Second World War was really celebrated, where history was close at hand. Prague was the first Continental European city I had seen (I had come from London) and it was almost weirdly intact, not modern. On the plane from America to London I had reminded myself that London would be modern; *my* England was so much a product of the nineteenth-century novels and poetry I'd been reading all my life that I knew I would be shocked to see automobiles. And in fact, nothing could prepare me for the slump I felt in London: I wanted the city of Becky Sharpe, of Daniel Deronda, even of Clarissa Dalloway, not the London of Frommer's guidebooks and the thrill of finding lunch for 5 pence.

Prague stopped my tourism flat. The weight of its history and the beauty of its architecture came to me first as an awareness of dirt, a sort of ancient grime I had never seen before. It bewitched me, that dirt, caught in the corners of baroque moldings and decorative cornices, and especially I loved the dusty filth of the long, grave windows at sunset when the light flared against the tall oblongs and caused them to look gilded.

I had arrived in a river city, just as I had left one in St. Paul. But the difference . . . On the right bank of the Vltava (in German, the Moldau) the buildings were old — to me. Some of them were truly old, churches and wine cellars and squares dating from the Middle Ages. But the real look, especially of the residential and shopping areas of Nové Město (New City — new since the fourteenth century when Charles IV founded it), was art nouveau, highly decorative, the Bohemian version of the Victorian. Across the river, in Malá Strana (Small Side — Prague's Left Bank), the city became most intensely itself, however; it rose baroquely up, villa by villa, palace crushed to palace, gardens crumbling and climbing, to the castle that ran like a great crown above it on a bluff.

The city silenced me. It was just as well I didn't know the language and was traveling alone. There was nothing for me to say. I was here to look.

My original intention in going to Prague was simple: to see the place my grandparents had come from, to hear the language they had spoken. I knew Prague was Kafka's city, I knew Rilke had been born here, and I had read his *Letters to a Young Poet* many times. I was a young poet myself. But my visit wasn't for them. Mine was the return of a third generation American, the sort of journey that is so inexplicable to the second generation: "What are you going to *do* there?" my father asked me before I left Minnesota.

That spring, the lines at the Prague Čedok office (the government agency that runs tourism in Czechoslovakia) were dotted here and there with young Americans looking for family villages. The young couple in front of me in the line had come from Cleveland. The man was asking a young travel agent, who was dressed in a jeans skirt and wore nail polish the color of an eggplant, how he and his wife could get to a village whose name he couldn't manage to pronounce.

"There does not seem to be such a place," she told him. She couldn't find a name on the map with a spelling that corresponded to the one the young man had brought from Cleveland on the piece of paper he was holding out to his wife. ("It's *his* family," she said to me. "I'm Irish.")

They decided to set out, anyway, for a village in Moravia that had a similar spelling. "I guess that's the place," the young man said, without much conviction.

I asked my father's question: "What are you going to *do* there?"

"Look around," he said. "Maybe somebody" — he meant a relative — "will be there."

My own slip of paper, which I'd brought from St. Paul, had the name of my grandmother's village ("spelling approximate," my cousin had written next to the name when he gave it to me), which was supposed to be near Třeboň, a small town in southern Bohemia. On the map, Třeboň was set among lakes (like Minneapolis, I had thought); here, the guidebook said, "the famous carp" were caught.

Suddenly, just then, as my turn came up, I had no heart for the approximate name of the village, for the famous carp, the kind of journey the Cleveland couple had set for themselves. ("We're going to do the same thing in Ireland," the wife said.) I stepped out of the line, crumpled up my piece of paper, and left it in an ashtray. The absurdity of trying to get to Třeboň, and from there to wherever this village with the approximate spelling was supposed to be, lay on me like a plank. I felt like a student who drops out of medical school a semester before graduation; I was almost there and, suddenly, it didn't matter, I didn't want what I'd been seeking. Apparently I wanted something else.

"Do you want to get something to eat?" I asked the couple from Cleveland.

But they didn't have time. "We have to split," she said.

"Yeah," said her husband. "It's a long way."

Perhaps, if you go to the old country seeking, as third or fourth generation Americans often do, a strictly personal history based on bloodlines, then, the less intimate history of the nation cannot impose itself upon you very strongly. History is reduced to genealogy, which is supposed to satisfy a hunger that is clearly much larger.

But if you go on a journey like this not to find somebody, but just to look around — then, in a country like Czechoslovakia (or perhaps only there, only in Prague), the country's history is infused with the urgency of the classic search for personal identity. The country itself becomes the lost ancestry and, one finds, the country is eloquent. Its long story, its history, satisfy the instinct for kinship in a way that the discovery of a distant cousin could not. For it is really the longing for a lost culture that sends Americans on these pilgrimages.

It seems a peculiarly twentieth-century unhappiness, this loneliness for culture. The Russian poet Osip Mandelstam who perished in one of Stalin's camps in 1938 was one of a group of poets before the First World War who called themselves Acmeists. When he was asked what, exactly, Acmeism was, Mandelstam said, "Homesickness for world culture."

This impersonal loss and the desperation it creates often are not appreciated in our psychological, personalized, society. "Masses of people," Richard Sennett writes in his book, *The Fall of Public Man*, "are concerned with their single life-histories and particular emotions as never before; this concern has proved to be a trap rather than a liberation." The reason Sennett suggests that "openness" and "being in touch with your feelings" and other such catch phrases of supposed authenticity do not work is that "people are working out in terms of personal feelings public matters which properly can be dealt with only through codes of impersonal meaning." In Mandelstam's phrase, this is the inverted effect of homesickness for world culture.

Countries like Czechoslovakia — the small, squeezed countries of Central and Eastern Europe — know this homesickness best. The first words of the Czechoslovak national anthem are, "Where is my home? Where is my home?" Strangely lost, elegiac words for a national hymn. (Sir Robert Bruce Lockhart, the British journalist and consular officer, thought it was the "least aggressive of all national anthems.") They are the words of a small nation that thinks of itself affectionately, as if it were a family. Except families don't have to worry about sovereignty.

❧

I put Třeboň out of my mind and spent the rest of the week walking aimlessly around Prague. If I had answered my father's question — what was I *doing* — I would have said I was sitting in coffeehouses, in between long, aimless walks. A long trip for a cup of coffee, but I was listless, suddenly lacking curiosity and I felt, as I sat in the Slavia next to the big windows that provide one of the best views of the Hradčany in the city, that simply by staring out the window I was doing my bit: there it was, the castle, and I was looking at it. I had fallen on the breast of the Middle European coffeehouse and I was content among the putty- and dove-colored clothes, the pensioners stirring away the hours, the tables of university students studying and writing their papers, the luscious waste of time, the gossip whose ardor I sensed in the bent heads, lifted eyebrows — because of course I couldn't understand a word.

In Vienna the coffeehouses — not all of them, thank God — lose their leases to McDonald's and fast-food chains. But in Prague the colors just fade and become more, rather than less, what they were. The coffeehouse is deeply attached to the idea of conversation, the exchange of ideas, and therefore, to a political society. In *The Agony of Czechoslovakia '38/'68*, Kurt Weisskopf remembers the Prague coffeehouses before the Second World War.

You were expected to patronize the coffeehouse of your group, your profession, your political party. Crooks frequented the Golden Goose, or the Black Rose in the centre of Prague. Snobs went to the Savarin, whores and their prospective clients to the Lind or Julis; commercial travellers occupied the front part of Cafe Boulevard, while the rear was the traditional meeting place of Stalinists and Trotskyites, glaring at each other as they sat around separate marble tables. The rich went to the Urban, "progressive" intellectuals to the Metro. Abstract painters met at the Union, and surrealists at the Manes where they argued with impressionists. You were still served by the black-coated waiters if you did not belong, but so contemptuously that you realized how unwelcome your presence was. The papers in their bamboo frames and the magazines in their folders, an essential part of the Central European coffeehouse service, were regrettably not available to intruders. If you went to the wrong coffeehouse you were just frozen out.

But if you fitted in, socially, politically, philosophically, artistically or professionally, well, then the headwaiter and the manager treated you almost as a relative and you were even deemed worthy of credit.

"Rudolf, switch on the light over the Communists, they can't read their papers properly," old Loebl, manager of the Edison used to instruct the headwaiter. "And see that the Anarchists get more iced water." Once you had ordered your coffee you were entitled to free glasses of iced water brought regularly by the trayload; this was called a "swimming pool."

The water was still brought, as I sat at the marble table of the Slavia, though not by the trayload. Perhaps there were political conversations, even arguments: I couldn't tell. But the newspapers were the official ones of the Communist Party, including, in English, the *Daily Worker*. When I asked someone

I'd struck up a conversation with, who was quoted as a source on American news, I was told, "Gus Hall," the chairman of the American Communist Party. "As a typical American?" I asked incredulously. "As the voice of the people," I was told. It struck me as funny, not sinister, although later I realized I was annoyed.

I walked around Prague, hardly caring if I hit the right tourist spots, missing baroque gems, I suppose, getting lost, leaving the hotel without a map as if I had no destination. I just walked, stopping at coffeehouses, smoking unfiltered cigarettes and looking out from the blue wreath around me to other deep-drawing smokers. Everyone seemed to have time to sit, to smoke as if smoking were breathing, to stare into the vacancy of private thought, if their thoughts were private. I was in the thirties, I'd finally arrived in my parents' decade, the men's soft caps, the dove colors of Depression pictures, the acquiescence to circumstance, the ruined quality. For the first time I recognized the truth of beauty: that it is brokenness, it is on its knees. I sat and watched it and smoked (I don't smoke but I found myself buying cigarettes), smoked a blue relation between those coffeehouses and me. For this sadness turned out to be, to me, beautiful. Or rather, the missing quality of beauty, whatever makes it approachable, became apparent in Prague. I could sit, merely breathing, and be part of it. I was beautiful — at last. And I didn't care — at last. I stumbled through the ancient streets, stopped in the smoke-grimed coffeehouses and added my signature of ash, anonymous and yet entirely satisfied. I had ceased even to be a reverse immigrant — I sought no one, no sign of my family or any ethnic heritage that might be mine. I was, simply, in the most beautiful place I had ever seen, and it was grimy and sad and broken. I was relieved of some weight, the odd burden of happiness and unblemished joy of the adored child — or perhaps I was free of beauty itself as an abstract concept. I didn't think about it and didn't bother to wonder. I sat and smoked; I walked and got lost and didn't care because I couldn't get lost. I hardly understood that I was happy: my happiness consisted of encountering sadness. I simply felt *accurate*.

Finally, one day toward the end of my week's stay, I bestirred myself, found my guidebook at the bottom of my suitcase and paged through until I found a gallery, a bona fide tourist destination. I went there: the St. George Monastery in the Hradčany, which has a spectacular collection of medieval art.

I brought a notebook, as I usually do to museums, and walked from gallery to gallery, looking, sometimes jotting down notes. The place was quite empty, the museum guards (most of them were women) were gossiping in the hallways and smiled at me when I went by. I ended up in a large room filled with altarpieces and icons, the gold foil background of medieval religious paintings glowing from each picture. An old man, as dove colored as any pensioner in the Slavia, was in the gallery, standing so close to a painting his nose almost touched the pigment. He put his hand up and touched the picture. I looked around: no guard. I decided to ignore him. It didn't seem to me a dangerous sort of touching. I was actually pleased he'd gotten away with it. I continued looking, jotting notes of my own wounded Christ. The old man shuffled past the painting he had stroked and was going out of the gallery, past me. I looked up and smiled. He looked surprised, and it occurred to me he might be confused and wonder if, because I had smiled, he should know me. I thought he was gone out of the room when suddenly, from behind, my arm was grabbed and he was crying, "An American, an American girl! Are you American?" I told him I was and he put his arms around me and hugged me. He was very old.

He told me he was very lonesome, that he was from New York. (Originally from Prague, he said, as if it were self-evident, but he was a shoemaker so of course he had gone to New York at the time of the First World War. I didn't quite get the connection but he seemed to think it was obvious.) His wife had died six months before. I told him I was sorry.

"May I kiss you?" he said. "Excuse me, but I'm so lonesome."

What with the wife and the old age and the loneliness, I leaned over, pecked him swiftly on the cheek and was pulling away, saying, "Of course you're lonely. That's normal, it's natural to be lonely." But he wanted to keep hugging, kept saying how terribly lonely he was, how glad he was to see an American.

"How did you know I was an American?" I asked.

"I peeked over your shoulder," he said, pointing to my notebook. "You were writing in English."

"Do you like the paintings?" I asked, trying to engage his mind somehow — away from loneliness, away from kissing.

Yes, he said, but it was lonely looking at them all alone. I suggested we look together. He liked that.

Suddenly all the paintings looked shockingly suggestive, full of half-clothed bodies. The old dove-colored man (he showed me his passport, as if to prove his existence: he was eighty-five) hardly looked at them. He looked at me, kept trying to stroke my face, occasionally sighed loudly and said how good it was to see an American — could he hug me again? I thought there had been enough patriotic hugging. I was a little alarmed. He reached out to embrace me again and I dodged him, looked up to see myself being regarded by two West German tourists, impeccably, coolly dressed. I found myself grinning foolishly, guiltily. They looked fleetingly around the gallery, didn't venture in, turned and left the room. I wanted, crazily, to run after them and explain my innocence. They think I'm his girlfriend, maybe a prostitute, I thought.

I might have left him before the German couple saw us, but oddly enough their hauteur, their cool judgment — I could see it on their expressionless faces — made me stonily loyal to him, to our encounter. He is perfectly harmless, he is a lonely old man alone in a foreign country, I thought, turning back to him and joining him in front of a writhing, bloody, ecstatic Christ. I don't think he saw the Germans.

He did not attempt to hug me. He wanted now, it seemed, to tell me his story. Did I mind if he told me — private things?

I did not mind. Well, with his wife it had not been easy. It rarely is, I said, wise and expansive now that he was off the hugging. No, he said. He meant in bed. In bed, I said dully, sensing we were not after all moving away from the hugging. Sex he meant, he said. Yes, I said.

He couldn't explain why — maybe I could understand it — but he had never been able to get *his* thing into his wife's *place*. It was like glued shut and he couldn't get in.

This is perfectly normal, I thought. I was brought up a prude, but this is the time not to act like a prude. This is in fact *wonderful* that an old man can speak so frankly, so simply to a stranger about something so personal. And he *was* talking with rare naturalness, no drama, no shame, the only emotion seemed to be a faint bewilderment that made his comments seem harmless, innocent, as natural as if he'd been speaking of the cross pollinization of flowers.

He showed me a picture of his wife. They had come back to Prague together several years before and now, because they had planned this trip together — who would have thought she would die, he said — he had come alone. His friends in New York had convinced him he should make the trip. "You have to come back to life," he said, obviously quoting.

His wife, in the picture, sat at a table in a beer garden. Under other circumstances, she would not have struck me: simply an old lady, neatly dressed. "She was a good-looking woman, yes?" he said. But I was thinking vaginas.

The thing was, he said, putting the picture back in his wallet, he couldn't sleep alone. *Couldn't.* I suddenly felt exhausted, as if I could not protect him or me from whatever twist his grief was taking — for I had, in some way, thought that by force of will I was keeping alarm (that is, sex) at bay.

And maybe I was exercising some kind of power, prude power, because just then he said, humbly, courteously, "You don't mind do you? You're an American girl, a modern girl, you don't mind . . ." It was a singsong, rhythmic, enchanted, and I knew, even before I looked down, what I would find.

"Not here!" I said severely, as if somewhere else would be better.

"Oh excuse me, oh not here," he said, as if he had forgotten himself, tucking his penis — a *young* penis, I thought, as if I knew a difference among types — back into his trousers. I have never seen a face as vulnerable and bewildered, coming, perhaps literally, out of a dream. I realized he had been playing with himself for some time and that only my stoical prudishness, old-fashioned and perhaps coquettish to his mind, had kept me from doing what any "American girl, modern girl" would have done: looking right at him, penis in hand, and telling him to cut it out. He seemed suddenly very old, very befuddled, as if he didn't know where he was, how he had gotten here. And I suddenly began to wonder the same thing: certainly he wasn't here all alone.

He had relatives in Prague; they would come back in an hour to pick him up. He and his wife had liked the medieval paintings and so he thought . . . but he was tired now, he said, and wished he could go right home. Would I walk him home?

But I was all firmness and fright now. I steered him out of the gallery, into the hallway and the safety of the matronly guards. I explained, in English, in French, in my menu-card Czech, in the sheer desperation of wanting to abandon him, that this old gentleman was tired and needed a place to rest. The miraculous courtesy of the Czechs, their formality and graciousness — certainly they are a people who say please and thank you more often than any other — took over, delivered me from my ancient sex fiend. And I left the place, giving the old shoemaker immigrant a hug — because he asked for it and because the matronly guards were clucking and demanding it too, it seemed, as a courtesy of youth to age between countrymen.

I met only one other American, a priest who was doing research on a medieval manuscript. He wasn't wearing clerical clothes because, he said, he was sure "they" wouldn't let him do his research if they knew he was a priest. He was a Jesuit, in fact. He asked me to call him Professor, not Father.

He worked in the library, he said, at a table next to a rabbi from Prague who was studying another manuscript. He had asked the rabbi if Jews in Czechoslovakia were given religious freedom. The rabbi looked at him, he said, and said quietly, "Do not ask me such questions," and then turned back to his manuscript as if nothing had happened.

The priest and I were sitting after the opera in the Hotel Paříž restaurant, having a drink, when he told me this. The Paříž is art nouveau, inside and out. At the time there was rickety scaffolding covering the entire facade. At home the hotel — all of Prague, I sometimes think — would be called funky. When I had arrived, an elderly porter who looked like a professor of something abstruse and pure rode all the way up in the tiny cell of the elevator with his eyes closed: rising in the mind, I had thought, to other regions.

That night the restaurant was crowded. Two German women sat at the table with us, following the European custom of sharing a table with strangers, using all the available chairs. They had been to the opera, too. The older one, blonde, wearing a red satin dress and a lot of possibly real jewelry, leaned across the table and said in English, "Yes, and this is my country. In 1945 they kicked us out. Everyone. We had to go, no exceptions, no matter if you're innocent. I had to leave my homeland."

She had tears in her eyes, which were heavily made-up. She was a little drunk. Her friend — perhaps her daughter — seemed embarrassed; she wasn't drunk.

"It was terrible," the older woman said loudly to us. "You can't imagine how terrible it was. I was a refugee. I had nothing. I lost my homeland. It was my homeland."

"Yes," said the priest, looking down, turning his glass around in circles on the white tablecloth. The younger woman said something in German, softly, urgently, to the older one. The two of them began to talk together again, in German, about the opera.

The priest and I started to talk about Vietnam. It was the week the American army left Saigon. The priest said he was glad the war was over; he'd been against the war. Still, he said, it didn't have the feeling of the end of a war, did it? I said I didn't know, it was the only war I'd lived through, even from a distance.

"It just seems to be stopping," he said. "You don't have the feeling of peace in the air."

It was less than a year after President Nixon's resignation. This event seemed to interest the Czechs I met much more than the end of American involvement in Vietnam. One woman, a secretary I talked to at a coffeehouse on Václavské náměstí, asked me if Nixon had *really* been a criminal. I said yes, it looked that way. She wanted to know how this was discussed in America.

"Do people just say, right out, 'Nixon is a criminal'?" she asked me.

I told her some people did; most people, in fact.

"But is this said publicly, by anyone?"

"Yes," I said.

"We don't *say* things," she said.

I left Prague the next day, on the train to Paris. I happened to sit in a compartment with a woman from Slavkov (Austerlitz). She spoke English. She spoke, in fact, eight languages ("It's my hobby; I'm a widow"). The compartment smelled strongly of garlic sausage, which she said she would share with me. She said I must not go to the dining car: it was too expensive. I didn't go to the dining car then or later, it was a matter of loyalty, and she was, immediately, the sort of person who demands loyalty, that things be done her way. Besides, for a long time, I had faith in the sausage.

She had been crying when I first came into the compartment. As we introduced ourselves ("Ružena, call me Rose") and she offered me ("later") the garlic sausage, I saw the tears on her face.

"I don't think my country will survive," she said. Just like that, without missing a beat after the offer of the sausage.

"What do you mean?" I said. I knew what she meant, but I couldn't believe she was talking to a stranger this way.

"First one thing, then the next thing. Russians, Germans, Germans, Russians," she said. "We can't make it. I have the scars from both of them."

"Scars?" I said.

"From the Germans, then from the Russians."

"What did you do?" I asked her.

"I don't know," she said. Then a moment later, "My husband was a soldier." It was impossible to know if that was meant to be an explanation; she said it musingly, as if thinking of it for the first time. She pulled her blouse open slightly, and there, above her breast, was a shiny, puckered, too-pink blotch of flesh and several thin dead-white lines. "The other ones are on my buttocks," she said.

Then she asked me, as she buttoned her blouse, if I liked the Beatles. "I love Santana. I love Frank Sinatra," she said. We talked about pop music all the way to the border, except when we went slowly past a certain dusty little town. The train had had to make a detour; it wasn't a town on the usual run. She looked out the window as we passed through (I didn't see the name of the place) and said, "Why do we come *here?* This is where I was in prison for a year."

"Because of your husband?"

"I don't know."

Then she asked me if I worried about black men marrying white women. I said I didn't. She sighed and said they had terrible problems themselves on this score.

"With blacks marrying whites?" I said, astonished. I had only seen a few black foreign students in the coffeehouses.

"Gypsies," she said, shaking her head sourly as if she'd bit into a lemon.

Being a good liberal, I decided to act like one. I told Ružena that I thought it was just fine if blacks and whites married. This seemed to hit her as an absolutely novel approach to the subject, one she simply hadn't thought of but which, now that I brought it up, she clasped as her own.

"Oh Vlastička, you must teach me," she cried. "You're so smart." But she added, did I understand the Gypsies were dirty? I was back in the embrace of racial nerves: the rag sheeny was dirty, the Gypsies were dirty, and we — we were clean.

Ruzena said shrewdly that my father must have known what he was doing when he named me. Patricia, she said, was Vlasta in Czech. And Vlasta came from the word *vlast,* which means "homeland." I said I didn't think my father knew Czech well enough to have thought that; anyway, nobody had ever mentioned it. They just liked the name and I was born near St. Patrick's Day. No, she said, shaking her head, looking wise, "I know your father, I know he's Czech and he names you Vlasta because he's Czech." Oh, you don't know my father, I thought. He thinks I should spend my vacation in northern Minnesota, which is paradise. But the truth was, I sort of liked the idea myself.

The conductor came in to stamp our tickets. I held mine out, but instead of taking it, he grabbed my hand and turned it palm up and began jabbering in Czech, poking his index finger insistently around my palm, glancing now and again into my face, *into* it, looking deeply into my eyes, searching and wild with discovery, it seemed. I couldn't understand a word, except that I thought I heard a single familiar one: "Kafka."

He didn't let go of my hand, but kept prodding it and saying what seemed to be urgent things to me.

"He says," Ruzena told me, "that you will have a long life, a happy life. He says you should know he isn't crazy. He says he is a psychic and . . ."

The little intense man interrupted her and said clearly, unmistakably, "Kafka, Kafka," in what seemed to me a perfectly crazed way. He kept hold of my hand but was swinging around between Ružena and me, looking at her, then at me, as she translated, as if he could assess the accuracy of her translation by keeping track of our expressions.

"He wants you to know that he is not crazy. He wants you to know he works with Dr. Kafka," Ružena said.

"Dr. Kafka?" I said wildly, and pulled my hand away.

They jabbered some more between them, and then Ružena said, "There is a Dr. Kafka, a famous professor, he says, who works with psychics in Prague at the Charles University. He works with him. He is a bona fide psychic, he says. He wants you to know he is intelligent."

I smiled at the man; he was shorter than I was and his uniform made him look childish, like a student at a military academy, although he must have been forty. "Tell him thank you," I said to Ružena. "Tell him I'm glad to have the good news."

She told him. "He wants to tell you his philosophy," she told me. "Maybe he's crazy anyway." He began to explain his philosophy, with Ružena translating grumpily; it seemed to be a grab bag of Eastern religions and a steady faith in the powers of clairvoyance. "He wants to impress you," Ružena said, right in front of him. "He wants to impress an American. Who knows what he is?" He gave no sign of understanding this.

Finally he left, with his silver ticket punch (we had to remind him to punch our tickets) and his absurd little blue suit. He said he would come back later to explain his philosophy in greater detail.

But he didn't come back. We never saw him again. At the border, about an hour later, Ružena became nervous. She was worried that at the last moment "they" wouldn't let her across the border because of the sausage, which she was convinced was contraband. She was going to visit her son who was married and living in Belgium; he had been out of the country in August 1968 and had simply not come back. The sausage was a present for the son, deprived, she felt, of proper sausages by his exile. I began to wonder whether I would get any of it. "Later, we will have some," she said, as if reading my thoughts.

The border station was an Iron Curtain cliché: barbed wire, a barren no-man's-land strip of stubble, even a weather-beaten wooden watchtower. I hadn't noticed these things on the way into the country the previous week.

The passport officials came through and everything went all right. No mention of the sausage. Ružena breathed again. But a few minutes later, three men came to the door: two policemen and a young man I recognized as the cashier who on my arrival into the country had exchanged my Western currency (American, British, Belgian) into Czech crowns. He was the first Czech I spoke to and I remembered him. They were looking for someone. The cashier saw me through the glass door, pointed, excitedly told the policemen something. They crowded into the compartment and began talking rapidly in Czech.

Once again Ružena was the translator. As she was talking, she leaned down and slid the bag with the sausage back behind the fold of her coat, which was hanging from the edge of the seat.

I had been given too much Czech money for my Western currency when I came into the country the week before, they were telling me— Ružena was telling me. A clerical error. I now owed them $75. I asked to see some sort of proof. I was told to get off the train and "wait for the next train sometime tomorrow" if I had any questions. I said something about wanting to speak to the American Embassy, but I don't think Ružena translated that. The cashier looked miserable. The $75, he told her to tell me, would come out of his salary if I didn't pay it. I said they couldn't just *do* this. Ružena said, "Be calm. *Soyez tranquille.*"

Ružena said, as if it were part of the translation (nobody spoke English besides us), that I must pay the money, I mustn't get off the train. I took out my traveler's checks and signed over several of them, and the three men left. The cashier and I actually shook hands before he left.

"Hard currency," Ružena sighed sadly after they'd gone. She pulled the sausage bag out from its hiding place. "You see," she said shrewdly, shaking a finger at me, "he was an agent." She meant the clairvoyant conductor. "Who else would they let go to the border on the train all the time."

We crossed the border in silence. It seemed to be a long passageway, rather than a simple dividing line on a highway. Finally, we were on the other side. I wanted to ask Ružena if she thought the conductor might really be a psychic, in spite of everything else. ("You will have a long life, a happy life.") But just after we went through West German customs, I heard several doors open along our corridor. Three middle-aged men were standing at our door. They knocked politely, as if the compartment was a house and they were making a call.

Ružena told them, in Czech, to enter. They bowed to her, all of them cramming into the little compartment in their drab suits. Each man, in turn, came up to me, took my hand and shook it and said something in Czech, something formal, it seemed. I smiled and shook hands. Then they left. I could hear the doors of their compartments slide open and then shut as they returned to their seats.

"What was that all about?" I asked Ružena.

"They say they are sorry; they are ashamed that such a thing should happen in their country. They say you have been robbed, but to forgive their country."

"It's not their fault," I said.

"But when it's *má vlast* . . ." she said, smiling, hands open, palms up. "My homeland" — the Smetana tone poem that inaugurates the Music Festival. My homeland — that music, the Sudeten German woman who was kicked out, the rabbi turning back silently to his medieval manuscript, the shoemaker immigrant coming back, still looking for sex, Ružena smuggling out a sausage. Even myself leaving — and gladly — that secretive, spooky country of my ancestors.

Before she got off the train Ružena wanted to exchange rings: a token of friendship. I thought she meant my grandmother's Bohemian garnet, but she had her eye on a cheap ring I'd bought in a Minneapolis head shop for a couple of dollars. I liked it, but I could part with it. Her ring, which was also cheap, was garish, a mud-yellow stone, a pebble, pasted (you could see the glue) on an ugly band; the band was adjustable. We exchanged rings, addresses, promises to write.

"Of course," Ružena was saying, holding her hand out, admiring the little violet pebble of her new ring (I held my hand out too, but I could not admire), "those men, they had to wait until we're over the border. They can't apologize back there." She said it with contempt, tossing her head in the direction of her country, dismissing it. But I wondered why should she be contemptuous — she who had been terrified about a sausage? And I was still hungry.

2 ❦

I HAD MADE the traditional wish ("to return") at Rabbi Loew's grave in the Old Jewish Cemetery, but I didn't expect to be back in Prague very soon. It had seemed, even before my train trip out of the country, when I stood alone on the Charles Bridge with its statues of saints ("the most beautiful bridge in the world"), that that city and the entire country had little, after all, to do with me. History, for people like me, I decided, begins in America. For the grandchildren of the late-nineteenth-century immigrants, Europe is an opaque peasant historylessness, full of towns we can't pronounce and languages we will never speak. The people who go in for folk dancing and ethnic cooking are, perhaps, doing all that can be done to "reclaim their heritage," I decided.

I went home to Minnesota and got a job teaching a poetry class to old people (the Leisure League) at the St. Paul Jewish Community Center. I got a letter from Ružena, who was back in Slavkov. She apologized for her "scribal errors" in English, and said that she knew I must be laughing at her letter. But I wasn't laughing; her English, in any case, seemed quite fluent. "From Vienna," she wrote:

> I heard very often many lovely songs with the American singers and I saw also in the TV some shows with Elisa Minelli, Johny Mathis, Harry Bellafonte — my darling — jose Feliciano, Trini Lopez, Dean Martin and Percy Sledge.

But from all I am happy to hear Santana and the orchestra Mahawishnu. I looked for them — that means for the discs in Belgium, but it was impossible to find them.

I am very content and grateful to you for the lovely post-card with the Indians and from your country. All my live I wished to have the possibility to read about the Indians, but like a child I read only Karel May, and that is a phan-tasie, *rien plus*. I thank you very much for such lovely gifts, like the postcards from your country. You know, I was al-ways thinking that America, this are only the skyscraper, and it is also a country full of beauty and poesie.

I had sent her some postcards of the Minnesota lakes, my father's paradise. She wrote that she was "so afraid to loose your friend-ship because of my delay" in writing. She was not happy. She thought my parents were lucky to have me near. "I implore them to let in your heart a small place also for me. I am so lonely here, really. I never thought I shall be so lonely. In such a small village I cannot find the friends and the culturel life I am ac-customed." She wrote that she was going to send me — "not now, soon" — some Czech music on records and some tapes for learn-ing the language. And, in many ways, she said again and again, Write me, write me.

I did write. And I sent her a Santana album. We wrote back and forth; I never got the records or the tapes, but I thought perhaps she had forgotten. I think she had.

I began, without much application, to take Czech language lessons from an eighty-year-old woman, recently widowed, who had escaped (her word) in 1948, the year of the Communist ascendancy in Czechoslovakia. I clipped articles about Czecho-slovakia from the newspaper ("In Modern-Day Czechoslovakia, Medieval Look Is Alive and Well," "Manifesto Charging Rights Violations in Czechslovakia," "Kohout and Other Czechs Facing More Questions on Rights Petitions").

I started to keep a notebook. On the cover I pasted a Czech postage stamp, and wrote "Czechoslovakia" on the flyleaf. The stamp showed a delicately colored sixteenth-century painting of the Hradčany. The St. Vitus Cathedral spire rose up from the fortress on the stamp just as it does in reality. But on the stamp the castle is on a green, pastoral hill; the city hadn't surrounded it yet. It had the look of a giant manor house.

I hardly recognized all this activity as obsessive. I just did it: the clippings (I considered hiring a clipping service, which did strike me as obsessive and I dropped the idea), the notebook with passages quoted from books and with my own thoughts, the weekly Czech lessons with Mrs. Beranek. Her husband had been an officer in the Austrian and later the Czechoslovak army. He had believed, she told me, that everything might have been different for their country, for all of Europe, if the Czechs had been mobilized after Munich. He thought they might have won, might have beaten Hitler. "It was a good army," she said.

She and her husband had met Tomáš Masaryk ("a beautiful man"); they had known President Beneš. ("I never liked him. He was so narrow, narrowly Czech. And he had a high, squeaky voice, not a man's voice, a *silly* voice.") Mrs. Beranek had graduated from Charles University, had studied music with the original Delilah of Saint-Saëns's *Samson and Delilah,* had "almost" become an opera singer herself, was related in some intricate but genuine way to Smetana. She taught English, French and German in Prague between the two wars as a pastime. She and her husband had lived in a luxurious apartment in old Prague, had a maid, and she hadn't the slightest idea now what she did with her time then. "Practiced the piano, I guess," she said, "and did embroidery. I did a lot of embroidery. And I had to plan dinner."

She lived now in a low-rent high-rise on the edge of I-94, the freeway between Minneapolis and St. Paul. The rent, for senior citizens, is exactly 25 percent of their income. In her case her income was her social security check. She paid $75 for a one-bedroom apartment. I came once a week, on Friday afternoons, for my lesson. I had good intentions about studying every week, yet every week I came without having looked at the textbook, *Colloquial Czech.* She never scolded; she commiserated. And she pronounced the old charm, *Come eat.* We began the lesson with cream puffs and coffee-and-cream, the sugar bowl much in use. I tried to explain that I *liked* my coffee black. She knew better: I was trying to save her sugar, trying to save her money, and she spooned in three heaping, expensive mounds of hospitality. And two of cream, which she sometimes whipped and placed in a glass bowl. She watched me eat; she did not eat, but she drank sugary coffee too. It was good, she said, to have someone to cook for. And so, because the cream puffs were one of the stages of her grief (the husband had only been dead a few months) and anyway, they were terrific cream puffs, I ate and ate. I was briefly zippy and ready to take on the unstudied lesson. But then, it all ebbed away, the cream puffs, the rich coffee, my phony confidence, and I was very sleepy, hardly able to keep my head from falling onto the white tablecloth of the dinette table where we had the cream puffs and the lesson. I was so sleepy I almost wept. And so we went on to the lesson and I learned nothing of the language from my pensioner who had made her own Slavia in the high-rise next to the freeway.

Most of the residents of the high-rise, when I first began coming for lessons, were old people and black people. By the time I left for London in 1977, with the money from an "Individual Artist's Grant Awarded for Poetry" in my pocket (almost the first outside evidence that I *was* a poet), it was possible to notice a new population group moving into the high-rise. The Vietnamese refugees had begun to arrive.

I wanted to keep an account in my notebook of all my reading, my thoughts, anything at all that had to do with Prague and Czechoslovakia. To be anything close to accurate, I should have started the notebook much earlier — not only to record my trip there in 1975 and all the reading I did before going, but to connect my current interest with the more unconscious past. To connect it with my childhood, in fact, even to my father's childhood, which somehow grew up alongside my own because I used to beg him for stories and he always told me something. Those stories, or descriptions of the West Seventh Street Czech neighborhood were like a shimmering companion-childhood to my own much more American childhood. That immigrant neighborhood glittered before I ever knew the word nostalgia or could imagine the idea of loss. I was always aware of that community, of the people who lived there, that they spoke two languages, that there was right here in prosaic St. Paul another, almost exotic city, lying like a kernel near downtown. I saw the vegetable gardens, the streetlights, the women gossiping; especially I saw (it's still there) the brewery down the block, with its red brick, the blink of its sign, its presence in the neighborhood as a "major employer," the picture, from the Depression, of the entire work force lining West Seventh outside the brewery, when my uncle's funeral procession went by: those soft caps in hand, suspenders, rolled-up shirt sleeves, the dove color, the mouse of humility under the red sign.

Uncle Frank's death there, before I was born, "before the War," stood over my childhood and colored it strangely, beyond logical proportion, even emotional logic. The lavish, inappropriate grief I felt over the loss of someone I didn't even know was the first indication I had that sorrow has a life beyond individual experience. Sadness lingers, loss can be inherited.

It was as if that neighborhood was intact and fully alive for me, as well as for my father. As if it were my neighborhood, my home and past. My life. It was, in a way. But only in the fragmented, partial way that a grandmother's house is another, shadowy family home to a child. I spent a lot of time there; the family life tended to revolve around that house on Webster Street for years. But I had to go all the way to Prague, I had to stand on that exact *other* piece of earth, to find out there wasn't a thread holding the two places neatly together, in spite of my grandmother crying over the album of Prague views in her kitchen fifty years after she'd left Europe forever. Or the relation between the two places has become entirely ironic: the brewery *is* a kind of Hradčany, a castle hulked over the neighborhood.

The more I have read of the history of "the Czech lands," the more I have been struck by the country's symbolic power, the will to live. Not the will to change, which was the phrase of my university years, the attempt to "make the personal political." But the will to stay the same, to exist bluntly and undeflected from *what you are:* my grandmother's way. My grandmother, that small powerhouse of love and hate, was my companion when I started out on my travels, my historical ghost. But even she waxed and waned in significance. Her feudal past, her ignorance and the solid assurance she had of her ability to work and that, working, she would surely survive — these things floated in and out, sometimes far away, from the city itself, the country and the light of Prague which steadily burned into my eyes as I walked, drifted really, through the city and listened to people in the coffeehouses.

I saw my grandmother a hundred times a day on the streets and in the villages where the train stopped. I saw her as I had known her — an old woman, small, round, white haired and bowlegged from rickets, the incarnation of labor. I saw her also as she'd been as a girl: the plump face, the coquetterie of the fin-de-siècle girl, the dizzying lusciousness of the servant girl. That was she. And she walks still in the streets of Socialist Prague. The women there do in fact, like so much else, seem to be oddly out of time. Even their modernity, their attempt at fashion particularly, is somehow off kilter. (I mean the average woman; there is a population of young women — some of them prostitutes, some less clearly so — who hang around the larger hotels. They dress up-to-the-immediate-minute and would seem completely in step in Paris or New York; the idea of the effort it must take for them to get their cowboy boots, their cigarette-leg leather pants, boggles the mind.)

How fragile is the touching desire for significance that fashion represents. There is real beauty and bravery in the tatty edges of style. It is impossible to see this when a fashion is in vogue. Even the nostalgia that has been the ruling aesthetic in women's clothes in recent years does not expose this quality. Because nostalgia has become modern, witty, immediate. In Prague everything has the haze of not-quite-rightness. It is Europe, it is familiar in a way — a city with traffic jams and pollution, but the glamour a country imagines for itself reveals, in part, its private thoughts. And in Prague, the style is several steps behind the West. Soon not just the women waiting in the hotels for hard currency tourists, but the women rushing for groceries will be wearing cowboy boots. And Paris will be onto something else. In spite of everything — the Soviet Union, Socialism, a Slovenic heritage — Czechoslovakia remains *Central* Europe: It looks West and East. Especially, with wistful curiosity, to America and the unreachable, flashy life of style.

Maybe I will never understand the passion I feel about Prague. I've just finished Marcia Davenport's memoir *Too Strong for Fantasy.* She never understood her obsession with that small arrow of a country. The fascination was there, for her, from the first. Her relationship with Jan Masaryk came later. He said she must have some Czech ancestry: her love for the place could only be explained that way, he said.

But that doesn't explain Jopi, the Amsterdam telephone operator I met at breakfast one morning at the Paříž. She told me she knew she should travel somewhere else, should spend her holiday in another place, "But I have to come back. Always back to Prague. Why is that?" She was genuinely bewildered. Maybe there are affinities for other places that amaze the people who find themselves enthralled. Prague, a friend of mine who loves Rome told me, is gray. It *is* gray, I suppose. The grime and ancient dust that cling to old stonework and that houses itself in the ornamentation of baroque palaces is burned off in Italy and the south by the sun. In Prague the winter grinds its fist into the old buildings. Nothing ever looks really clean. And then there is the Iron Curtain, the gray metal that is over thirty years old now and that an entire generation, my own, has felt itself looking through to see, as Philip Roth calls it, "the other Europe." Prague is as gray as it is golden. (Zlatá Praha, it has always been called — golden Prague, perhaps in honor of the misty, gilded light or perhaps for the alchemists who once made it their capital.)

Czechoslovakia is different from the rest of baroque Europe. It is "the heart of Europe"; it is the sadness of the continent. It is the intersection of East and West; the two great trade routes of medieval times crossed exactly in the Old Town Square: the north-south "amber" route and the east-west route between the Frankish Empire and Byzantium. Geography is irrevocable, and Czechoslovakia is dead center. It gets in on all the trouble. "Whoever controls Bohemia, controls Europe" — Bismarck. Hitler too, although not in those words. And now, definitely, the Soviet Union, but with hardly any words at all. The swagger has gone out of colonization, but there it is, all the same.

The country's beauty is its greatest sadness, a final irony and perhaps a national consolation. On the train into Czechoslovakia, the man in my compartment (oh, the people riding those trains!) said over and over, "It is beautiful. Isn't it beautiful?," as we rattled past the fields where the hops are trained up thin wires in summer like string beans. "Poor, but most beautiful country," he said. "More beautiful than America. Yes?" And I said yes, not because it was true, but because it was true at the moment.

The beauty is part of the fascination, the broken beauty of that city and the still-lovely nineteenth-century quality of the farmland. But there is something else too, something beyond the European beauty and the rounded-down edges of age. The other allure is political. Prague presents any decent person with the deep ambivalence that must be felt in the face of the choices West and East present for the future and for justice — which are suggested by Socialism. Socialism which, after all, is one of the important political ideas of modern times, which proposes how we are to live together.

My own background is petite bourgeoisie. My father is a florist. The happiest heritage of Czechoslovakia is also bourgeois: the Masaryk Republic of 1918–1938. I cannot really leave that fact when I think of politics. It connects me to the basic old democratic ideals of my own country (just as it did Tomáš Masaryk, who married an American). But the frightening truth that is emerging from this century of frightening crimes is that democracy may come to be a pointless word in the West as well as the East. The Left in this country had no energy, no *imagination* I'm tempted to say, for Czechoslovakia in 1968 when the Russians invaded — even as we protested against our own war in Asia. The Right was worse: while saying the United States was "fighting Communism" in Vietnam, the hawks didn't lift a finger to help Czechoslovakia in August 1968. We had given that piece of goods to Russia. It was that simple. We had no real faith in the brainless, shopworn anti-Communism that had been our "ideology" for the previous twenty years.

And yet, in Prague, the people I met in 1975 said, "Don't forget us." They didn't mean me personally; they meant America (always "America," never "the United States"; "America" with that money-in-the-streets ring to it) should remember their country, should "do something." I almost laughed. Certainly, I came home a more ironic person; my earnestness had acquired a gloss of irony. I was too ashamed to tell them, "Listen, when I said I was coming to Czechoslovakia, a lot of my friends told me to have a good time on the Dubrovnik coast. They don't even know where you *are*. You're peanuts."

How is it possible to have a coherent political philosophy, something besides good intentions, with such currents swirling about? In my generation, the Left (to which I was naturally drawn) did not gaze long at Europe. North Vietnam, Cuba, the Third World, China were the places to think about, the places of the future. These were all countries — especially China, which was most revered — about which information was least definite, most imprecise, full of blanks ("Who are the poets there?" I asked. Blank, blank), and therefore perhaps, the places one could contemplate longest in utopian terms. For like the generations before us, we were American: utopians, in search of an *idea* because there wasn't the finer satisfaction of a culture. We were a lot like our parents after all, in spite of the generation gap we were rather proud of having caused.

The experience of Vietnam, in particular, made it difficult to feel anything but disgust and shame over our own ways of controlling our piece of the world, our "colonies." I suppose I wanted to be a liberal democrat, a believer in individual rights and the sovereignty of nations. I wish it were possible to believe these things, that they aren't pathetic stands against the inexorable defeat of the liberty the world has believed in, at its best, for centuries.

In 1970 when Jim Moore, the man I live with, went to prison for resisting the draft I was surprised when a friend very active in the antiwar movement told me it was a big mistake. I'd heard, read, about strange defections, weird turns to the Right; I thought perhaps I was witnessing one. But it wasn't that. "Going to prison," he said, "is a completely moral move." (Actually he said, "Going to prison is, like, a completely moral move," but that makes him sound worse than he was or than I perceived him).

"Yes," I said, proud of my man.

"Yeah, and so where is he now? He's in prison. I mean, it's admirable and all that, but we need people on the streets. Going to prison is, like, it's a very personal thing, you know? It's not political."

I began to understand that I knew very little about politics.

It is not only the technology of destruction that makes all the old values of liberal democracy fearfully vulnerable (my friends and I came to adulthood thinking of ourselves as radicals — mainly because the liberal press called us that — and the word *liberal* still signals reproach, although of course very few of us were radicals. But the word lingers). The technology of communications is even scarier at times. For it can destroy a culture, the one place an oppressed group can hide when its sovereignty is taken away.

But all of this is far from Prague, from the people I met there, from whatever is located within the heart of the heart of Europe, the Europe so few people even think of as Europe. All I knew for certain as I began my second trip was my fascination with the place, a fascination that had grown, rather than abated, since I first went there to set my curiosity at rest. I didn't find my grandmother — or I found her and she was wearing a mini-skirt. I didn't find the goose-down pillow of history; and even the European beauty, which I'd dreamed of for years, like the provincial I am, was not what I expected. Prague finally lifted me out of the self-absorbed female preoccupation. I saw there that the beauty of the Old World is broken, and that this brokenness was what I had been missing, not the beauty itself. My father was right when we went fishing: this probably is paradise, right here.

I also have a sense that my fascination with Prague is not simply a quirk, but that it represents something deeply rooted in the history we are still living out from the past, a past we thought we were done with. This history is like the long, rever-berating chime from a cathedral bell, which moves through the air by feel, by vibration, rather than by actual sound, long after the tone itself has dissipated, and everyone assumes there is silence.

3 ❧

IN MAY 1977, I went from London, where I was staying, to Prague, again during the music festival. In the two years since my first visit I'd come to feel that the significance of Czechoslovakia, specifically of Prague, had something to do with the curious emptiness that has been the subject of Western literature at least since the Second World War, perhaps since the First World War. (The Acmeists gathered together before the First World War, but Mandelstam gave his haunting, faintly ironic, definition of Acmeism — *homesickness for world culture* — afterward, when, as he saw, the European civilization he considered his own was beginning its century-long death.)

The sense I have, as someone born immediately after the Second World War, is that I — or anyone born after 1945 — was born into an elegy. The first half of the century was spent in killing, destroying the cities and nations that represented our own culture. Now, during the final quarter, the quarter in which my generation will live and work and tell what it sees, we are in mourning for that very loss — even as we turn to other cultures (Asia, the Third World) for our battlefields, and, paradoxically, also for spiritual direction.

The grief of Europe is often unacknowledged or buried. In 1949 the Swiss writer Max Frisch, then in his thirties, was already noting in his diary that a friend had chided him for his "forcible attempt to keep wounds open" through his preoccupation with the devastation of the Second World War. Four years after the worst war Europe has known, only a year after Czecho-slovakia became a Communist country (Frisch went to Prague several times during these years and was concerned about the struggle there, especially among artists), in the midst of Stalin's last brutalities — and already the desire for silence, the appeal to forgetfulness. The reason Frisch's friend gives — the classic reason and obviously a sincere one — is that attention to pain creates, or extends, the pain. The point is "to heal."

One thing that seems to be clear, now that we have had over thirty years to heal that particular wound, is that whether or not the pain is acknowledged, whether memory is invoked or not, a residue of grief, a haunted quality, remains in Western culture. The grief, even if it is denied (for the best reason: for the living), is there, waiting for the next generation like an inheritance from someone we never knew. Often the heirs, even while pursuing this grief almost obsessively, are unaware of it: Jopi who goes to Prague on her yearly vacation the way a salmon goes up the Columbia and simply walks and walks around the city and doesn't know why. She isn't the only one. I had met another tourist like her.

His name was Kenth; he was a Swedish medical student. He had gone, as I had one May afternoon, to U Fleku, the fourteenth-century brewery, to drink the famous black beer in the garden courtyard where the horse chestnuts were in blossom. The flimsy white and red flowers were falling on the heads of the waiters who were dressed in white jackets. They looked, with the blossoms caught in their hair, like a roving gang of bridegrooms in a folk opera.

Kenth had been to Prague, he said, eighteen times in the previous six years. Like Jopi, he had no personal associations with the city, no family or friends, no interest in Socialism. Like Jopi, he said he loved music and painting; he liked to walk around the city. That was all. "I have to be here," he said. "I come whenever I can. This is Europe — what's left of it. You can still feel it here, here more than anywhere."

Young Europeans like this, who have not turned to American

pop culture or to Oriental religions, represent the values of Western culture as it was known before the Second World War. But American culture is the vital one. "It is incredible to me how Americans disparage their culture, as if it were cheap or inferior," the West German film director Wim Wenders said in an interview in the *Village Voice* when his movie *The American Friend* came out in 1977. "This is a movie about internationalization," the review of the movie said, "about the interrelationship between American culture and European life." And the tone of the movie was elegiac.

"I don't know if you can understand what American culture meant to me," Wenders says in the *Village Voice* interview. "I was born in '45, in Dusseldorf, two months after the war ended. Everything about German culture was suspect. There was great insecurity about our culture, about any national feeling.

"The first thing which was really important to me was sitting, listening to Chuck Berry on a juke box, in a place where I was not allowed to go. When I listened to rock and roll over the Armed Forces Radio Network — AFRN — it was a culture which was not approved of by my father's generation. I even had to hide my first Elvis Presley records."

The interviewer finishes by saying, "For Wenders culture did not flow from Europe to America. It came from America to him."

I went to see *The American Friend* several times; I thought it was a wonderful movie, an elegy, evocative of Mandelstam's homesickness. He is at the head of the mourners, and these others — Jopi, Kenth, perhaps even Wim Wenders — are at the end of the long black line. It is such a long line, stretching almost the length of the century, that those at the end hardly know consciously what it is they are regretting. They just come instinctively, Kenth, Jopi, to a place they sense is theirs.

Beyond recognizing this elegiac impulse, I wanted to know about — it seemed important to understand — the contemporary life of a poet in a country where, unlike our own, poetry is taken seriously.

It is rather difficult to get into serious trouble in the United

States by writing poetry. There are exceptions: in the late 1960s, it was not at all clear that those who formed American Poets Against the Vietnam War and who went around the country giving readings, would not be prosecuted for their actions. Many younger poets — or simply young men who were writing poetry — did, in fact, go to prison precisely because of the relation they saw between poetry and politics. In the letters to draft boards that I saw during those years, either as friend or as teacher who wrote accompanying "character reference" letters for some of these young men, it was interesting to see how frequently they quoted Whitman. Literature, not political theory, was what they invoked. Thoreau was about as theoretical as anybody got. The impulse was, in one sense, essentially aesthetic: the war was *ugly;* it was somehow repellent. These young men — and I myself as part of the antiwar movement — were not only *angry,* as the press so often said, about this war; we were miffed by it, by its very existence as an ugly blot on the rather attractive, unreal picture we'd been given of our country by our liberal education.

But, for the most part, poetry in this country is essentially a private matter; its public is small, isolated, not usually considered dangerous. In fact, this sort of freedom—the freedom of the ignored — is exactly what American poets often find so exasperating. Nadezhda Mandelstam, the widow of the poet, has written in her memoirs about poets from the West who visit her and say that "at least" poetry *matters* in the Soviet Union and Eastern Europe. She, naturally enough, is not impressed with their reasoning. Her husband mattered altogether too much.

But to a Western poet, or any Western writer, there has developed a romance, a fascination about the poet in Eastern European countries, a fascination that says more about the helplessness of Western writers in the face of mass culture (which creates a climate in which our literature is "free" but doesn't "matter") than about the actual status of poets and poetry in the East. It is exactly here, at the intersection of personal statement and mass society, that the poet stands — whether the poet matters to "the people" or not.

I decided to return to Prague to walk the dreamlike streets of that beautiful, broken city and to talk to poets, if I could find any, who walk there not as visitors, but as residents in the heart of the most elegiac city of Europe. There were, as well, the other poets with whom one inevitably walks in Prague: Kafka, Rilke, the native sons of the golden city, its poetic ghosts.

Before I left London, I had to get a travel alarm clock for the trip to Prague. I went down West End Lane in West Hampstead where I was staying to a shop that sold luggage. I'd noticed a few small clocks displayed in the window, along with all the suitcases, valises and backpacks. Inside, the shop had that hushed feeling of a cloister which some small, not-much-frequented shops have. It was dark and hivelike. The place was crammed with luggage, cheap steamer trunks stacked to the ceiling, smaller tough plastic and metal suitcases, plaid canvas bags and very small cosmetic cases, rucksacks and coin purses. But no sign, inside the shop, of a clock.

At first, my eyes were not accustomed to the light; the place seemed darker and more cavernous than it really was. Then, I was able to see, amongst the piles of luggage at the back of the room near a curtain, a small man with a sweeping head of black hair that had lines of gray going through it in a bold pinstripe. He was eating a sandwich. His face was lined. A face with a history, I thought automatically. His accent was Central European.

I said I needed a travel clock. The price range was six or seven pounds, he said. "And there's one for four pounds, fifty pence." I said I'd take that one. He went to the room behind the curtain and came back with a small box, took out the clock, demonstrated how to wind it, how the alarm worked, how to set it up on its stand. It was a simple mechanism that anyone could figure out but he seemed to feel the demonstration came with the purchase.

As he wrapped the parcel I told him I needed the clock because I was going to Prague for the Music Festival. "Praha!" he said. "A beautiful place." I asked him if he knew it well. Oh, yes. And smiled as if there were a private joke in my asking such an absurd question. But he didn't say anything.

"Were you born in Prague?" I asked. He didn't say anything for a moment. I was pushing.

"Oh, not far from there," he said, and fluttered his hand, as if all directions were one direction. "Not far. The other side of the mountains."

He held the little parcel, which he'd finished tying with string, and began naming the landmarks of Prague that I must be sure to see: "The Charles Bridge, the Hradčany, all the twisting streets of Malá Strana, all the palaces, the baroque architecture. Very beautiful. You have nothing like that, nothing so old in your country," he said, acknowledging my own accent. "It is something quite different for you, is that right?"

I found myself saying, idiotically, "Well, of course, we have Indian culture."

"Yes, but we've destroyed all that, haven't we?" he said, gently. There was something comical, something touching, about this gallantry in the face of genocide: he said "we" so naturally. It was the automatic gesture of one who has the habit of tallying disasters, like a private scorekeeper, an amateur historian. This is a highly moral, civilized impulse — to keep naming the lost, the destroyed, the buried; as if honor, in our century, had been pared down to keeping vivid the exact details of disintegration. We had moved by now to the doorway of the shop, and he had handed me the small parcel with the clock in it.

Suddenly, just as I was about to step out of the dark shop, he said passionately, "We have destroyed the manmade things — this is bad, very bad enough. But now, now we have begun on nature. Now we are destroying nature. And that," he said, holding his palms up, "is the end." He was very angry, almost frantic.

But just as suddenly as he'd begun, he snapped out of it. "No, forget this," he said, shaking his head and waving his hand in that dismissive way he had before. "Enjoy the music. Go for the music." He looked old; his beautiful thick hair, which was rather long, flowed gracefully from his temples in subtle waves. In the light, I saw it was grayer than I'd thought before in the shop.

"Don't think about it," he said. I had heard this before, at the Jewish Community Center in St. Paul, from the old people in my poetry class. Some of them had escaped from Hitler; at lunch one day, after class, I noticed the man and woman across the table from me had those blue numbers tattooed on their arms. These old people had invariably told me they liked to read "happy poems." They, like the shopkeeper, did not want me to "think about" Europe "during those years."

It's as if those who have lived the worst of this century in European history are intent upon protecting the rest of us. We aren't survivors in the literal sense that they themselves are, but to them we are because we have been passed over. We are, for them, the scant pickings and leftovers of innocence. Americans especially, with our inexperience as a nation of what the War really meant, are fabulous creatures to men like him. We appear on the horizon — strange, attractive, even dangerous in our unmarked eagerness for life, our appetite for our roots.

We stood for a moment at his doorway where the division between the brightness of the street and the darkness of the shop was sharp and severe. He made a deprecating grimace and fluttered his hand again. "Forget this," he said, as if he had confided some awful story to me. "Enjoy the music. It's the city of Mozart."

He went back into that dark room full of suitcases and clocks, as if he were in charge of the emblems of exile and history. I went back to my flat and packed the red leatherette travel clock in my suitcase. I might have been stowing away an explanation, the reason I was drawn, like the telephone operator from Amsterdam and the Swedish medical student, to that city, to the heart of Europe, the sadness of the century.

4 ❧

THE PLANE was late. ČSA (Czechoslovak Airlines) is nearly always late. Its international flight designation is OK, which just about says it. Czechs themselves who travel between Prague and London try, according to a Czech friend of mine, to book a British Airways flight because they are more reliable. ČSA flights *go;* they just don't take departure time very seriously. The rumor was that our plane was being held for some African diplomats. But, then, rumors are very Czech. I had the feeling, as I waited in one of the flight lounges at Heathrow, that I had already been gathered behind the heavy draperies of bureaucracy that are not only the entrance to Prague but Prague itself.

We were given vouchers for the airport restaurant while we waited (over three hours, although no one ever said it would be that long; they inched us along in twenty-minute delays). It was easy to spot the Prague passengers in the cafeteria line because we all had the pale green vouchers in our hands.

I took my tray to a table where a young American student and a grandmotherly woman (both green vouchers) were sitting. The woman had been through all of this before, she told the student and me. Just relax and enjoy your tea was her idea. She was English, but since 1945 she had lived in "Czecho," as she called it. Her husband was Czech, a doctor who because he was Jewish had gotten out of Europe in 1938. He spent the War in England where they met and married.

They went back to Czechoslovakia in 1945 — "to help," she said. "My husband was an idealist. He thought they'd need medical people. I thought being in the center of Europe, I would see a lot. I thought we'd go everywhere." Then the rueful Central European shrug: "But of course there hasn't been much traveling." She had a curious accent; the native English and the Czech she had spoken for over thirty years conspired to create a kind of unplaceable, comical brogue.

She had been in England for two months to visit her daughter who had just had a baby. At first, she said, she had been depressed when she came back to England: she watched the TV and felt terrible because of all the strikes, all the reports of poorly made houses, all the *complaints*. The news on the television depressed her badly and she wanted to get back to her village near Karlovy Vary. "Then I got used to it," she said.

Her daughter had left Czechoslovakia, legally, in 1969, to study in England. She was able to get several visa extensions, but was finally told to come back to Czechoslovakia in order to renew the permit. By this time, she had met her future husband and was afraid to go back, for fear she might not be allowed to leave again. She ignored the summons.

She was sentenced, in absentia, to a prison term. She still cannot go back, perhaps never will be able to go back. Besides her parents, she has a sister who is married and has a family in Czechoslovakia. Now she carries a British passport, but she is a fugitive in her own country. Her mother, who has British and Czech passports, is able to visit her, but her father cannot. "Actually," the old lady said to me and to David Beseda, the American student (who told us he was going to Czechoslovakia to see if he could find any relatives), "we've been quite lucky."

❦ ❦ ❦

Notebook entry (written on the plane):
It seems, to me, a broken and terribly displaced life. Perhaps I forget that there are people who want very much to see themselves as "European," not as "British" or "Czech" or "French."

She went to Czechoslovakia in 1945 with the happy thought that she would be in the heart of Europe — Bohemia has always been "the heart of Europe." Her idea that Czechoslovakia was the "center" is telling, and gives a yardstick with which to measure the radically altered idea most of us have developed in the last thirty years of what Europe is. "Europe" has shifted dramatically to the West. It does not include, to our minds, very much besides France, Germany (West), Italy, Scandinavia, Spain, Belgium, the Netherlands, Austria. Penguin Books has an Eastern European fiction series, edited by Philip Roth, called Writers from the Other Europe. Exactly.

But in 1945, when this woman went to Czechoslovakia, it must have been different. That's why so many people ended up living far different lives than they expected. Mrs. Beranek living in that blank shaft of a silo building next to the buzz of the freeway, for example. Or this woman with her off-kilter accent and her dazed acquiescence to the break-up of her family. Still, in 1945 Czechoslovakia would still have been the right place to settle if you wanted to be "a European," if you wanted to be smack dab in the middle of European culture — if you believed it could still be fanned back into life.

Historically, its central location has been Czechoslovakia's main trouble. Bohemia and Moravia are called "the historic provinces," with a nice ambiguity that does not say whose history is meant — perhaps history itself. The usual trouble has come from German-speaking nations; there was a long, sentimental pan-Slav tradition in reaction to the three-century Austrian rule, which made Russia, for many Czechs, an attractive ally even in the days of the czars.

But generally, the Czechs seemed to take seriously the idea that they were in the middle — neither fully Western nor entirely Eastern. Most of the citizens of what, in 1918, became the Republic of Czechoslovakia were probably pleased with Masaryk's idea that their new state should strive to be "a higher Switzerland." This phrase had the advantage of sounding harmless *and* sovereign. It was an elegant idea.

Tomáš Garrigue Masaryk — how strange he isn't better known, isn't revered in the West. Perhaps not so strange after all: his country doesn't exist anymore, his plan failed, his own son, Jan, played out an agonizing Hamlet-like role in the years leading up to the Communist ascendancy in 1948. Masaryk's idea for his country was that it must take seriously its identity as a small country. "The problem of a small country," he said, "is somewhat like the problem of a little man. His human dignity must be respected without regard to the material differences in bigness." Masaryk's idea was to *shame* the big countries into giving his country sovereignty.

This is an odd way to look at nationhood, a curiously polite and highly moral way of attesting to sovereignty. It is also, as all courtesy fundamentally is, an admission of the barbarism implicit in human relations, and the need for something more powerful and inbred than law to control it. Seen in this way, Masaryk's strategy was that of an entirely cynical, fearful man, a man who *must* be fearful, who *must* anticipate the worst. The problem of the small nation is that push too often does come to shove. And then no appeal to morality, to courtesy or decency works because war takes over.

František Palacky, the nineteenth-century historian who has been called the Father of the Nation, was Masaryk's guide for a Czech nation. "Palacky anticipated," Hans Kohn says in an essay titled "The Historical Roots of Czech Democracy," "already in the middle of the last century, the progressive unification of mankind as a result of technical and economic developments; he was convinced that the time of small states had passed and that mankind was drawn irresistibly toward the creation of very large political and economic units . . . Thus for him a small people could exist only on the strength of its intellectual and moral achievements. 'Whenever we were victorious,' he used to remind the Czechs, 'it was always more as a result of spiritual forces than of physical might, and whenever we succumbed, there was always the insufficiency of our spiritual activity and of our moral courage responsible for it.'" (*Czecho-slovakia*, the book in which Kohn's essay appears, by the way, has its own historical significance. It was first published in 1940 as part of the United Nations Series, and consists of chapters by various scholars, all writing with the shadow of Nazism, the overthrow of the Masaryk Republic and the War itself, falling over what they wrote.)

This emphasis on the moral, on the spiritual, might be simply, contentedly bourgeois in other circumstances, but not when a nation must in fact return to these facts over and over through defeat. The man in the luggage store who sold me the clock said of American Indian culture that "we've destroyed all that, haven't we?" And it's true that what happened was genocide and that the Indian culture ("a traditional life" as it is called by Indians) was brutally attacked. But not destroyed: the culture in fact absorbed the genocide, and became more sacred, more spiritual. And, necessarily, more secretive. An American Indian, one who lives traditionally, told this story to a friend of mine: He went to a museum of Indian artifacts in Georgia and listened while the guide (a white) explained that "no one" could seem to agree on the significance of a certain sculpture, a bird with huge wings. Some anthropologists, she said, thought the bird was an eagle; others argued that it was a vulture. She explained the talismanic significance of each bird. But the Indian who lisened told my friend he knew it was neither an eagle nor a vulture. It was in fact another bird altogether, one now extinct and whose name he knew from the ancient songs handed down in his tribe. It had to be this extinct bird, he said, because the song was explicit and so was the sculpture. The songs, the poetry had kept the facts straight.

What happens when a small nation is squashed? It is left without sovereignty, but what after that? Certainly it is left with an even larger sense of its identity as a civilized people, a *wronged* people, in clear distinction to the foreign intruder. (Americans can perhaps get something of a feel for this cultural fact when we consider the Southern emphasis on courtesy, on a way of doing things that puts Yankees in the position of being unattractively gauche.) A destroyed people is a cultural people — not simply cultivated in the superficial sense of the word, but passionately attached to something Richard Sennett, in his book *The Fall of Public Man,* calls an "impersonal code of meaning." This makes literature central, necessary. For literature is the people's picture of itself and its way. And then, too, the necessity of being fearful — as a nation — must become a deep national emotion. The sense of dread. What can people do but simply shrug it off? One does not *live* in such a situation; one lives *as if* — as if everything were all right, as if life were normal. Kafka, Hašek and his good soldier Švejk, the Czech shrug.

But this woman leaving her daughter in England and returning to her village near Karlovy Vary — is *she* afraid? It didn't seem so. She sat in the airport, pink cheeked and English, taking solace from her tea in that way only the English seem to, telling David Beseda and me that, "actually, we've been quite lucky. We've had very little trouble actually." Stirring her tea, musing at the cup as if it were an old but very reticent friend about whom she ponders and wonders. "Of course, there's Elena [her daughter], but really, we've been very lucky." And then she explained the excellent terms of her husband's pension and her own pension which, she said with satisfaction but no greed, includes time she worked in England before the War. She had no complaints, she said.

All this depressed me. Did I want an old woman to get on her high horse and be angry at what had happened to her? (She was angry at the TV in London — she was confused by it and all the complaining and strikes.) Yes, I did want her to be angry. Apparently, I didn't want to be angry alone. I didn't sit with her on the plane.

Prague was gray. At the airport terminal at Ruzyně outside of Prague, we were told to line up at the *banka* to exchange money. Czechoslovakia, which maintains its own idea about the value of its currency on the world market, allows no Czech crowns in or out of the country, and demands that visitors spend at least $10 a day while in the country. A dollar is worth, officially, about ten crowns; on the black market, you can easily get twenty.

David Beseda was behind me in line. He had sat with the old woman from London, telling her, he said, about his grandfather who had emigrated from Moravia to Texas, and who had died there recently. He had the name of the village in Moravia and was going to make a trip there. He said he wished his grandfather knew he was making the trip. He wished he spoke the language, at least a little. I gave him the name of my hotel and he said he would call me when he got back to Prague.

Zdenka Nováková, a friend of a friend, was waiting for me on the other side of the frosted-glass doors that separated the arrival and customs area from the terminal lobby. We had never met before, but our mutual friend (who was really only an acquaintance of mine in New York) was an old friend of hers and had arranged for Zdenka to meet me at the airport. Zdenka had a car. "She'll want you to stay with her," my New York friend had said. "But don't do it. It isn't good for her and it won't be good for you."

Zdenka was holding a bouquet of lilacs. They were wilted, drooping out of the tin foil that was wrapped around them. Her sixteen-year-old daughter, Elena, was with her. The two of them, clearly mother and daughter, seemed in some way to have reversed their roles. Elena was reserved and maternal; Zdenka exuberant and girlish. She thrust the lilacs out to me and at the same instant hugged me, so that the flowers got crushed between us. "The plane is *late*," she said dramatically, as if this were remarkable, even wonderful, news. She had beautiful brown eyes.

She couldn't find her car keys, which she had certainly *had* —

she'd *gotten* here, hadn't she? Furthermore, my hotel did not *exist*. "I know all the hotels. I've never heard of this *Garni*. I've never heard of anyone *staying* at such a place as this *Garni*." She said this loudly, in alarm and disbelief, as if the very pronunciation of the name of the hotel was hard evidence against its reality. Her brown hair was cut short in a kind of mop, the hairdo of a woman determined to be practical, who has decided looks don't matter. She kept pushing the front part of the mop out of her eyes where it kept falling. It was a very impractical haircut.

Elena shook my hand shyly; she almost curtsied out of excessive politeness. "How do you do?" she said precisely. "I am pleased to meet you." She seemed a little startled that this mass of odd sounds made perfect sense to me; she smiled with relief and pleasure.

"Elena is going to speak beautiful English," her mother said. "Aren't you, Elena?"

Elena found the car keys (they were in Zdenka's purse). She tried to beat me to my suitcase and carry it to the car, and spoke quietly and calmly to her mother in Czech, apparently suggesting a rational course of action about the nonexistent Garni. She guided us out of the building to the car, put the suitcase in the trunk, motioned me politely into the front seat, and squeezed herself into the back where she began studying a map of the city.

I wished she was driving. Zdenka seemed, quite literally, not to know how to drive. She lurched onto the highway and was astonished, it seemed, to find other cars there, cars which themselves were in motion and which posed an endless, maliciously unpredictable series of threats. She said, "I'm a terrible driver," as if she was at least meeting the situation halfway by being honest. I was terrified and thought, "How strange to be killed in a car accident because I'm too polite to say anything." But I didn't say anything.

Zdenka was talking animatedly about the Garni and the

absurdity of my staying there. She looked away from the road and over her shouder to Elena as she talked, heaping sarcasm, it seemed from the tone of her voice, on the miserable Garni. She was driving very fast, especially for someone not looking at the road; we sailed past rows of people waiting for buses. They went by in a blur of drab clothes and splotches of lavender: everyone seemed to have a branch of lilac.

"I tried to get a room at the Paříž," I said because I was in the front seat and thought it would be an improvement just to get her looking toward the front. "But the Paříž was full."

"The Paříž," Zdenka said expansively, raising her hands off the steering wheel for a moment in her enthusiasm. "Everyone knows where the Paříž is."

She and Elena jabbered over the map, Elena thrusting it forward into the front seat, and her mother twisting sideways to see and comment. Elena didn't seem troubled by her mother's driving. Maybe they all drive this way, I thought.

Abruptly, somewhere within the city, Zdenka slowed down. This was almost more alarming; the cars behind us came down on us fast and, at the last moment, swerved into the other lane to pass. "I never know about these brakes," Zdenka said. "It's best to go slow. It's safer that way."

They had not found the Garni on the map, which seemed satisfying to Zdenka. "We will go to our house first," she said decisively, but turned to look at Elena who nodded approvingly. "We will make inquiries about this *Garni*. We won't just go where there is *nothing*."

I thought, I could just take a taxi from the apartment. I thought, all we have to do is make it to the apartment. Certainly we'll get to the apartment.

Elena smiled encouragingly at me. "We will telephone," she said soothingly, as if she were patting my hand which was clenched in my lap.

"Yes," said Zdenka enthusiastically, turning in her seat to look proudly at a child who was so clever. "Yes, we will telephone from the flat." Or maybe she was delighted with the thought of the telephone, an invention which, when she pronounced its name, sounded marvelous and exotic.

Zdenka was a doctor. She had lived in New York during the Second World War when her parents, both Jews, had emigrated there. She had returned to Prague, she said, because "once a refugee, always a refugee. You have to have your own country — even if it's Kafkaland." She was divorced.

"Here is my life," she said as she cut sandwiches for us in her kitchen, "in this order: I am mother to Elena, I am *father* to Elena, I am a doctor, I am a lover of music, and my greatest love — to translate Italian books into Czech." She said that, left to her own inclination, she would just be mother to Elena and translate. That was her great love, she couldn't say why.

Her flat was an old, roomy one in the Kampa, a little island on the Malá Strana side of the Vltava. A romantic location and a choice one. The flat itself was in need of repair; the electricity and plumbing were faulty, and the whole place needed plastering and painting. But it didn't matter; the dusky colors of the walls — possibly peach, possibly pink — and the faded upholstery and fringed rug were as smudged and lovely as the old buildings out the window. The furniture was heavy, full of claws and curlicues and very dark. There was a massive bouquet of lilacs in a jar on the sideboard; some of the flowerets were falling on the blackish wood.

I was tempted to stay. Zdenka had invited me, as my New York friend had said she would. "We just go to the police station. We say you are staying with me. That's that. You stay with me," she had said in the kitchen. But I held firm about the Garni. I didn't want to go to the police station. I said maybe later, when I came back from a trip I was making to Slavkov to see Růžena, I would stay with her.

I had brought presents for both of them. Penguin paperbacks for Zdenka, a pair of blue jeans for Elena. The blue jeans didn't fit; they were too small. Elena said it didn't matter — she didn't really like blue jeans.

"Elena has her own mind," Zdenka said. "Here everyone is jeans crazy. It's jeans, jeans, jeans. But not Elena." Zdenka was delighted with her paperbacks. One was a biography of Dorothy Parker. She thought that would be a good one to translate, although her own English, she said, was not good enough for the job.

It was late when she called the Garni. She seemed annoyed that, in spite of everything, it had the temerity to exist. "But," she said with satisfaction, "it is located very inconveniently." She insisted on driving me there. Taxis were too expensive, I mustn't spend my money. Besides, she really wondered if this *Garni* would have a room after all.

Elena shook her head indulgently at her mother. She said she would come wtih us. "My navigator," Zdenka called her.

Prague is one of the most beautiful cities in the world. It is strange that it has never really been a tourist city. Even in the days of the Viennese Empire and the Baedeker tours, it wasn't a standard part of the grand tour. It retained its provincial, essentially bourgeois, personality. In certain ways, the Prague of those days might be compared to Montreal today. It was a dual-language city — Czech, the language of the larger population of native people, was not the ruling-class language — and it had the cultural and political febrility of such crossroads cities.

The thirty years of Socialism have deepened the city's isolation, and the two languages are gone: the German population, which was 80 percent Jewish, was destroyed by the War. It is today even less of a tourist town, more intensely introverted. But it is a loved city, loved by its residents and by those who do visit it. A Western tourist feels quite alone in Prague; it is an exhilarating, surprising sensation after the sometimes deflating familiarity of London or Paris. Perhaps the city is even more loved now than it ever was, for it does not belong to Europe, and maybe never will again. It is part of Eastern Europe, that loneliest of geographical designations. It is a good city for walking; and walking is a good way to feel love.

Petru Popescu, the Rumanian writer, is perhaps typical of the Eastern European intellectuals who came to feel a special love for Prague. He wrote this brief memoir, which appeared in *The Index on Censorship* in 1976:

For artists who grew up behind the Iron Curtain (a curtain that deserved its name in the strictest sense until the early Sixties), Prague was a city of many personalities, an embodiment of many intellectual dreams . . . It . . . had a rhythm of peaceful common sense, the bourgeois patriarchality of back gardens and trellis walls, tiled floors and uneven stairs, on which the dignified citizens stumbled up and down, through beer-mist, in a landscape so untouched by history that it became incredible, miraculous. The noble towers, the middle class drinking evenings, the proletarian outskirts combined in a vast social lesson, just like the Catholic Slavs brewed slowly, allowing in their midst energetic German streaks and melancholy Jewish islands. Heavy, peaceful heart of Europe, beating towards the ruthless North, the devious East, the Latin South. The most complete city of Europe, patinated by time and drowned in music, profound like a requiem and disarming like a miniature, was the harbor of our travels in the mind. We spent here our unlived lives, we visited untouchable shores and we enjoyed the most delicious and sad kind of freedom, the freedom of the past.

Alas, these lines have spelled themselves in the past tense already. Where is all this now? Still there, in the city's eternity, and yet buried under all the narrow streets with cobblestones wounded by tanks. Thirty years after Munich, another outbreak of opaque, cretinous hate. Not only the musical romance and the baroque landscape were crushed. Curiously, from under the Russian tanks, Prague revealed itself as a solidarity of workers, as an old school of social-democracy and human popular management, of teacherish left-wing ideals. Fragile and myopic like the consumptive revolutionaries of yore, the heretic Communist party of what was before the war Europe's most hard-working and sincere democracy produced a wing of dedicated visionaries who, pushed forward by the stream of an exasperated nation, agreed to give up their police power and to govern by trust alone. Killed in the bud, this last hope of a working-class state seems to confront the world with another moral Spain. Alas, this republic was not able to enlist the help of international brigades. Normalised by the objectivity and realism of guns and tanks, Prague slips back into the past, its eternal refuge, while the people of Prague continue their imaginary lives. And we, the witnesses of this assassination, in a world more and more prepared philosophically to accept the rape of conscience.

I intended to take some notes from Marxist texts. It seemed the next step in acquainting myself with Czech intellectual history. I felt a great resistance to this reading and, before I came to Prague again, I had only read the *Communist Manifesto* and Trotsky's *My Life* — which doesn't count anyway, according to a friend of mine who has read *everything*, because "it's just his autobiography." I realize now what my resistance has been.

For one thing, the real imprint of Socialism in Eastern Europe has not come from Marxism, but from orthodoxy: form, not content. This is a simplification. But we can see, from the lives of the poets and intellectuals who perished in Lenin's or Stalin's time, that they were not a counterrevolution; they didn't have some other political alternative in mind. Typically, those who perished were faithful ideologues themselves (for example, in Czechoslovakia, Rudolf Slansky, the secretary general of the Communist Party) or, in the case of poets, they were "clouddwellers." (Stalin is supposed to have attached to Pasternak's secret police file the directive, "Do not touch this clouddweller.")

Ideologues and the poets who perished so absurdly together had in common perhaps only a single thing: the work of language. One could say they met in their devotion to language: a religious impulse.

Ideology and the bureaucracy it spawns create "a new language." How happily, in fact, the word *new* is used in the whole canon of revolutionary politics: Socialism offers nothing less than the opportunity to create "a new man." Who, wishing the best for the world, could be against that?

It is a stunning idea, and combines brilliantly, in a single image, the familiar, reassuring shadow of Christianity and the heretofore frightening — but at last domesticated — spectre of faceless technological life. The Industrial Revolution *seemed* (to Blake, to Wordsworth, even as late as Lawrence and to ourselves in the West) to be the end of "man," the breakup of the individual-at-home-in-the-world. But no, don't worry, there is a way out: one need not be a "man"; it is possible to be "a new man." The phrase acknowledges terror, even as if defies it. To be a new man is to leap the barriers of history, perhaps even of biology, and (this is the part that matters), to feel no loss, no strangeness. No absurdity.

In our own country, the misuse of language has gone straight to absurdity, without benefit of ideology. The worst evidence of our crimes in Vietnam was not that Curtis LeMay said, We'll "bomb the North Vietnamese back to the stone ages." That is the ancient and entirely familiar cry of the warrior. Much worse was the infamous statement made by an Air Force pilot: "We had to destroy the village in order to save it." This statement is haunting because it is utterly rational and utterly crazy. Our grief is that this reasoning made perfect sense to our government.

Those caught in the web of ideology in the Soviet Union and Eastern Europe perished, perhaps, because in the end they could not manage the hair-splitting language of orthodoxy which was the only language they recognized. No one could say for certain what the new man was, but it and other such abstract but highly charged phrases had to be defined over and over. And one person's definition was the next person's evidence against him. The history of Communism in Eastern Europe is full of "confessions" — leading to prison terms and executions — for transgressions against the new language.

George Steiner, in his essay "Text and Context," discusses this. "Marxism-Leninism and the ideological idiom professed in communist societies are 'bookish' to the root. The scheme of origins, authority and continuum in force in the Marxist world derives its sense of identity and its daily practices of validation or exclusion from a canon of texts. It is the reading of these texts — exegetic, Talmudic, disputative to an almost pathological degree of semantic scruple and interpretative nicety — which constitutes the presiding dynamic in Marxist education and in the attempts, inherently ambiguous as are all attempts to 'move forward' from sacred texts, to make of Marxism an unfolding, predictive reality-principle."

Poets, on the other hand — I'm thinking particularly of Mandelstam — are devoted to language at least partly because of its history, its peculiar ability to be the unconscious storehouse of a people's culture, values, point of view. Poetry is the richest form of language because it is the most concentrated utterance. It is immediate *and* ancient. Its ancientness is implicit: language truly is, always has been, *handed down* from parent to child. When a child in one of Kenneth Koch's poetry-writing classes wrote "Rose, where did you get that red?," he spoke a precise, contemporary thought, and also attached himself, unconsciously, to a long tradition — of roses and of poets.

Philosophically, too, poetry is attached to ancient values because the materials of the emotions remain what they have always been. Even when Pound said, "Make it new," he could not deny the ancient: the *it* stands for all there is to make new.

Mandelstam is emblematic not because of his typically tragic death, but because of his wistfulness. He was wistful for poetry.

He wanted, he said, to "pronounce for the first time the blessed word with no meaning . . . in the Soviet night." In another poem, written in 1930, he says

> *I could have whistled through life like a starling,*
> *eating nut pies . . .*
> *but clearly there's no chance of that.*

What he is saying, I think, is: let me out of the ideological mind and the insanity of abstracted language. Mandelstam is not a new man; he is an ancient.

Even in our country where poetry is not read, as we're always told, the poet symbolizes the personal voice, so individual, so far from the abstract rationalism of the ideologue, that the Western stereotype of the poet is that of the divine crazy, the romantic (the word is used imprecisely, dismissively, even by poets). But the stereotype betrays a longing. I've never told anyone I write poetry without, after an initial shyness, getting the same reaction: respect, fascination, wistfulness (they too write poetry, or used to, or wish they could, or know someone who "can put words on paper"). The wistfulness of the grocer in St. Paul who said to me, "Poetry. Now that's something. That's a life." Not "that's the life" — he didn't think I was a bum. He meant it was work of value: *a life.* His wistfulness was not so far from Mandelstam's, a longing for a culture that sustains the imagination.

I haven't taken the notes, haven't read the classic theoretical texts that I intended to. I sense they can't explain the reason our civilization has been sliced in two, into Europe and "the other Europe." "The gestures of the individuals," Muriel Rukeyser wrote in *The Life of Poetry,* "are not history; but they are the images of history." And that is what I must study. The things I want to "observe perpetually" expose themselves in every contemporary gesture, just as poetry has always known, as it busies itself with roses.

5 ❦

I WILL CALL the poet I met Jaromil. I won't say how I met him, and his name isn't Jaromil. I don't know if it is necessary to go to the trouble of giving him this pseudonym. I do it instinctively and a little fretfully, anxious to do the right thing. I wanted to ask him if I could use his name when I wrote about him, but some diffidence held me back: I didn't want to compel him to say directly, "no, please don't mention my name." Or perhaps I sensed he would say, "You decide. Just act normal." He often said, when I asked him about his reaction to political situations, that he "just tried to act normal." He said this briskly, like a soldier who keeps a single clear command in mind.

We are familiar by now with this aspect of accounts from the Soviet Union and Eastern Europe — the false names, the obscured identities. But something not usually considered happens when a pseudonym is given in place of an actual name and when personal details are changed in order to safeguard someone. The real person recedes a bit, but the focus, strangely enough, instead of becoming blurred, is refined and made sharper. This man, given a pseudonym, is no longer a particular person enveloped by the swarm of his biography and his minutely individual identity. He becomes, instead, "Jaromil," a character. In this case, he is The Poet. He stands for that. For that is all that remains of his biography. A repressive society, one that takes the voice seriously enough to silence it, may obscure and deny many of the particular stories and details of its national life, but as it does so it automatically clarifies and intensifies the significance of utterance.

Jaro, in Czech, means "spring," a word and season firmly associated by now with Prague because of the Prague Spring of 1968. (The official title of the music festival is also *Pražské Jaro,* Prague Spring.) There is another reason I've chosen this particular pseudonym. Jaromil is the name of the hero of Milan Kundera's novel, *Life Is Elsewhere,* a story of a poet enthralled by the cult of the new man and ideological purity. In this respect, Jaromil proved to be a very different man, a very different sort of poet, although he came of age at the same time as Kundera's poet — immediately following the Second World War, at the time of the Socialist ascendency in 1948. He was a university student then, as Kundera's Jaromil was. But unlike that young man, he did not burn with the revolutionary spirit. He did not want to be the new man. He wanted, he told me often during the walks we took through the old city, to "act normal, just act normal."

❦

We took our first walk at night, a couple of days after I arrived. Prague is no more beautiful at night than it is during the day, but it is more haunting. It is amazingly silent; one doesn't think of cities being capable of such silence anymore. Václavské náměstí, which is a sort of squat Champs-Élysées (it is the main street of downtown Prague), is busy late into the night, and it has the noise and activity one expects of a capital. Quite a few hotels are located there, and some of the restaurants and sausage stands stay open late. But the rest of the central city — Staré Město, Nové Město and Malá Strana — is dark and surprisingly still.

Jaromil met me at the Garni. It is a B-plus annex to the larger class-A Olympik Hotel (the reason, Zdenka said, *no one* had ever heard of it). It is located outside the older central city in a gray industrial area, on a good tram line. The trams, which are often crowded, run late into the night (to accommodate late factory shifts) and are cheap; a one-crown (ten-cent) ticket takes you anywhere.

I seemed to be one of the few independent tourists in the Garni. The parking lot was filled with tour buses, mostly from East Germany and the Soviet Union, some from Poland. Every morning the lobby of the hotel was crowded with people waiting for these buses to take them around the city in great herds. Prague, for most visitors (because most tourists are from neighboring Socialist countries), is a city of the guided tour and the large, gawking group.

In the evening, however, the hotel was quiet. We had arranged, when we spoke on the telephone, to meet in the lobby at 8 o'clock. Jaromil was on time. He was dapper; that was the immediate impression he made. Like all dapper men, he looked a little comical at first glance. He was not small, but had an elfin, gamin look, even with his thinning hair, which set him apart from his clothes, as if they were a smart uniform and he simply a green recruit. He was wearing a snappy plaid jacket — I never saw one better cut in Prague — and astonishing shoes. The shoes were red, the deep polished red of two candied apples. They had raised heels, and the toes were rounded and a little bulbous, reemphasizing the apple motif. It was clear that they were meant to be very stylish. They were a mild version of disco shoes. No adult with a Ph.D. and even the most harmless sense of his own importance would wear such shoes in the United States. Yet he — a professor and a major poet — wore them; he didn't wear them in the witty, self-conscious way that stylish people sometimes dress in the West. Those shoes were no joke. He was dressed for the evening. He was dressed, I sensed, to meet an American.

I was wearing a flower print skirt, the sort of thing that is called a peasant skirt, suggesting that it is worn by milkmaids in happy Central European landscapes. I'd bought it in Minneapolis. They were showing a lot of them in the stores before I left. I even wore a fringed shawl.

We took the tram to Staré Město. Jaromil was pleased that I

wanted to walk: that was the thing to do in Prague, he said. He asked me what I thought of the city. Beautiful, I said. I wanted to tell him I admired his poetry, which I'd read in translation, but I sensed he wouldn't like a direct statement. I said again that I thought the city was beautiful, just beautiful. He nodded. "But too much traffic," he said. "You can't get around."

We walked from the tram stop down Celetná Street to Staroměstské náměstí (Old Town Square) where the big Jan Hus monument stands. I said this was one of the walks Kafka and his good friend Max Brod used to take. "Kafka is everywhere," he said. We stood by the old astronomical clock, one of the landmarks of the city. We had just missed the hourly performance when the clock tolls the hour and the twelve apostles and the other carved statues, including the figure of Death, march woodenly past an open window above the clock's face. But we stood there looking at the clock anyway. Jaromil explained how to read its various dials, and told me that the man who had made the wonderful mechanism had his eyes put out by the man who commissioned the work so that he could never make another one. I'd read this in my guidebook. I thought it was probably just a legend, but he told the story in a ceremonious, satisfied way, as one does with the lore of one's place.

I wanted to sit somewhere and talk, but Jaromil hadn't made reservations, and all the *vinárny* around the Old Town Square seemed to be full. Prague has many of these wine cellars, some of them many centuries old. They are popular, especially with West German tourists who, unlike the East Germans, tend to travel in smaller private groups. There are Czechs in these places too, of course, and in the beer halls.

We finally found an empty table at a *vinárna* near the Charles Bridge after walking for a long time around Staré Město, Jaromil pointing out landmarks and curiosities. On a wall in a narrow street someone had scrawled in large letters Alexander Dubček's name. "Only look," Jaromil said, "it's spelled wrong." The name read Dubcek. Jaromil liked to point out this sort of thing; he seemed to feel the little absurdities and contradictions of the city were its essential fascination. "See, see," he said with relish, "Kafka."

We drank a bottle of red Hungarian wine at the *vinárna*. Jaromil talked about why he liked America; he'd never visited there but he followed American news as best he could. "Energy," he said, holding his hands in front of him as if he were illustrating the collision of molecules. "America has so much energy."

"It's all misdirected," I said.

"You think so?" he said, surprised at this apparently.

"Look at the Vietnam War."

"Yes," he said expansively, "but look at everything else."

I didn't like this. I wasn't used to poets passing over the Vietnam War this way. I felt he was being frivolous. Yet I knew he wasn't frivolous. He had lost his job after the Russian invasion in 1968. He wasn't allowed to publish in his own country. I expected a little moral indignation. I was used to it — I grew up on it. I spent the first ten years of my adulthood, along with many of my generation, telling the older generation to stop the war, telling them that the war — and they themselves — were immoral. Perhaps, like others of my generation, I'll never get over having been right.

"The Vietnam War was genocide," I said. "It was worse than anything," I said severely, but I sensed I sounded oddly prim.

"Really?" he said quizzically, not disagreeing.

We spent the rest of the evening walking around old Prague. The silence was absolute in the city, unless we happened to go by a bar or *vinárna* where people were crammed into the small rooms that were filled with the haze of smoke and were very noisy. Hardly anyone seemed to be on the streets. They seemed to have been assigned to their respective bars and stayed there, perhaps day in and day out. Maybe Jaromil purposely guided our walk through empty, silent streets so I could feel this ghostliness. But I think we were both wandering, without plan.

He pointed out landmarks — Kafka's family home (scaffolded for repairs, with an angular bust of Kafka mounted on the wall); the clock in the part of town that used to be the ghetto, the face was marked with Hebrew letters, the time going, it appeared, backward; and churches, a lot of churches.

There were hidden landmarks too: he showed me the building — one of them — for the secret police. "Now this is wonderful," he said with relish. "Here we have the secret police. And here we have the street — St. Bartholomew Street. You see? This is Kafka, everything is Kafka." He looked at me doubtfully. "Do you understand? St. Bartholomew — the day of the religious massacre. And now politics is religion. You understand?" I said I did.

He took me past the passport and visa office, an unmarked building that looked like an auto body shop and didn't seem to have any identifying sign. "We know where it is," he said. The passport office was also on some significant street, but I've forgotten the name and forgotten the tidbit of Kafkian pleasure he explained was to be had from contemplating the location of the passport office on that particular street. We went around the city like this, perhaps for a couple of hours, Jaromil pointing out a building or a corner, and telling me, with his elfin relish, how this too was another brick in the great Kafkaesque castle of the city.

Finally, we went back to the tram stop, near the National Theater and the Slavia, the big old coffeehouse in the Central European tradition. Its window tables provide one of the best views of the Hradčany in the city. The Writers Union building is around the corner from the Slavia. We stopped in front of the long display window, full of books written by members of the union.

"You see all these books?" Jaromil said. "Not one is by a writer."

"You mean, they are . . ."

"No real writers publish here anymore. None. These are the people who could not make it before. They are second rate. They were jealous. Now they ride around in big cars. Here it is the opposite from you in America. You have the establishment and you have the underground. Here the underground *is* the establishment." This too he said as if it were a mot, a witty one-liner. There was no sadness; he didn't even seem to bear anyone a grudge. This too, apparently, was Kafka, and to be relished.

"You know," he said as we rode back to the Garni on the tram, "the Czechs have a different sense of humor. I went to a movie here, and there was a scene that takes place in a new suburb. The apartment buildings are tall and modern and everything is finished. But there are no sidewalks anywhere. Everywhere is mud. The people in the film must put on galoshes to walk from their cars to the apartment; then they must pull off the galoshes and put their shoes back on. Every time they go anywhere this happens. In Prague during this film everyone is laughing so hard — they're on the floor. It's so funny, you can't hear what the actors are saying — everyone is laughing. Then, later, I saw this same movie in London at a film festival. And nobody laughs. It's not funny. I laughed, but nobody else thinks it's funny. It's Kafka."

He brought me back to the Garni. The door of the hotel was locked and I had to pound on the glass until the desk clerk came to open it. It was like being let into a dormitory after hours.

The next day was Sunday. I'd planned to take a long walk alone. I wanted to walk around the city as Kafka had — not as he had with Max Brod, but as he and Gustav Janouch had. Janouch was a young boy, the son of one of Kafka's coworkers at the Workers' Accident Insurance Institute. He wrote poetry which he showed to Kafka. Kafka said, "There is too much noise in your poems." But this criticism, which was not, according to Janouch, harsh or cruel, but somehow impersonal and even humble, began a friendship between the young boy and the writer he admired. They took walks together through Prague; Gustav Janouch kept a diary in which he recorded Kafka's conversations. Many years later, after his own life had been "turned away," as he put it, from poetry, he published his *Conversations with Kafka.*

"The living Kafka whom I knew," he writes in his postscript, "was far greater than the posthumously published books . . . The Franz Kafka whom I used to visit and was allowed to accompany on his walks through Prague had such greatness and inner certainty that even today, at every turning point in my life, I can hold fast to the memory of his shade as if it were solidly cast in steel . . . Franz Kafka is for me one of the last, and therefore perhaps one of the greatest, because closest to us, of mankind's religious and ethical teachers."

I thought I would retrace some of these walks. But I slept late, and woke to a gray day. I didn't want to go anywhere. I went downstairs and ate a lot of crescent rolls and drank coffee; I watched the East German tourists drink beer with their breakfasts. Then I went back to my room. I was exhausted, as if I'd put in an entire day tramping through the city. I threw myself on the bed and stared out the window at the factory across the street. It was draped with one of the red and yellow banners in honor of the solidarity between Czech and Soviet brothers.

I spent the rest of the day there, reading a memoir by Flora Thompson about Oxfordshire at the end of the last century, when England still had the remnants of its peasant culture. I read steadily all day. I only left the hotel once, at dinner time, when I went next door to the glittery Olympik for a heavy meal, lavishly spending my meal tickets, as if the whole thing were free, though of course I'd paid in advance. I ordered every course, from soup through dessert and coffee, alone at my table with linen tablecloth, the excessive formality of Czech hotel service buzzing around me. I experienced a little gust of hysteria in the middle of the meal when the waiter brought out a covered silver dish, whisked the oval cover off, and began serving me large dollops of plain, peasant sauerkraut in the French style, wielding the serving fork and spoon in one hand with grave formality.

Then I went back to the Garni, exhausted, as if, as my aunt used to say, I'd worked hard. I didn't go to the evening concert, though I had a ticket. I didn't want to go into the Old City. I just wanted to sleep.

In the morning I took tram number 22 to the castle. I had

dreamt during the night of a stag and a bear; what they had been doing, I couldn't remember, but the stag had been heartbreakingly beautiful there on his hill full of berries and the bear had been up to no good. Bohemia and Russia, I decided, but I didn't bother writing the dream down — it didn't seem to be a *dream,* just that brief picture. But I did make a note of the idea of *hunting,* how Bohemia has always been a land of the hunt. One of my few familial facts about this homeland of mine was the legendary one: Rudi, my grandmother's brother, her favorite, had been shot in the leg for poaching. Even the wild belongs to somebody.

I used to write down even dream fragments, but in recent years I pushed my dreams away, ignored them. I did not like the period when I was most attentive to my dreams, writing them down meticulously, studying them, reading books about dreams. This activity was most intense when I lived, with my friends, in the farmhouse in western Minnesota, after our university years. Since then, I had come to feel that dreams, treated in this watchful way with the best of intentions became less rather than more attached to the pulse of life. Perhaps for Jung (who was more our model then than Freud — Freud does not suit feminism easily), perhaps for other people, the concentration on the dream yields a deeper relation between inner and outer life. For me, though, it narrowed life, separated inner and outer reality, and made me grouchy in a way similar to my period of perpetual observation in high school. Lately, I moved, often memoryless, through my dreams, images snagging here and there on my waking self, all the more startling and satisfying for their being broken bits, abbreviated figures without narrative, especially without explanation. I liked, simply, that all that stuff was *in there,* in me: the weird bucking animals, too-luminous flowers, the many birds I saw nowhere else, bright, alert, flying around, the mud of back yards in glowing pools.

The time when I attempted to understand my dreams was a bleak one of broken friendships and ruinous (sometimes downright silly) ideological feuding. Maybe I stopped writing down my dreams for the worst reasons, out of pique against that time or from self-defense, being fearful of bad news about myself.

But for another, unrelated, reason I don't regret the turn my dreaming took. I have always had the feeling — how else to put this — that "real life" is itself dreamlike. Not only that it is odd and often as unlikely as dreams can be, but something more elusive, which has to do with the floating quality of reality. The effortless, unbidden, the *delicious,* sensation of being mixed up in the fiber of other things is the floating quality of reality shared by dreams and waking.

The attachment I feel to Prague has a lot to do with the city's being, more than any place I know, a landscape of this real-life-in-dream. A quality that salves conscious and sleeping mind, creating harmony. And so I walked the streets, and so I smoked — I who don't smoke — in the *kavárny* among the dove-colored pensioners. And just as I rarely know anymore what my dreams mean (because I rarely have anything but fragments when I wake which I allow to rise or fall on their own strength), in Prague I was a sleepwalker, aware of bright episodes, moments, gestures, but not in possession of the whole meaning. And that seemed right. This relation between dream and waking has been more useful to me, though probably it is inexpressible, than the pages of notes I used to take and the analyses I labored over.

The tram was crowded, as trams in Prague usually are. I had to stand at the back, wedged in with a lot of other people. Lilacs everywhere: old women stood holding huge bunches of them in both hands as if the bouquets were solid posts that helped them keep their balance, and outside people who appeared to have no time to waste, rushed from vegetable stand to butcher shop with bunches of lilacs stowed, like a staple item, in their shopping sacks.

Then I saw, very near to me, the falconer and his bird. A man, dressed in green like a true man of the forest in knee pants with high leather boots and a green leather short jacket. On his head he wore a cap of soft velvet, possibly suede, with a feather on the side. But most incredible was the falcon that clove to his gloved hand with its lacquered claws, its head covered with a tiny leather mask topped, as the hunter's own cap was, with a small, stiff plume. They looked as if they had just stepped out of a mille-fleur tapestry for their tram ride — or were still in the tapestry, set among the lilacs of the other tram passengers.

Where, I wondered, could these two be going, where were they seeking prey and the open sky, here in the middle of the city on the city tram? The falconer seemed perfectly at ease in the back of the crowded car. When he got off, at the Slavia stop, next to the National Theater, and stood waiting for a connecting tram, it was the rest of the world and not he that looked inappropriate. I was reminded of my first trip to Prague in 1975, when I saw a peasant woman from the country standing in Malostranské náměstí (Small Side Square) in her local costume. She was the best-dressed woman I saw in Prague. And she stood somehow apart, *correct*. She was either lost or frightened; she looked bewildered. But still her bewilderment was like the falconer's calm: she was *what she was*. It was there to be seen, and beyond that, beyond her confusion or his confidence, nothing else was of much concern. In their different ways they struck me as emblems of the nation. As such, they are less odd, less fantastical than many other things one is likely to see in the city. They are genuinely mythic; they express certain essential qualities of the national psyche, what are called by Jung archetypes.

The enthusiasm for Jung's psychology in the United States, in fact, is based at least partly on a hunger for myth. But it has always seemed, when I read the poetry inspired by it or work my way through the studies of endless fairy tales, to be an unsatisfying, essentially remote exercise of the intellect. It is as if the acknowledgment of archetypes, cross references from private dream to various folk tales and myths, was meant to be a kind of consolation for our having no folk life or folk culture of our own. The uses of the psychology are stretched too far and often become pretentious or precious.

But the figures of fairy tale and myth came really to life, when

I rode the tram jostled by mille-fleur figures, watching the falconer and his bird. Fairy tale came to life and assumed power. For there he was: the tall, lean, blond falconer dressed in the color of the forest, his deadly bird strapped to his wrist, riding the tram in the middle of Prague. And his fellow passengers cast only the most casual eye upon him, holding to their lilacs, as he left the tram and stood in the street, the cars zipping dangerously by him. He came to life, as the figures of fairy tales do, amid the strange loveliness of the gardens and water-dalles and castles, the moats and ducal cities of fairy stories, but also amidst the underlying dread and the stern passionate pedagogy of myth, as if the very earth were teaching.

I arrived at the Hradčany. It is often called simply the castle. *Hrad* means "castle" in Czech. But like the Tower of London, which is not a tower, the Hradčany is not a solitary castle. It is a medieval fortress, a whole walled area, with churches, courtyards, streets, back alleys, monasteries, gardens, palaces and vestries. This giant bulk seems to hang on the edge of a bluff overlooking — even overseeing — the city. A small, impacted world raised over the real world.

"I cannot comprehend," Kafka's friend Willi Haas wrote, "how anyone could understand Kafka who was not born in Prague between 1880 and 1890." It is still possible to come to a sort of intimacy with Kafka (and thereby with fairy tale) by walking through Prague. Kafka hardly mentions the city in his work; certainly he did not memorialize Prague as Dickens did London. But to see, for the first time, the Hradčany from across the river, to see it hanging there, a massive structure poised over the lyrical haze of the winding Vltava and the baroque houses and old gardens on the descending hills, is to see the landscape of Kafka.

You recognize instantly that this is the city of the Western mind, the perfect model to express our psychological reality, which is the reality Kafka wrote of, and is also the reality that has turned so many Western writers to him and his stark litera-ture of myth and quest. Absurdity, in a way, only makes complete sense in Prague where the architecture of fairy tales collides with modern history. The city has the filled, jumbled history of European architecture; it was virtually untouched by bombing from the Second World War. Unlike the center of Paris or Vienna, it is also largely unmarked by the Americanization and patchiness of plastic, fast-food places, and advertising. The core city, which is quite large, is even untouched by modern archi-tecture (that is, by anything much newer than the Masaryk Republic) except for a few hotels and stores. (Of course, in the more suburban areas, even as near as my hotel, this is not so; and there are people in Prague who argue passionately that some ancient areas *must* be torn down — the tenements of Vinohrady, for instance — and that contemporary urban planning must be brought into play. People need places to live.) Besides the city's gothic and baroque treasures, which are often mentioned in the guide books, Prague has perhaps the richest and largest repre-sentation of extant art nouveau building and decoration in Europe, certainly much more than Paris, the city usually asso-ciated with the art nouveau movement and period.

Prague was for Kafka, and it remains today, a spiritual city. Absurdly spiritual. Its architecture was spared by modern war and by modern vulgarity. It remains powerful, as if the landscape of a dream had been brought to life. It is not simply beautiful, as I began to understand when I spent my first trip walking and smoking my days away in coffeehouses staring at it: the beauty is broken. And this draws the heart out of you to it. It is a city that demands relation. The Hradčany is not only the city's major landmark; it is the accumulated presence of the city's many aspects cast above it, enthroned, as power classically is. Perhaps because of this, it is not a site you *visit*; there is the definite sense that you journey to the castle. The long, steep walk up narrow streets from Malá Strana emphasizes this sense of pilgrimage.

I arrived, however, by tram, having taken the number 22

which winds through Malá Strana and up behind the fortress, making its Hradčany stop near the side entrance, by the castle gardens. I walked through the second courtyard of the castle. Many large groups of escorted tours were wandering through the courtyards. I followed behind one, at some distance. St. Vitus Cathedral, perhaps the central tourist attraction in the castle — it is crammed with golden monstrances and medieval art treasures — was ahead. The approach to the cathedral is broken by an arched passageway leading to the third courtyard. The cathedral is suddenly *there*, huge and intricate with decoration, little ghouls and goblins leering out from corners, immediately beyond this covered walkway. I remembered this from my first trip. You can see the spires from the outer courtyard, but the church still comes as a surprise because, for a moment, the passageway cuts off the view.

There were two covered passageways. The one on the right was crowded with several tour groups from East Germany and Russia. The left one was practically empty. I went through it. As I reached the end of the passageway — it wasn't long — a Czech soldier came up to me, blocking my view of the church. He spoke in German, then immediately switched to English.

"Good morning, madam," he said loudly. I decided he was some sort of guide, offering a tour.

"Good morning," I said. "I just thought I'd look around on my own."

"Did you not see the sign?" he asked. He was pointing toward a white placard, printed in five or six languages, which was posted at the side of the passageway I'd just come through. It said pedestrian traffic was prohibited in this passageway; the passageway was for maintenance trucks and cars only.

I apologized, and told the soldier I hadn't seen the sign at the other end. "I'll be sure to use the other way out when I leave," I said. I began to walk toward the church.

He snapped to attention, blocking my way. "You must go out," he said, pointing to the passageway, "go out, and come back the other way."

He didn't want me to go out the *legal* passageway (as a punishment), and then return through it. He was insisting that I retrace my steps through the (clearly illegal, as he'd pointed out) passageway for vehicles, and *then*, I was to come through the pedestrian walkway next to it.

"I don't believe this," I said, pointing to the sign. "Certainly you don't want me to go back through *this* way. The sign here says it's not for pedestrians. I would just be doing the wrong thing twice."

A small group of tourists had begun to gather around us; most of them were speaking German, explaining the situation to each other. The general feeling seemed to be that I should do as I was told.

"This is absurd," I said loudly, to anyone. "The sign on this end says NOT FOR PEDESTRIAN USE and the sign on the other end — which I admit I didn't see — says the same thing. I made a mistake. But it doesn't solve anything to have me break the rule again. I'll be sure to go out the right way," I said cheerily, firmly to the soldier. I moved toward the cathedral.

He took hold of my arm and pushed me toward the not-for-pedestrians passageway. "You *go* — there," he said. He was not happy about this, but apparently it was not possible for him to back down. He was young, blond, red faced, and beginning to perspire. The little crowd of tourists didn't like the part where he pushed me — ever so hesitantly. He was nervous. But he held his ground. "Go back. Go back where you came from."

I entered the passageway and retraced my steps. He called after me, "You must go back and do it correctly."

When I got to the end of the passageway and was in the wide, open, second courtyard, I looked back and saw him at the other end, clearly framed in the arched opening at the far end of the passageway. A few of the German tourists were still there, gathered behind him, watching too. He was standing in the sun, as I was: brown uniform, red decorations, the blond head. He looked satisfied, but he wasn't smiling. He motioned impatiently for me to come through the other walkway.

I was halfway through, among a crowd of Russians on an escorted tour, and I realized that I mustn't go any farther. More than the cathedral, more than the ninth-century St. George Church, more than the monastery with the collection of medieval art, even more than Zlatá ulice (Golden Street) where the alchemists were supposed to have lived and where Kafka really did live one winter, more than the beauty I had come for, I wanted to deprive that self-satisfied creep of seeing me emerge from that passageway.

I almost turned around and walked out. I don't know why I didn't. Somehow it wasn't permitted, or maybe I felt I'd only be spiting myself. Certainly, it wasn't because I felt the whole thing was silly and not worth fighting: I was so furious, I felt practically weightless, as if I might rise off the ground and levitate sheerly from rage.

I came through the passageway, into the bright sun. The soldier was standing there; his arms were folded. He nodded, but he did not smile. Nothing was forgiven on his side either. I passed by. I was now in the heart of the castle.

I spent the afternoon looking at medieval church art in the St. George Monastery where it was cool and silent, and the pictures were flooded with gold. Later, I followed a tour of schoolchildren down a sunken stone staircase into a dungeon where we were told about medieval torture, and were shown the tiny, absolutely black hole where especially recalcitrant prisoners were kept, sometimes for years.

6 ❧

ZLATÁ PRAHA the city has always been called: golden
Prague. When I first saw it, in 1975, it *was* gold — misty,
hazed with late afternoon sun which struck the dust of the tall,
grave windows of old apartment houses and picked up the glint
of the gilt knobs of the Powder Tower and the decoration of the
art nouveau buildings like the Hotel Europa. The air itself
seemed golden, as if the haze were filtered through a thin gauze
of gilt mesh. This, I had thought, is the gold that floods the back-
grounds of medieval religious paintings, the gold of icons which
takes the place of the more modern technique of perspective.
The gold, in these medieval paintings, refuses to remain simply
a background but instead becomes the very subject of every painting. There are the familiar forms of course: the virgin, the
madonna and her wizened (or fleshy) baby, the Christ suffering
or teaching, serene or in agony. But the gold takes over; it is the
unending form that begins as foil and is embossed and decorated
with the tiniest, most attentive of patterns. The artists (always
anonymous, always "Master of" this place or that) never seem
to tire of pricking the gold foil with their minute tools in constel-
lations of flowerets, circles, spirals and swirls, squares and diamonds. The haloes of each holy person are only the first of the
many intrusions of the gold into what is called the foreground.
The head of each person is illuminated by these private suns
which rise as emphatically and gracefully as a peacock's tail behind them. Sometimes the figure is just a fall of darkish drapery

above which the halo is set like a great platter. In a group portrait there will be three or four gold dinner-plate haloes whose perfect roundness is interrupted only slightly by the fact of three human heads.

I was very taken with the gold. The gold of the medieval paintings, but especially the gold of the city, the way the city seemed to glint. I asked someone I met in a coffeehouse about this strange, glittery light. He said it was pollution and I suppose it is. But the initial impression remained.

At one time Prague was the European capital of alchemy, whose study was encouraged by the philosopher-king Rudolf II who reigned from 1576 to his death in 1612 — to us, the Elizabethan, Shakespearean time. Rudolf moved the imperial court of the Holy Roman Empire from Vienna to Prague, and the city became "a center for alchemical, astrological, magico-scientific studies of all kinds," according to Frances A. Yates, whose book, *The Rosicrucian Enlightenment,* is a fascinating study of esoteric thought and its influence in the period immediately preceding the Thirty Years' War, the time that almost brought an end to the Czech nation.

"Hiding himself in his great palace at Prague," Yates writes, "with its libraries, its 'wonder-rooms' of magico-mechanical marvels, Rudolf withdrew in alarm from the problems raised by the fanatical intolerance of his frightened nephew [Philip II of Spain]."

Prague became, she says, "a Mecca for those interested in esoteric and scientific studies from all over Europe. Hither came John Dee and Edward Kelley, Giordano Bruno and Johannes Kepler. However strange the reputation of Prague in the time of Rudolf it was yet a relatively tolerant city. Jews might pursue their cabalistic studies undisturbed (Rudolf's favorite religious adviser was Pistarius, a Cabalist) and the native church of Bohemia was tolerated by an official 'Letter of Majesty.' "

This native church was, in fact, the first reformed church in all of Europe, founded by Jan Hus one hundred years before Luther. Hus was, and remains, the greatest figure in Czech history and one of the great men of Western civilization. He preached in the Czech language, not in Latin, and compiled the first Czech grammar. Language, for him, was culture, and culture was the nation. He was burned at the stake as a heretic in 1415. His attachment to language as the cornerstone of national identity and independence was the beginning of a long Czech tradition. It is, perhaps, typical of small, vulnerable populations in general: the mother tongue is the essential home, the one clear barrier between themselves and the stronger, conquering nations.

Rudolf even extended his protection to the Bohemian Brethren, a mystical sect attached to Hussite teachings. "Prague under Rudolf," Yates writes, "was a Renaissance city, full of Renaissance influences as they had developed in Eastern Europe, a melting pot of ideas, mysteriously exciting in its potentiality for new developments."

It did not turn out so well. Rudolf died in 1612. After a brief reign by his brother Matthias ("an old man and a nonentity," according to Yates), the Bohemians offered the crown of their country (which they considered an elective monarchy) in 1619 to Frederick, Elector Palatine. Frederick and his wife, Elizabeth, daughter of James I of England.

Frederick and Elizabeth seemed the perfect successors to Rudolf — "the Shakespearean pair," Yates calls them. *The Tempest* was performed at London as part of their marriage celebration; there is some thought that the mystical nuptial masque in the play was added to the original version specifically for them. In any case, no one could have missed the connection between the Miranda-Ferdinand marriage and Elizabeth and Frederick's. The aura of their court at Heidelberg was magical, steeped in the ambiance of hermetic study and the romance of science, a word that then had almost the same meaning as magic.

Elizabeth and Frederick were destined to be only "the winter king and queen of Bohemia," as they were later called derisively. Their coronation ceremony, at St. Vitus Cathedral in the Hradčany, was conducted by the Hussite clergy. It was the last great national religious event of the independent Bohemian church which, along with the rest of the nation, was soon to be crushed. On November 8, 1620, Frederick's Protestant army was defeated by Catholic forces led by the duke of Bavaria at the Battle of the White Mountain, outside Prague. This was the beginning of the Thirty Years' War.

For Frederick and for Bohemia, "the defeat was total," Yates writes. "In Bohemia, mass executions or 'purges' exterminated all resistance. The Bohemian church was totally suppressed and the whole country reduced to misery."

It was, among other things, the end of Prague as the alchemical capital. It was the defeat of the Czech nation, but can also be seen as one of the moments when the Western world lost a chance for the development of a holistic civilization. Exactly here, one might say, at the Battle of the White Mountain near Prague, is one of the places where science and religion were broken apart from each other, wounding Western consciousness profoundly.

Science, torn from its spiritual root, meant the end of alchemy, but also the end of a civilization with a united mind, a consciousness that could hold together ancient spiritual, psychic values and the newer progress of the analytical process. The mind-body split is not the essential wound in Western consciousness. It is the mind-spirit split, the intellectual severing that prepared the ground for the worst results of this rupture: the atrocities of "rational ideologies" that our own century has experienced in abundance. Central Europe is, after all, the land of the concentration camp and the "final solution."

"It is one of the more profound ironies of the history of thought," Yates continues, "that the growth of mechanical science, through which arose the idea of mechanism as a possible philosophy of nature, was itself an outcome of the Renaissance magical tradition. Mechanism divested of magic became the philosophy that was to oust Renaissance animism and to replace the 'conjuror' with the mechanical philosopher.

"This fact is not yet generally understood, and whilst awaiting its recognition it is important that we should try to discover and understand all the circumstances leading up to this momentous change in man's attitude to nature."

This change in attitude was the split in consciousness with which we continue to live and from which modern Western culture has developed. The gold of the alchemists was, of course, spiritual and transformative. Gold was the token of exchange, but it was also the substance of *change;* that is, of spiritual transformation. It is interesting that the popular (and orthodox) modern view of alchemy disparages it not only as a pseudoscience, but also attacks it morally — as evidence of the common avarice of the kings and princes who were greedy and credulous enough to employ magicians for such outlandish purposes. This double attack (it is *stupid* and *wrong*) is suspiciously eager to wipe out any speck of value, to make alchemy just another "wrong track," like bloodletting.

The golden light of metaphor, which is the intelligence of poetry, was implicit in alchemical study. To change, magically, one substance into another, more valuable one is the ancient function of metaphor, as it was of alchemy. The savage suppression of hermetic studies that occurred after the Battle of the White Mountain in 1620 ended the slow progress toward a unitary modern consciousness based, at least in part, on the intelligence of metaphor. Such a mind might, in our own day, have kept science (more specifically, technology) attached to the spiritual hunger that is its ancient source. But as it is, the suppression by force of the magic sciences "affected the tone of thought in the early 17th century," Ms. Yates says, "injecting into it an atmosphere of fear."

This intellectual fear is familiar to us in its modernity. It is the fear of mystery, of the wisps of life that refuse to be pinned down, that will not "make sense," that are irregular and do not *fit.* This fear has justified every atrocity in our immediate history: against Jews, against blacks, Asians, against the victims of the abstruse ideologies of Communism and anti-Communism. It is the response of consciousness stripped of its old allegiance to spiritual values. It has made us think of gold as glitter. Even a phrase like "the golden age" suggests an era not simply past and gone, but one that never existed — a "figment of the imagination."

In this way, the imagination itself seems not to exist. It becomes a phantom, instead of the golden background that connects the various figures of the mind as they evolve through history. The thick gold of the medieval icons, the background out of which the religious figures emerge, is what we have lost. It seems, as one stands looking out over Prague and its gilt haze, to have dissipated but not altogether disappeared in this city that is so often, these days, described as gray. We have come to think of all of this part of Europe as gray; it is the result of thinking of it for thirty years as existing behind an iron curtain. But that is a more recent image. The gold and its history persist even as a phantom.

We must be starving for beauty at home. The next day I walked across the Charles Bridge ("the most beautiful bridge in the world," the guidebook says) with its statues of saints. I thought, for some reason, of the new Washington Avenue Bridge over the Mississippi in Minneapolis, the bridge John Berryman jumped from. If this were his city (crazy thought), would he have jumped (crazy thought)? I don't think people jump off bridges for the same reasons here. In fact, they jump from windows, not bridges: defenestration, the peculiarly Prague form of suicide and assassination. Jan Masaryk jumped or was pushed from a window to his death in 1948 — and his death echoed back to earlier defenestrations in the nation's history.

Berryman wrote a poem about Minneapolis which was published after his death. "Site without history!" he called the city.

> I've lived here off & on for sixteen years
> and can't tell if — inspired at last by him —
> I bend my art to it
> whether to deplore or celebrate your essential nonentity.

He was angry at the blank surface, the clean slate of a city full of granaries and computer corporations, whose only real history ("the red man") lies drunk in a gutter, as he says in the poem.

> And who, I enquire in vain
> at the corner of 5th and Hennepin, was Hennepin?
> Professor Toynbee speaks of "the rudiments of a soul"
> that you must have evolved in order to become a "city."

The fact that it's not a good poem doesn't matter; his testimony is clear. Even someone in Minneapolis, who might know Hennepin, but not Toynbee, would see the point. In Minnesota, a lot of the poets say they are "regional poets." The prairie is an ocean, they say. Or the prairie is an analogue, as the ocean is, of the imagination — the waving grasses, the unbroken sheet of landscape. This, in spite of the fact that there is virtually no virgin prairie left and we will never see for ourselves how overwhelming the high grasses were to the pioneers who saw them and cut them down.

These poets don't write much about Minneapolis. Or if they do, the sentiment is Berryman's, although perhaps less harsh, less cranky. They don't talk about Minneapolis. Yet, Robert Bly said at a poetry reading a few years ago that there are more poets in Minnesota than in any state outside of New York or California. An unverifiable, silly statistic, but he has something: Minneapolis prides itself on its "cultural life." There are many theaters, professional music and dance companies, art galleries, a lot of money to support the arts. Yet Minneapolis, as Berryman says, is not a real city. It does not have the ghostliness; it doesn't have "the rudiments of a soul."

I was about to say this is because it is still raw, new, and nothing has happened there. But a lot has happened: the Midwest contains the story of the pioneer, which is the essential story of American identity. The pioneer presents, in a single image, the idea of the pursuit of happiness through individualism and the inevitability of massacre. Berryman saw "the red man" lying

drunk in the gutter on Washington Avenue in Minneapolis.
And James Wright, who also lived in Minneapolis, came to hate
the city too:

> But I could not bear
> To allow my poor brother my body to die
> In Minneapolis.
> The old man Walt Whitman our countryman
> Is now in America our country
> Dead.
> But he was not buried in Minneapolis
> At least.
> And no more may I be
> Please God.

Minneapolis is not beautiful. It isn't even ugly; it is just
awfully clean. Berryman and Wright were annoyed because
Minneapolis reminded them of nothing; it refuses to be a
metaphor. The prairie grasses (which are gone and ghostly) are
the swaying rivulets of the mind. That *works,* poetically. But
who will bite down on "the essential nonentity" of a city that
has enough corporate money to support the arts? The blandness
is too threatening for words.

Berryman lived in Minneapolis for years, running up, he
told us in his classes at the university, gigantic phone bills to his
friends in the real capitals of the country because "that's what
you get when you live in a place like this." He felt, I think, on
the extreme edge of national life.

He taught in the humanities program at the university, not
the English department. His subject was the Western classics,
not contemporary poetry. He taught Homer, Virgil, Dante, to
large crowds of undergraduates. I don't remember any comments he made in class; he didn't explain anything or make any
stunning analyses, as I recall. He just read aloud to us from
Homer or the Bible, whatever we were studying. That's how I
remember his classes: he read, we listened. One day in particular
comes back: he read us Andromache's farewell to Hector, the

scene before Hector is killed in battle. Everyone in the room was crying by the end; he was crying too. "Go home, children," he said when he was finished, and we were all just sitting there in that ugly room (the architecture building, oddly enough) with our overshoes making black puddles under the desks and our mufflers and heavy coats dangling around our chairs. We didn't move. He said it again: "Go home, children. Get going." It didn't seem odd when he called us children.

He had limitless passion and imagination for loss, I think. Every death, every devastation, must have been vivid to him. Andromache's loss was — I remember how *real* it felt that day. We all felt grief, though we didn't call it that.

Perhaps it was an ironic fate that such an elegiac man lived in a city so unmarked by history, by all the devastation he sensed (all contemporary poets sense?) to be his nearest subject. At any rate, less than four years after that day, he was dead. He jumped from the new bridge, in miserable January. Is that how the rudiments of a soul are begun for a city?

And James Wright had moved to New York a long time before that. And he died there, far from Minneapolis.

In 1977, just after the New Year, a group of writers and other intellectuals in Czechoslovakia signed and published a human rights manifesto which they called Charter 77. It was published widely in the Western press. There were originally 241 signers; later this number more than doubled. By the time I was in Prague, the charter was five months old. One of its major spokesmen, philosophy professor Jan Patačka, was already dead — of natural causes, although some of his colleagues felt his health had been undermined by the tension of interrogation and political pressure against the Chartists. Zdenka told me she had gone to Patačka's funeral; she hadn't known him but he was a figure much revered by the entire country. His death, especially in its relation to Charter 77, was the first "national" mourning since Jan Palach, the young student, burned himself ("Torch

Number 1") in 1969 as a protest against the Soviet occupation and the suppression of the Prague Spring. But Patačka's funeral, unlike Jan Palach's, was not a great national event. People were more circumspect; the charter was not the deeply national event the Prague Spring had been. And Jan Palach's death had been so gruesomely symbolic. Anyway, Zdenka said there were men taking pictures at Patačka's funeral. That scares people away.

I met no one who had signed the charter, but there also seemed to be no one who was unaffected by it. For one thing, Czechoslovakia is a small country and one is frequently struck by the family quality of its citizenry, particularly its intellectuals. Almost everyone in Prague offices and institutes had to sign — or cleverly avoided signing — a declaration against the Chartists. These petitions were sent around, like an office memo, to the heads of agencies, institutes and departments. The supervisors were supposed to get their subordinates to sign the statement. Jaromil and his wife and I had visited an editor who said she had been very lucky: her superior had simply signed the statement himself for the entire staff of the office, thereby taking the burden away from individuals.

Later, Jaromil said, laughing, that it was a good thing: the editor had a tendency, he said, to brood over the moral decisions that came her way. "What to do, what to do, that's all she talks about," he said. "No work gets done. It's the same everywhere. Everyone thinks, should I do this, can I do that. Just act normal, that's what I try to do."

This same editor had tried to convince another writer, a friend of Jaromil's, to divorce his wife. The wife had been frightened after the Prague Spring ended and, without telling her husband, signed his name to a denunciation of the liberal reforms of the Dubček government. The husband had been dismayed, but this is the sort of thing that happens in Czechoslovakia. And he didn't want to leave his wife. The editor, Jaromil said, saw it as a moral imperative, and hadn't forgiven the man for not divorcing his wife.

The editor was clearly suspicious of me; she spoke some English but the conversation, as we sat drinking homemade slivovitz, tended to be routed through Jaromil, in Czech. She wondered what brought me to Prague. Just to see it, I said, and Jaromil translated. She raised her eyebrows, a thin, watchful face. I wanted her to like me, but I could tell that the answer had not been the right one. It must be nice to travel just because I wanted to see something, she said and Jaromil translated, somewhat sheepishly. Here, she said, people had reasons for what they did. Her husband, quiet and beaming with affection the way shy people sometimes do by way of hospitality (the slivovitz had been his idea), clouded over. But the editor steered just on the safe side of courtesy, and then smiled and made a self-deprecating joke. And everyone relaxed. "I hope you enjoy your grand tour," she said, in English, as we stood at the door later, about to leave.

"Were you against the charter?" I asked Jaromil when we were walking around Vyšehrad a few days later; it is an even older fortress than the Hradčany and is positioned on the opposite side of the river, at the other end of the city, on a high bluff.

"No, no, of course not," he said. "It is a very good thing, but you see, it will make no difference. Still, it is a good thing to say these things."

But he had not signed. Like many Czechs, his family was certainly part of the reason. As the playwright Pavel Kohout (who has since had his citizenship revoked and lives outside the country) is quoted as saying in a piece Tom Stoppard wrote in 1978 about the charter, "If it wasn't for fear of spoiling their children's education, far more people would sign the charter. So they conform, and they tell their children not to take any notice of certain things their teachers are forced to tell them. So the children are taught that lying is an ethic — say one thing at home, another at school. Of course it's understandable, but it is also our tragedy. 'I did it for the children,' is the Czech problem."

Jaromil never tried to explain himself or excuse his not signing; he didn't present special circumstances. He admitted, rather embarrassedly, that he did not much *like* Vaclav Havel personally. ("He's a little . . . pushy, I'm afraid," he said sadly, as if this were unfortunate rather than annoying.) Havel is one of the leading playwrights in the country. He was in jail for his part in Charter 77 when I arrived in Prague, but was released while I was there; Jaromil heard through the grapevine, first, that Havel had recanted, then later, that it was a lie and he had done no such thing.

On the other hand, Jaromil's admiration for Jan Patočka was, like most of his countrymen's, practically reverent. (Tom Stoppard who, in spite of his name, was born a Czech, has compared Patočka to Comenius and Tomáš Masaryk as one of the three truly great world philosophers the Czechs have produced.)

Beyond family considerations and whatever effect (probably very slight) his personal dislike of Havel had to do with Jaromil's not signing the charter, the real reason, I think, had to do with a particular view he has of poetry. He has a fear of genuine literature getting lost somewhere between the ideological battles of the orthodox line and the repetitive, exhausting soul searching of people like his editor friend who try to muddle along, keeping their jobs and their self-respect.

We were walking around the Vyšehrad Cemetery. It was a cold gray day and a mean wind was blowing. He was telling me, because I had asked him, how he wrote his poems. "I work always from the detail," he said. He held his hands out in front of him, as he had when he was talking about America's energy the first night we met. His hands seemed to be grasping something very small, and he appeared to be regarding it closely. "Always, always, the detail," he said, looking at his hands and then at me to see if I understood.

He became very excited and animated as he explained what he meant. He used the words "concrete detail" and "very specific" as if they represented a new, startling method, rather than the stock in trade of every freshman composition teacher. In all our walks around the city, he had never seemed as serious, as unlike his usual elfin, ironic self, as he did then as he tried to explain, as we stood by the grave of Božena Nemcova, the importance of "working from the detail."

A detail is a fragment. In any language, detail is the unsorted accumulation of a culture. But in a country like Czechoslovakia where ideology has rubbed culture bare, the detail is precious perhaps because it is idiosyncratic and has not been codified or processed. It has not become part of the orthodoxy.

The real problem with Socialism for most artists in this century has not been with its analysis of social and economic conditions; literary history, at least since the Russian Revolution, both East and West, is filled with writers who welcomed Socialism, often at the expense of personal privilege, simply because they thought it was morally right, or because it made sense or suited their view of historical process. Later, many of these writers changed their minds and became anti-Communist. But for imaginative writers, the problem was not, usually, with Marxism: they didn't know Marxism. The problem was orthodoxy.

Arguments against Socialist realism, the orthodox method for "people's art," have been made not only in the bourgeois West, but in the Socialist countries themselves. The International Kafka Conference, which was held in Prague in the mid-sixties, was, in a sense, a statement against the orthodoxy of Socialist realism. Especially after the Second World War, Socialist realism seemed thin gruel, a completely inadequate way to express psychological reality — and psychological reality (perhaps most starkly portrayed by Kafka himself) was clearly the direction of post-War literature.

Czechoslovakia, in particular, which had been highly industrialized before the War and which was a small bourgeois country, had little context or tradition, as Russia had, for the panoramic social novel. There had been no Czech Tolstoy. Czech literature in 1948 could look back to only a little over

100 years. Before that, the language and its literature had just about disappeared during the 300 years following the Battle of the White Mountain when the country was part of the Hapsburg Empire. Czech was reduced to a peasants' language, a language whose literature was practically nonexistent.

The romantic movement and the spirit of the 1848 revolutions came to the Czech lands in the sudden, dramatic (and still echoing) Czech renaissance. Božena Nemcova, whose grave Jaromil and I stood by, the historian František Palacký (who is sometimes called the Father of the Nation) and other writers of the period, turned to the folklore, the songs and traditions of the peasantry in an effort to bring to life an almost extinct national culture. They wrote, they translated, they published — in Czech. In a sense, they were doing all over again what Jan Hus had begun in the fifteenth century when he preached in Czech: they were attesting nationhood — first in language. Later, Tomáš Masaryk, working very much out of the cultural energy of the Czech renaissance, brought the people to political nationhood, after the First World War.

Translation was perhaps the greatest effort of the Czech literary renaissance: the world was suddenly brought to the Czechs in their own language. Dickens, Shakespeare, Pushkin, all the classics of the world languages appeared in Czech for the first time. The irony of this situation is that once again the Czechs showed their essentially conservative nature: for them, the final effect of the 1848 revolutions was not revolutionary, but intensely bourgeois. It became clear for the first time that there was a Czech middle class. It was for this class that Shakespeare was translated; for them, the romantic tales of Nemcova's *Granny* were written — in the idealized pastoral language and style that only a culture moving away from real peasantry and rural life finds congenial and flattering.

The relation of Czech culture to folklore is clearer and more immediate than it is in other European countries because of the long Hapsburg domination that drove the culture into the peasantry. Milan Kundera, perhaps the best known of the current

Czech novelists (he has been living in recent years in France), has written about this aspect of Czech literary history in his novel *The Joke*.

The joke of the title concerns one of those unfunny Czech lives: an ardent young Communist, in love with an even more ardent young woman who is spending the summer at a Communist study camp (the time is the late forties), writes her a postcard, ending "Long live Trotsky!" as a tease to her political earnestness. He ends up in prison and later in a work camp. When he gets out, years later, and is putting his life back together, he goes back to his home in Moravia, which has always been the heartland of Czech folklore traditions. He meets there his boyhood friend Jaroslav who has spent his life performing in a cymbalo band, teaching and researching the folk music of the country. Jaroslav's son Vladimir has no time for the cymbalo bands and his father's reverence for folklore. He wants to ride a motorcycle and listen to rock music. Jaroslav's speech to his son (which he never in fact delivers) explains how Czech culture emerged in the nineteenth century and why culture, for the Czechs, is the uniquely powerful force that it is.

All nations have their popular art. But for the most part it can be distinguished from their culture without much difficulty. Ours cannot. Every western European nation has had an unbroken cultural development, at least since the Middle Ages. Whereas in the 17th and 18th centuries the Czech nation almost ceased to exist. In the 19th century it was virtually reborn. Among the older European nations it was a child. It had its past, and rich culture too, but these were separated from it by an abyss of 200 years during which neither nobleman nor burgher had spoken Czech. The Czech language retreated from the towns to the countryside and became the exclusive property of the illiterate. Among them, however, it never ceased to continue creating its own culture – a humble culture, completely hidden from the eyes of Europe. A culture of songs, fairy tales, ancient rites and customs, proverbs and sayings. And this was the only narrow bridge which spanned the 200 year gulf. The only bridge, the only crossing point. And so the men who at the turn of the 19th century began to create a new Czech literature and music grafted it upon this existing culture. That was why the first Czech poets and musicians spent so much time collecting fairy tales and songs. That's why their early poetic and musical efforts were often only a paraphrase of folk poetry and folk melodies.

Vladimir, if only you'd try to understand this. Your father isn't just a crackpot folklore addict. Maybe he is something of an addict but he goes deeper than that. He hears in popular art the sap without which Czech culture would have dried up. He is in love with the sound of its flowing.

This love of mine began during the war. They wanted to show us that we had no right to exist, that we were only Germans who spoke a Slavonic tongue. We had to assure ourselves that we'd existed before and that we still exist. We made a pilgrimage to the source . . .

We awoke folk song from its deep slumbers. Those 19th century patriots had transferred popular art to the songbooks only just in time. Civilization began rapidly to displace the popular traditions. So at the turn of the century we had to take folk art out of the songbooks and restore it to life again . . . The folklorists couldn't revive traditions as rapidly as civilization had been able to bury them — at least not until the war reinvigorated us.

There are certain merits to having one's back against the wall. A war was on, and the life of a nation was at stake. We heard the folk songs and we suddenly saw that they were the most essential of essentials. I dedicated my life to them. Through them I merge with the stream which flows deep below . . .

One might think that the nearness of this folk culture would have made "Socialist art" (an art of the people, in the way folk art is) more genuinely the art of the country after the 1948 coup than it was in postrevolutionary Russia. But even to the casual observer, it is clear that the Czech national character —

if one exists — is deeply bourgeois. The Czech renaissance, even as it collected the culture of the peasants, was the evidence of a middle class. Perhaps during the long period when the language was almost lost, the Czechs learned without being told but from the implacable authority of oppression that, for them, the middle class was a lifesaver. It was the class that sustained nationality and language, that is, culture, through its writers and intellectuals. And culture turned out to be requisite for survival — it *was* survival.

Although culture often is a handmaiden of nationalist ideology, there are times when the nation is so powerless politically that the makers of its culture (especially writers because literature is the bearer of the national language) have special significance. Culture becomes essential, not, as it is in our own country, an entertainment or a luxury. Art, for such a nation, is a spiritual experience. That is, the people are *conscious* of the spiritual qualities of art.

There were passionate nationalists among the Czech writers both before and after the establishment of the Czechoslovak state in 1918. Karel Čapek, who is perhaps the best-known Czech writer of the century, was one such nationalist, and a good friend of President Masaryk, whose ideas he helped to popularize. But the curious thing is that, once the Czechs had their nation, the poets, on the whole, became less distinctly Czech, less provincial. In the coffeehouses of Prague, where intellectual life was carried on, the poets (according to Kurt Weiskopf's book, *The Agony of Czechoslovakia*) fought the fights of surrealism, Dadaism and modernism — Western bourgeois art battles, specifically French.

(Although the English, in the memorable person of Chamberlain, have come to represent the sellout of Czechoslovakia at Munich in 1938, the French were there too. And the French betrayal may have been the more painful one to a man like President Beneš who was a Francophile. It was the French, my Czech teacher Mrs. Beranek told me, who had come to the newly formed state and trained the officers, including her husband, for the new army. Many people who came to her for lessons wanted to study French and English, not German or Czech, the two languages of their own city.)

According to Kurt Weiskopf, who was a young trade union representative in Prague just before the German invasion, the intellectuals of Prague were absorbed in arguments about surrealism versus impressionism, the merits of Matisse and Cocteau in 1937–1938 when their nation was falling around them, under the stirred up hatred of the Sudeten Germans (a designation dating from the Nazi era, by the way). Psychoanalysis, rather than economics, was the discipline of the coffeehouses.

Jaromil was just a boy then. Later, he did not become the romantic poet twisted by ideology like the Jaromil in Kundera's novel, *Life Is Elsewhere*. He never joined the Party; he remained aloof, probably by using the most sophisticated method — by maintaining his childlike manner. His wide-open eyes, his slightly comical puppet look — all of these conspire to make him the sort of man you smile at, for no particular reason, and not with contempt. Perhaps Stalin would have recognized him as one of the cloud-dwellers.

We walked around the small, dense Vyšehrad Cemetery where "everyone," it seems, is buried — all the great figures of Czech literature and music. (Smetana's grave was covered with flowers and wreaths, most of them wilted, in honor of his May 12 birthday.) The great ones of Czech science, history and law were there too. I didn't recognize many of the names, but Jaromil pointed them out to me, translated their epitaphs, placed them for me in the country's history.

It is a strangely moving place. One realizes in that small cemetery the smallness of the country, the kinship of its intellectuals and their mutual life, cast adrift as they are on the small island of their complex, impossible-to-learn language. There are only about 10 million native Czech language speakers, and here, in this spot, the makers of their culture are laid close together. It is an ancient place, much older than the Hradčany. And unlike the Hradčany, Vyšehrad is not intact; it is a ruin, emblematic of the country's culture itself, so often built, then broken, then partially rebuilt again.

We left the cemetery and walked toward a view of the river, which was far below. There was a park nearby and we walked in it. Jaromil was talking still about details, how he never liked to say anything abstract, how he waits for the specific fragment of conversation or a gesture to begin a poem. He wanted me to understand that, he said. Perhaps his passion for the detail is part of the elegiac sensibility and stands in opposition to the ideological good cheer of Socialist realism. Ironically enough, it is also in opposition to the self-congratulatory smoothness with which the current regime has exploited the mysterious national folklore (which Kafka seems to have brought into modern world consciousness — Kafka, who knew Czech).

We stood high above the Vltava; we were looking down at a tennis court in the park and from there to the bend of the river. Jaromil had stopped talking. He smiled and pointed to the people below who were playing tennis. "In the fifties," he said, "that was a bad time. Everybody spent a lot of time deciding this is good, this is bad. Tennis and sailing, for example, were bad; they were bourgeois sports. It could be dangerous to go sailing, to even admit you liked tennis. That was when Dvořák was bad — because he wrote the *New World Symphony,* and Smetana was good because he wrote 'Ma Vlast.'"

A couple was playing tennis below us, and farther down, on the river, we saw several white triangles which were the masts of sailboats. "Now we can play tennis," he said smiling radiantly and ironically; it is part of his charm that he can smile both ways at once. As we walked away, back toward his car, he said, "But you know, it may actually be much worse now. Now it is more subtle. We do it ourselves."

We drove back to the Slavia where he let me out. I spent the rest of the afternoon, as I often did, walking back and forth across the Charles Bridge, between the statues of the saints.

What is it like to live in a city whose architecture is so old, it feels inevitable even in its quirkiness — the endless rococo moldings, the streets that go off like stray thoughts, the piled up crowd of centuries of urban life, the arched passageways that could lead anywhere and are purest Kafka. Nothing is planned. It is the opposite of what is probably the most consciously planned form of public space, the shopping center.

The first enclosed shopping mall in the United States was constructed in Minneapolis in the 1950s. The architect and planner was Victor Gruen, an Austrian who spent thirty years of his life working in the United States and who has since returned to Vienna in his retirement. His latest activity is, interestingly enough, protesting the construction of shopping malls, especially those in rural areas.

What he had in mind, Victor Gruen said in an article by Neal R. Peirce that appeared in the *Minneapolis Tribune*, when he first sketched out the shopping mall in 1943, was something "more than just selling machines." The malls were "to include medical offices, rooms for club activities, circulating libraries and post offices in addition to shops." They were intended to be closely related to nearby housing — "spots of urbanity in the long suburban stretches."

But, as Gruen says, "there was a tragic downgrading of quality." Profits, "development," and the breathless consumerism of America conspired to create leaching monsters that threaten the city they attach themselves to and which are "wed irrevocably to the automobile" precisely because of their remote locations. The attempt to transpose the life and vigor of a city, the community aspect of human life, to suburban settings has created "selling machines," entirely phony "centers," which are the center of nothing and can be ruinous to true centers. The city is threatened; the wonderful plan is a terrible mistake, and the "downgrading of quality" *is* "tragic." In Prague, things are different.

Nothing is planned. Yet the presence of intelligence, the intellect of the dream, is apparent everywhere, and it is enormously satisfying. Marcia Davenport recognized it when she first came to Prague in 1930 to research her first book, a biography of Mozart. She went for a walk (this city for walking!) her first morning, without a map, not knowing the city, simply wandering. Like anyone who comes to Prague and loves it, her attachment went beyond an appreciation of its strange beauty. Like me, she called it recognition:

> I walked on, full of a rising sense of contentment that was altogether new in my experience of strange places. Without hesitation at the bottom of the boulevard I crossed Na příkopě, the broad modern avenue that meets it, passed through the arcade of a nearby building and emerged, as I had sensed I would, in the eighteenth century, standing in Ovocný Trh (The Fruit Market) and looking at Stavovské Divadlo, the theatre which was the central landmark that I had come to see, where *Don Giovanni* had had its first performance.
>
> To this moment I can recapture the surge of delighted recognition with which I felt myself transported back into the world where my mind for so long had been living.

Where *had* her mind been living? Not simply in the past, but in a particular concentrated past moment — Mozart's creation of *Don Giovanni*, which is one of the high points of Western culture. She was at home.

She was devastated, later, by the Communist ascendency in 1948. It was worse, for her, than the Hitler years, perhaps because there was no war to end it. By then, she was a close friend of Jan Masaryk; they were to be married in London where he sent her in the last hopeless days of the old Republic and where he said he would join her. But he was already dead — either pushed or jumped from a window — while she waited for him at Claridges. Her meeting with him and their friendship came years after that first walk through Prague. Her initial response to the city was no different in essence from the Swedish medical student's or the Amsterdam telephone operator's.

"The city and the country," she writes, "for twenty years held for me that fertile mystery which we call inspiration. A very large part of that has been unconscious . . . Some of this may be atavism. Some may be romanticism. All of it is truth and therefore much of it is tragedy."

When she returned for a visit, to lay the past to rest, in 1967, Prague was not beautiful. It was robbed of its Bruegel markets, the intense clutter of shopkeeperly life. The red and yellow banners hanging from the baroque buildings appalled her. The "tender butter-yellow" stucco of the baroque houses of Malá Strana were gray; the quaint old signs for butcher, greengrocer, shoemaker, were gone. Prague was gray and gone for her.

But, not having a pre-War picture with which to compare it, the essential beauty is there for me as compellingly as it was, at the beginning, for her. More so, perhaps. The very shabbiness of what was once so gay is appropriate to recent history. Prague is beautiful, but it is broken. There is no point in coming to Prague if you only want loveliness and grace. Even the occult fascination old Prague had for the German romantic writers — the legends about the golem (the robot who ran amuck in the ghetto and is supposed to haunt the city), the lingering haze of the magicians and alchemists and the unreachable *something* that the occult attests to in human intelligence — all of this, since the War, has found a firmer, less airy, significance. "The only definite thing," Kafka told Gustav Janouch on one of their walks through the city, "is suffering." Prague was mystical. (It had the golem, the alchemists, Rudolf and its hermetic thinkers.) Prague was gay. (It had Mozart, whose greatest success came from this city; "My Praguers," he said, "they understand me.") Now its beauty has extended itself out of the tender butter-yellow eighteenth century, out of the mistiness of the occult, into this harsher beauty of sadness. The city is sad. I wanted Jaromil to break under it and *be* tragic. I didn't want any more irony. I was tired of Kafka (I found another Kafka on my own; there is a plaque at the American Embassy; Kafka lived there too. But that's a joke it takes an American to appreciate; when I told Zdenka she just smiled vaguely. She didn't get it.)

Perhaps all beauty is sad at the core. Solemn beauty, that is, not the light beauty of youth and untouched form. Human physical beauty cannot reach this depth. Only a city can sustain the truth of this fact of beauty — the brokenness — because, unlike an old woman who was once beautiful, a city can perfectly balance, in its architecture, the fresh loveliness of form *and* the ruined, irreplaceable qualities of age.

I had all this in mind, sketchily, while I was walking around the Kampa. I ended up at Zdenka's. She was flailing around in the kitchen, making the noon meal. She wanted me to stay. Elena was in the living room, sitting on the windowsill, drawing the steeple of a church and the masses of lilac and trees that cut off the rest of the church from view.

In the kitchen where we were alone, Zdenka suddenly stopped beating the veal cutlets with a hammer (a regular hammer — she said she couldn't find the wooden mallet). "I meant to ask you," she said softly, shyly, "would it be possible to try again about a pair of blue jeans for Elena? After all, she wants them. The jeans craze," she said, shaking her head and gesturing with the hammer. "It's hard for them to live without jeans. This is what it is to be young." I said I would send another pair from London when I went back.

"Oh good," she said, and went back to hammering. "Be sure to wash them first."

"Why?"

"So you can send them as used clothing. I could never afford the duty otherwise. These *jeans*," she said, hammering and, it seemed, angry.

7 ❦

Several nights later I went to a concert in the Smeta-nova Síň (Smetana Hall) of the Obecní Dům, a building which on the ground floor and basement has a smoky *kavárna* and two old-fashioned restaurants, the one in the basement decorated with large art nouveau mosaics. The whole building is art nouveau and was considered, by some people, a disgrace when it was built. It has some of the only Alfonse Mucha murals extant in Prague. The *kavárna*, which I visited during the day, did not seem to be a tourist hangout, although it was centrally located. Most of the foreigners were students, usually Arab or African, who were in Prague studying at the Charles University or an agricultural institute. During the day, the other patrons were elderly. At night, people sometimes stopped for coffee or a beer before going upstairs to the concert. This is what I did.

I was looking forward to the music. The Prague Spring Music Festival is not the most famous music festival of Europe, and this year a number of performers from the West (including Leonard Bernstein) had canceled their scheduled appearances in protest of the harassment Czech officials were giving signers of Charter 77. But Prague has always been a great music city; it was once "the conservatory of Europe." And there is no better way to feel part of a country whose language you are cut off from than to sit in a concert hall and listen to music. For once, you understand the sounds that are coming at you, just as the natives do.

The orchestra that night was the Slovak Philharmonic; the program's major items were Beethoven's piano concerto in G Major and, after the intermission, Dimitri Shostakovich's Symphony no. 3, the *First of May* Symphony, which commemorates the workers' holiday.

The Smetanova Síň looked like a dolled-up high school auditorium; it was bright, and the flat wooden floor stopped at a plain proscenium box raised at the front. There were some waxy looking statues at the sides of the stage. The seats were hard and made squeaking noises when anyone moved. During the Beethoven, nobody seemed to move much. The performance wasn't exceptional, but we applauded at the end for quite a long time.

After the intermission, only a little over half the audience had returned to their seats. I didn't see this happen at any other concert, and at first I wasn't sure what to make of it.

The *First of May* was the only work in the second half of the program. It is probably an example of what, in literature, is called Socialist realism: a lot of cymbals, a lot of kettle drums, a lot of "triumph." As music, it is a little repulsive.

We didn't clap much, those of us who were, now, a rather scattered audience. We clapped so little and so feebly, in fact, that the conductor (whose name, according to the program, was Mr. Slovak, as if he represented the nation itself) finished taking his bow in scattered clapping and chair squeaking, and he walked off the stage as the audience went silent. We were barely polite. American audiences rarely make things so clear.

We weren't impolite to Mr. Slovak; it seemed we were thinking, as an audience, of something else. In fact, the conductor, as he took his bow, had a look of complicity on his face. It was, I think, a deeply national moment, an instant when everyone in the hall knew what was happening and felt the same thing. It was a moment of connection — solidarity even — which none of the music had created among us. Or perhaps, ironically, Shostakovich had created it, sheerly by its vulgar (Russian, as everyone was thinking) triumph.

This was the picture: Mr. Slovak was bowing; his wry face had an odd half-smile as he bowed to us, who were hardly clapping in the half-filled room. It was his smile — an entirely intimate and savvy smile. He accepted, it seemed, and reflected back, the silence, the emotional aloofness that is at the heart of political resistance. He stood there before us, a formal black-and-white figure whose face was for the moment entirely ironic, the emotion beyond tragedy. And he bowed. He acknowledged something other than music, other than applause. He registered a profound national protest. We filed out of the hall and went our separate ways, quietly, into the wet Prague night, the streets gleaming black from the rain.

The next day I met Jaromil; I was walking through the city again with him. We were walking fast, through the newer part of the city near Václavské náměstí, dodging the crowds, trying to keep together as we weaved between shoppers and tourists and made our way around the scaffolding of the new subway that Prague had been building, with what Jaromil calls Czech slowness, for almost the whole of the past decade.

"Did it mean anything?" I asked him. "Half the audience left at intermission, and then everybody barely applauded after the Shostakovich. Did it mean anything?"

"Yes, yes, you're right," he said. "It means something. You're getting very Czech. Everything means something."

David Beseda, the American student who had come on the same flight from London as I had, was back from the country-side. We met at a *vinárna* near the Staroměstské náměstí and drank a bottle of Moravian wine. I was going to Moravia soon myself, to visit Ružena.

David had found out that day that his last name, in Czech, meant "a place for dancing and festivals." He was very pleased about that. He was pleased as well about his trip to Moravia. He had taken the train all day to the village his grandfather had emigrated from. On the train he had composed a note in Czech, which he printed carefully on a piece of notepaper, using a phrase book. The note said: "My name is David Beseda. I am from America. My grandfather came from here. Could you please show me where my relatives live?"

He got off the train in a tiny village, late in the afternoon. A young woman outside the little station seemed to be the only person around. He ran up to her, and held the note in front of her.

The young woman smiled, he said, and nodded a lot, and said various things, none of which he understood. But it was clear he was to follow her. She led him to a house not far away, knocked on the door, and when a middle-aged woman answered, talked to her briefly, showed her the note. And then the middle-aged woman threw her arms around him and pulled him into the house. She was his grandfather's niece, his second cousin. And that was that.

He spent several days with the family, he said. They managed to get somebody, a neighbor girl who translated technical manuals from English into Czech at a nearby factory, to act as interpreter.

"Did you talk politics?" I said.

They were loyal to the Party, he said. "The first thing they asked me when I asked them if they had freedom of expression, was what happened to people in my country when they got sick. They wanted to know how much a hospital room cost per day. They think they've got a better deal."

They didn't think freedom of expression was worth much if you had to pay $75 a day just for a bed if you got sick.

While we were talking a young Czech with very long hair, a real hippy such as you don't see much in the United States anymore, came and joined us. He couldn't speak English, but he wanted to talk. He grabbed David Beseda's phrase book, which was on the table between us. He wanted to say something about music and flipped through the book, piecing together his sentences. He loved rock music, he said. He made the motions of playing a guitar. He liked to wear blue jeans. He pointed to his jeans, which were very dirty. He liked long hair. He held out a clump of his hair, which was tangled and matted. None of these things were allowed, he said, flipping through the phrase book. He kept repeating a word in Czech, a word neither David Beseda nor I knew. He said it slowly, carefully; he repeated it many times patiently, as if we would finally get it if he just pronounced it carefully enough. He couldn't find the word in the phrase book.

Finally, David Beseda brought out a Czech-English dictionary from the book bag he had with him. The young man was delighted with the dictionary, and paged through it quickly, running a very dirty finger down the small print of the pages. Then he thrust the book in front of us. His finger was pointing to *svoboda*. Freedom. Then he made frantic hand-waving gestures and shook his head, as if he were communicating with the deaf and had to communicate through mime. He poked at the word in the dictionary and then shook his head vehemently.

"No freedom?" David Beseda said. *"Ne svoboda?"*

"Ne, ne, ne," the young man said, and shook his long matted dark hair. He sat back satisfied, relieved, as Virginia Woolf once said after a good day's writing, of his meaning.

The men at the next table, working men who were drinking beer and had been laughing, had fallen silent. They seemed embarrassed. The hippy said something to them, and they laughed, shrugged, and went back to their conversation. Then he said something to us. But we couldn't understand.

Finally, David Beseda said, "Yes, we understand. No freedom. *Ne svoboda. Rozumime.* We understand. No freedom." And the young man started to say something more, and then looked at us and laughed. He waved his hand in a gesture of futility.

"Rozumime," David Beseda said. "We understand. *Ne svoboda."*

The young man shook his head and went back to the table of men drinking beer. He didn't look at us again. When we left, he looked up and said casually, but in an odd pronunciation, "So long." He gave us a wry smile. He seemed to be

amused, himself, with his English. "See you around," he said.
The men at the table, none of them hippies (he was like their
mascot), laughed. We laughed. We decided later he must have
learned his English from rock records.

In 1953 the Polish poet Czeslaw Milosz published a book in
the United States titled *The Captive Mind*. Two years before,
he had broken with the Polish government which, after the
War, he had represented as a cultural attaché, first in Washington, later in Paris. He lives now in California where he teaches
and writes. He is a philosopher and a poet.

Milosz was never a member of the Communist Party, but like
many intellectuals in Central and Eastern Europe, after the
devastation of the Second World War, he had little desire to
look backward. And, as he shows, the West (particularly America) represented decadence and the past, the status quo, while
the Soviet Union presented a model that looked to the future
and believed in and urged the creation of the "new man."
After its people had witnessed the destruction of Warsaw and
of a whole pre-War way of life, the promise of a golden future
was more appealing, more reliable, than a return to the past:
there was no past.

Milosz's book may be the most intelligent and moving personal account and attempt to analyze of the impact of Socialism
on creativity that has yet been written. "My book," he writes in
the preface, "takes the reader into the world inhabited by the
intellectuals of Warsaw, Prague, Bucharest, and Budapest . . .
I seek to create afresh the stages by which the mind gives way
to compulsion from without, and to trace the road along which
men in people's democracies are led on to orthodoxy."

He does this against the devastated backdrop of post-War
Central and Eastern Europe. In fact, the corpses and the
bombed cities, the starved and brutalized populations of these
countries are never far from the bright, almost grotesque, image
of the new man. It is difficult for Americans, particularly those

born after the War, to understand the intimacy implicit between the fires of the War and the phoenix of the new man. In Prague one is not allowed to forget. Plaques and photographs are mounted on walls commemorating by name various citizens, usually very young people, who died in street fighting at the end of the War. There are usually jars of flowers placed on the little wooden stands nailed under these memorials. Most of these dead would, after all, only be middle aged today if they were alive; it is quite possible that their parents, not their children, place the jars of flowers by their pictures.

"Probably only those things are worthwhile," Milosz writes, "which can preserve their validity in the eyes of a man threatened with instant death . . .

"A man is lying under machine-gun fire on a street in an embattled city. He looks at the pavement and sees a very amusing sight: the cobblestones are standing upright like the quills of a porcupine. The bullets hitting their edges displace and tilt them. Such moments in the consciousness of a man *judge* all poets and philosophers."

In other words, such extremity of experience creates a lassitude toward literature. It encourages irony — for what *words* can transform (or should transform) such experience? "Dialectical materialism," Milosz writes, "awakens a response in them [writers of Eastern Europe who went through the War] because it is *earthy*." Writers with this huge weight of experience longed for, above all else, an "elimination of emotional luxuries." Even "sensitivity" was, for these writers, suspect; it was obscene. If the destruction of their cities and the brutalization of their people were going to "mean" anything, they themselves must be "worthy." They must be strong; they must be real. This called for nothing less than a new sort of human being.

Milosz's book is particularly valuable in stressing the compelling power of dialectical reasoning for the post-War artists of what later were called (still are called) the satellite countries. Milosz calls it "the Method" and says that it "exerts a magnetic influence on contemporary man because it alone emphasizes, as has never before been done, the fluidity and interdependence of phenomena. Since the people of the 20th century find themselves in social circumstances where even the dullest mind can see that 'naturalness' is being replaced by fluidity and interdependence, thinking in categories of motion seems to be the surest means of seizing reality in the act. The Method is mysterious, no one understands it completely — but that merely enhances its magic powers."

The Captive Mind is not a bitter, or even a polemical book. Its lucidity and care are astonishing, given its publication date in the early fifties in this country. It is, of course, ultimately anti-Communist. Milosz is one of those people, subtle and complicated by nature, who have not been able to live on the sidelines. He had to choose, and his lot fell with the West — and as he seemed to know even when he wrote this book, the lot went with capitalism and the particular injustices and contradictions and self-deceptions of Western democracy.

The political situation he writes about is the late Stalinist period, but it is the early Socialist period in the satellite countries. Czechoslovakia had been a Socialist country for only five years when the book was published. An entire generation has passed since then, but his book is valuable not only as a historical document; it also bears, to a certain extent, on the situation of Prague's intellectuals today. Because of the repression following the 1968 Dubček reforms, the Czech intellectuals have been thrust back into some of the more obvious and painful confrontations with state authority that characterized the Stalinist era. No one, as Jaromil said to me one day, is looking the other way.

There are differences in the climate an intellectual in Prague today faces from that Milosz describes in the immediate post-War era. For one thing, by and large, Prague intellectuals fear for their jobs, not their lives. The era of mass terror (which in spite of the famous Slansky trial was never as pronounced and devastating as it was in the Soviet Union) has not been the result of the Prague Spring overthrow. It is important to understand this distinction from the point of view of a Czech intellectual. Otherwise, if one looks at such distinctions (people are being harassed — badly, but not murdered — usually) as grotesque hair-splitting, one misses the significance and nuance of life today.

It is significant that, after 1968, Alexander Dubček and his colleagues were not executed (as Imre Nagy was in 1956 after the Hungarian revolt) and that Czech writers, journalists, film makers and other artists were not sent, en masse, to prison camps or worse. Several people (Jaromil was one), when I asked them about repercussions after 1968, said — with the thoughtful air of connoisseurs testing one era of repression against another — that, all in all, they had gotten off rather easily, considering what they had been up to. (More recently, the imprisonment of Czech signers and supporters of Charter 77 appears to have been stepped up; there are more trials, more direct harassment. Pavel Kohout, who was on a legal visa outside the country, was informed in October 1979 when he attempted to reenter that he had been stripped of his citizenship and could not return.)

What the country had been up to in 1968, in fact, had been another attempt to unite East and West in their land: "Socialism with a human face." The eight months of the Prague Spring began at least several years before January 1968 when Alexander Dubček was elected prime minister and censorship was lifted for the first time in twenty years. President Antonin Novotný, his Stalinist-era predecessor, had already lost his grip, at least in cultural and artistic areas. The films that made Czechoslovakia a leading film making country — films like *The Shop on Main Street, Loves of a Blonde* and *The Fireman's Ball*, were all made before 1968.

The landmark event, culturally, was the International Kafka Conference in 1967 in Prague. At this conference Czech scholars made an impassioned plea for the acceptance of Kafka into the canon of the nation's writers. They argued that Kafka did not represent Western decadence and murky, self-absorbed nihilism, but an essential voice of modern literature. They even suggested that it was possible to be alienated in a workers' state. To deny Kafka in his own land, they said, would be to put Czech (and Socialist) literature in a reactionary, isolated box.

The Prague Spring was a unique and fascinating phenomenon. It was not, as had been the case in Hungary, an uprising. It was not a military action (even in August, when the Warsaw Pact troops moved into the country, the Czech army was not mobilized). It was not even, at its deepest roots, a political or economic revolt, although the economic policies of the liberal economist Otto Sik certainly were a major part of Dubček's program. (Part of what it meant to give Socialism its "human face," in fact, meant giving the population access to Western consumer goods.) At its core, the Prague Spring was a cultural phenomenon. It was created — as a thing of national beauty — by its writers and journalists and intellectuals and students, not by the politicians. Dubček was the man of the moment. He was able to *respond*. As a result, he was very popular. Perhaps anyone who abolished censorship would have been popular. In a country like the United States where the question of freedom of expression has in recent years been debased to a matter of the rights of publishers of hard-core pornography it is difficult to appreciate the passion in the struggle against censorship.

The eight months of the Prague Spring seem to have been spent not creating new, uncensored works of art that were somehow new and broke the old patterns; rather, it seems as if the country spent that brief period chatting. There were TV and radio panels almost every night, with writers and other artists discussing strategy and tactics, values and goals. The country's intellectuals seemed to spend the eight months talking to each other, and, like everybody else, watching and waiting to see what would happen. The main discussion revolved around the issue of how swiftly the new reforms should be implemented.

Now, everyone says, they should have gone slower. Jaromil said this — and he had appeared on the television panels in 1968. This is perhaps the most bitter irony of the years since the end of the Prague Spring: the writers and artists who were at the center of the reforms in 1968 find themselves criticizing *themselves*. If we had done this, if we hadn't done that — this sort of self-examination, rather than simple fear, perhaps explains why Jaromil and others have not signed Charter 77. An episode like the Prague Spring is not something that comes about because of good planning or even good intentions It emerges from the impacted sadness of history. "You think," Kundera writes in *Life Is Elsewhere*, "that just because it's already happened, the past is finished and unchangeable? Oh no, the past is cloaked in multicolored taffeta and every time we look at it we see a different hue."

For long periods, the past comes back sadly, elegiacally. Then something happens, something imperceptible, as if the whole nation had sighed involuntarily, and the usual weight of sadness and irony shifts slightly, and the impossible happens: the past comes back as the force and reason for change.

The worst aftermath of the crushing of this new faith and exuberance is the self-castigation it brings. To hate the Russians (and everyone seems to) is one thing, but to feel always nagging the thought that if we had done this or that *it* wouldn't have happened — this is the most debilitating effect of repression. To live over and over, in one's national history, the defeat of such risings of faith, is exhausting. The editor who had not liked me, who had wanted her friend to divorce his terrified wife, was exhausted with the effort of falling this way or that on issue after issue.

People come up with strange solutions to the problem. Zdenka had said, the last time I stopped by on one of my walks, that she had gone, the evening before, to a dinner for workers in her clinic in honor of the departure of a group of Soviet physicians who had been working there on a project for the past three months. There was a lot of drinking, toasting. She got along with the Soviet doctors just fine, she said — at work. "They are so crude, though," she said. They drank too much, got loud, were capable of pawing you, she said, as if this were behavior the Russians alone indulged in. She obviously did not like them at all.

"I proposed a toast," she said, "to the Hapsburg Empire." This, after the toasts to Soviet-Czech brotherhood and all the other half-drunken, half-sincere toasts, had been received with great hilarity. "They thought I was quite a wit," she told me. "What they don't know is, I mean it."

A bizarre toast for a Czech: the return of the centuries-long oppressor. "But," she said, "at least they weren't *beasts*. The Russians . . ." she trailed off. As František Palacky had said in the previous century, in a much-quoted phrase, "If Austria did not exist, it would have to be created in the interests of Europe and humanity." His statement is great-grandfather to Zdenka's toast, except of course the Empire did exist for him. There was a measure of safety (or nostalgically, it seems that way now) in the idea of *Mitteleuropa*.

"Perhaps," Milosz writes, "the era of independent states is over, perhaps they are no more than museum pieces. Yet it is saddening to say good-bye to one's dreams of a federation of equal nations, of a United States of Europe in which differing languages and differing cultures would have equal status . . . Must one sacrifice so much in the name of the unity of mankind?" Zdenka harks back to the Hapsburgs, only partly ironically, the domination that she feels could have, if luck had been with them, developed into a "United States of Europe."

The atomization of society, which we see all about us, and which has become the dominant psychological reality of the century (so that the current interest of Americans in their roots is probably at least partly an identification with the alienation of immigrant ancestors), has occurred alongside the paradoxical growth of a technology so advanced and sometimes so lethal that we are forced to admit we live in "one world." In other words, as the sustaining strength of culture has been lost and people feel "alienated," estranged and isolated, we are, for the first time in history, in control of the means to communicate with the whole world. It is an ironic, unsatisfying power. For we are left without the warmer circle of culture, an intimate and yet impersonal tie which, traditionally, created for its people the world entire, and was for The People a Way.

✤

"Are you going to write a 'Letter from Prague'?" Jaromil asked me one day as we walked along together.

"I'll write something," I said.

"I've read a lot of these 'Letters from Prague,'" he said. "What does it mean? A person comes, stays a week; he walks around and then he writes an article and says, 'The people seem contented — or discontented. Fresh vegetables appear to be plentiful, but the lines in stores are long — or the lines are short, but the vegetables are wilted. The people are well dressed — or the women don't have any sense of style.' Whether we stand in line, vegetables, what we wear — that's it. What do you think?"

"I noticed, as I rode by on the tram this morning, that a vegetable stand seemed to have wilted vegetables, mostly just kohlrabi and radishes — but it's only May. And the well-dressed women seem to be West German tourists. And I've noticed lines."

"That's what I mean," he said, shaking his head.

"I was joking," I said.

"Yes," he said, but he didn't laugh. We walked along together in silence.

✤

What *is* it possible to know? I mean, beyond the fact that there are or are not wilted vegetables, and that the women do or do not have nice clothes (is it possible to know even that?). This is the question that haunts modern times: *did you know?* Did you know about Auschwitz? ("Only a few people knew." "We didn't know.") Did you know about My Lai? Did you know about the CIA in Chile? Did we know? When did we find out?

There is, in this question, the lingering nerve of an ethical culture: if we know, then we are responsible. We still feel we must answer for our knowledge. But clearly, it is necessary, at times, for whole nations to be sure they do not know certain things. East Germany, for example, has worked out its relation to Second World War history in a way that acknowledges *and* denies reality: yes, the horrors of the camps existed, but the cause was Fascism, which has been boldly routed by Socialism. As a result, East Germany, unlike West Germany, does not pay reparations to Jewish survivors.

As for us, who knows what more, exactly, will emerge from the Vietnam years? Was America really surprised by My Lai? It strikes me that I, an ordinary citizen in the Midwest with no special information, was not surprised. Horrified — yes, I was sickened; I remember the pictures. But I wasn't surprised. The whole business stank to high heaven for years. Years before My Lai, *Life* magazine ran that full-color picture of a GI wearing a string of ears slung around his waist. That, I think, is when I knew — knew all a person needs to know. I knew then that it was worse than war; it was a perversion of the national self, as well as the destruction of another nation.

It was not necessary to be told much to come to the realization that I *knew*. Apparently, moral intelligence is subtle and wily; it finds the news. We do not need to be told that there are concentration camps dotting Central and Eastern Europe, and they are located here and here. We do not need the U.S. Army or the American press to give the "facts" about My Lai. Atrocities cannot be hidden. They appear first in language: *We had to destroy the village in order to save it.*

But in order "not to know," large groups of people, whole nations, have to find a way to blunt their intelligence. A way must be found not to know. The cost must be enormous. History is traduced, but perhaps it always is. Worse than that, people must deny over and over the intelligence of their senses. It is a denial of the most ancient poetic intelligence. It is a denial of reality. At its most extreme, it is madness.

We are haunted by history because we denied its reality

when it was the present. It keeps coming back, as Kundera says. It will keep coming back until we get the story straight. "During the war," Muriel Rukeyser says in *The Life of Poetry*, "we felt the silence in the policy of the governments of English-speaking countries. That policy was to win the war first, and work out the meanings afterward. The result was, of course, that the meanings were lost. You cannot put these things off." And therefore, the hunger for meaning increases.

But to answer my question, at least for now: what is it possible to know? Apparently, just about everything we need to know. This fact must be acknowledged: we do know when something vile and gigantically evil is happening among us. We may not know the names: Auschwitz, Buchenwald, Terezin (the "artists' concentration camp" that wasn't far from Prague), My Lai. But we know. It is impossible to believe otherwise.

Still, I often feel *wrong* to be approaching this history as I am — I who have been untouched by this kind of suffering. I go cold at the thought that silence *is* the only response, as so many of the real witnesses have said. I have felt, vaguely, that if I could get permission (I think of it that way) for this inquiry from the man in the luggage shop in London, that I would have my justification, my right to speak at all.

Why such timidity? It comes, I think, from the peculiar relation the "untouched," such as myself, must have to the Holocaust. It remains the central episode of our history, the horror against which all other atrocities are measured, even previous ones, and by which innocence is gauged. My relation to it is not one of personal or even national guilt (as, say, a young German might feel). Mine is the confusion, the search, of someone unmarked. *Nothing bad has ever happened to me.* Nothing impersonally cruel and ruinous — and that is an odd, protected history or nonhistory to have in this century. I can only proceed, assuming that to be untouched has some significance in the presence of the deeply touched life of this city.

Or perhaps I must be more emphatic: the value of my inquiry *is* that I am unmarked. I have no "story," no documentation of the camps, the tortures, the cruelties. I have not lived in the post-War world Milosz describes as "a hard school, where ignorance was punished not by bad marks but by death." Such a world (and it is a world where the War and the peace that followed must be seen as one thing) forced the intellectuals here "to think sociologically and historically." People like me are entirely different.

We are part of the evidence that all that raw material from survivors and witnesses has gone out of journalism, even out of the testament of history, and has plunged into the psychic life of all of us. The horrors and the sadness, the endless mourning, is floating there, careening in the imagination, looking for a place. Looking for some way to be transformed. Looking, in a word, for culture. As I am.

_____

*T*OWARD THE end of my three weeks, I went by train to visit Ružena. I was thinking about Jaromil on the train, and I was depressed. The day before we had met again, he the ever-dutiful tour guide. He felt I should see Karlstejn, a great medieval castle in the countryside. He also thought I should see the countryside, more than from a train. And it was beautiful, the fruit trees furred with blossoms so that you couldn't even see the black bark on the branches. It *was,* and without irony, the "romantic Czech countryside."

In the little village below the castle, I was charmed by the cottages, the small gardens and the vegetable plots raked neatly, the seeds in already but only a few green lines of shoots up yet. I saw a round loaf of bread on a window ledge outside of a house and wondered aloud what local custom this was — putting wheels of bread outside the window.

"But it's no custom at all," Jaromil had said. "Not everything you see is a 'Czech custom'; some things are just there — somebody puts a loaf of bread outside a window. I don't know what it means. It doesn't mean anything. It looks funny to me too." He wasn't annoyed, but there was a little exasperation. Being a tour guide was not always easy.

Later, back in Prague, we stopped for coffee at the Slavia, he giving in to my *kavárna* addiction. We were talking in English, of course, and, after a few minutes I noticed that a man — big and beefy, a sleepy-looking man — had moved to a table near us. Soon, he was leaning very near, his arm thrown over the back of the banquette, supposedly sprawling for comfort, as large men sometimes do in small chairs. But really he was listening to us. It was obvious; *he* was obvious.

When we were outside on the street, Jaromil said yes, the man had probably been listening; the police placed such people in various public places, like the *kavárny* where Czechs were likely to meet Western visitors. When they saw anything suspicious — two people speaking English, one of them obviously a Czech — they listened. Jaromil said it was quite silly really. He had had a better view of the man than I had, and he said he was convinced the man either couldn't understand English at all or couldn't understand it with the disadvantages of eavesdropping. And then — what had we been talking about? The medieval art at Karlstejn, the view of the Hradčany, other possible tourist sites for me to visit: harmless, blameless. But I was spooked.

"Do you think they have been following us all along?" I asked, using spy movie dialogue as naturally as if I knew what I was talking about.

For the first time, Jaromil replied to me coldly. "If you're afraid, don't be seen with me." He said he thought it quite probable that we had been followed. So what? These things happened. It was quite normal.

Later, I was troubled, worried that he thought I had asked if we were followed — and of course I had sounded frightened: I was frightened — because I wanted to drop him. I walked to his apartment, found him and his wife at dinner. I was welcomed, Jaromil's wife wanted to hear my impressions of Karlstejn. Later, when she had left the room for a few minutes, I told him why I had really come. "I was just surprised," I said. "I didn't mean I didn't want to take walks with you." We had never spoken in a really personal way before and I felt more embarrassed, partly because of the intimacy of what I was saying.

Jaromil seemed a little surprised. He, for his part, he said, had never meant what I had assumed; he had simply meant that if I didn't want to be risking the unpleasantness of being followed, that he would understand. He had meant nothing more. He was relaxed, casual, dismissive of the whole thing. I felt a little foolish, felt I had managed to make the whole thing bigger than it was. But I remembered his tone, the cold pride, the stern I-will-go-it-alone voice that I had been so certain of. And then, the other thing: he had said, politely, carefully, that he felt he ought to warn me about Zdenka. He didn't mean anything specific — as far as he knew she was fine, a fine person. But he just felt I should show discretion around her. Her flat, he felt, was a little too choice, the location on the Kampa too wonderful. How had she managed to get such a perfect arrangement? It didn't look right, that's all he wanted to say — and it was clear he had thought long about saying it, and perhaps said it at that moment because he wanted to show he trusted me, that all was forgiven. Or didn't need forgiving. I explained that the flat had been in the family. "But still," he said, and left it at that. I had already arranged to stay at Zdenka's flat when I returned from my visit to Ružena. My New York friend had said not to (for different reasons of course than Jaromil), and now Jaromil had said to keep my distance. But that was where I would stay my last nights in Prague, and I had been looking forward to it, to the Kampa, to living in a friend's house, as if it were completely normal. When I told Jaromil, he nodded. He understood, he said and didn't think I should worry at all. And then, typically, he shrugged. Just as Zdenka would have done. The national gesture.

Ružena met me at the station. She looked the way I remembered her: thin, attractive in a sporty way. She was about fifty-five but seemed younger. She wouldn't let me carry my suitcase. We walked along the platform, lurching it between us. People looked at us because we appeared to be fighting.

We had two hours before the train left Brno for Slavkov. We put the suitcase in a locker (she insisted on hoisting it in), and we walked into a sunny, broad street in front of the station.

Brno, the Moravian capital, is Czechoslovakia's second city. The country has two languages: Czech, spoken by the people of Bohemia and Moravia, and Slovak, spoken in Slovakia. The two languages are similar, however, and mutually understood. In former days, the rivalry between the two national groups was severe; it constituted a serious problem in creating a joint nation. The Czechs regarded the Slovaks as an uncultured peasantry; the Slovaks thought the Czechs were too slick, too citified, to be entirely trustworthy. My grandmother, a Czech, did not like the notion of someone being a Czechoslovak, a being as unlikely to her mind as a dog-cat. Nor did she like to be called a Bohemian, for that was, for her, merely a territorial designation and did not express what she *was*. Her identity was racial, not national in the more modern sense.

The history of the twentieth century has inevitably drawn the Czechs and Slovaks together in a solidarity that has more to do with tragedy and mutual isolation than anything else. Alexander Dubček was a Slovak (and therefore one of the minority) and he became the rallying figure of the entire country in 1968.

Moravia is distinguished from Bohemia by a more elusive cultural quality. Moravians think of themselves as the *real* Czechs. Joseph Wechsberg, a Moravian himself, says the attitude of Moravians toward the rest of the Czechs is rather like that of a Boston Yankee to the West. Ružena ran true to form. As we passed by a scaffolded old building, she pointed and said, "Older than Prague."

But, I thought, not a *city* as Prague is a city. Not as complicated and dreamlike. Dreamlike: not a sentimental reference but the effect of many rushing lives thrust together in a place concentrated by the past, a rush that provokes a confused sense of movement, hazy and not entirely explicable as in a dream. We stood waiting to cross a busy street and I felt, as I've felt in downtown Minneapolis standing next to the IDS Center: that the farmland, the green sheet of real countryside was very near, and that *it* was what mattered here, not this attempt at a city. Like Minneapolis, I thought, Brno is probably an easier city to live in — better "quality of life," as the corporations tell their executives when they move them to Minneapolis. But Brno is distinctly a provincial city which means a touchy city, a city everlastingly looking over its shoulder — to New York, to Prague, to the real city.

I suggested that we have lunch at a good restaurant — a celebration, I said, and my treat. I also gave her the little present I'd brought from London — a record, and a packet of postcards. She'd told me, when we met two years before, on the train, that she collected postcards.

Ružena wasn't sure, she said, about going to a good restaurant. We were walking down a busy street, she a little ahead of me because she walked so fast. "Keep your money, keep your money," she said over her shoulder. But she brought us to a hotel restaurant that had a decorative fountain and a small pool with carp swimming around in it. ("You choose it, you eat it — the very one," she said with civic pride.)

It seemed like a swanky place and that somehow put us at ease. The eating gave us something to do. We were, in fact, nervous to be together. We didn't really know each other. Who was she, after all? Someone I had met on a train, who had offered me a sausage when I was hungry but, inexplicably, had never given it to me. A woman who cried over *ma vlast*. Someone with scars, with whom I had exchanged rings (neither of us wore them, I noticed). We took a long time over lunch. We started with liver dumpling soup. Then roast duck and the spongy yellowish dumplings made of bread, not of potatoes as the German ones are. And beer, two tall cylinders of gold. Then Ružena ordered coffee and the restaurant's special dessert, a torte constructed of layers of thin, crisp cookies and a filling of whipped cream and ground hazelnuts. We talked about food; we said over and over, how good it was to see each other, how glad we were to be together again. But when she asked me how long I could stay, I said I had to leave in two days, although I'd originally planned on five. She just nodded and kept eating her hazelnut torte. She didn't try to get me to stay longer.

"Did you bring traveler's checks?" she asked me. She was drinking coffee; I was still eating the torte.

"Yes," I said.

"Perhaps you can do a favor for a friend of mine who has a sick baby?" she asked.

"Anything," I said. But I didn't like the sound of her voice. She was wheedling. I didn't like to think she was wheedling. Also, I wasn't used to anyone thinking I was a person with money. "Anything I can do," I said, but I sounded stiff, even to myself. But the funny thing was, I meant it too: anything at all.

"We'll talk about it later," she said casually. "No hurry. Just a kindness for my friend who has the sick baby."

I said fine, anything.

&

The train to Slavkov was filled with commuters going home from work. We walked from the Slavkov station to Ružena's apartment, which was in a newish, cinder-block three-story building. We walked up the dusty street, still tugging the suitcase between us. There didn't seem to be any center, just these few treeless streets, laid out like a half-finished subdivision in a lost Midwestern town, except there weren't any cars around. It was a cheerless, too-bright place, and the wind, which was blowing hard, was filled with dust.

This, I thought, was the site of the Battle of the Three Emperors. Napoleon had been here. Tolstoy had sent Prince André here to fight. He had returned from this place to Russia to ask his friend Pierre about the "eternal questions of loneliness and despair." I saw nothing that looked like a battlefield, and nothing looked old. It was a raw, dismal place, even in the spring.

Ružena had complained, during most of the hour-long ride from Brno, about her apartment — which was too small, and about Slavkov, which, she said, had no culture. "Without music, without books and movies, what am I?" she said. "I'm nothing.

Without culture, nothing. I must have that. Food, no. Culture, I have to have."

She opened the door of the apartment and motioned me inside. I entered a tiny room, crammed so full of objects that at first I thought it was a terrible, crazy mess. But, in fact, the room was fastidiously neat. It was simply covered — walls, floors, every surface, with *things*. Many, many books in cases running up the walls, books in all the languages Ružena speaks: Tolstoy in Russian, Flaubert in French, Shakespeare and Dickens in English, Goethe and Schiller in German, Italian poetry, American novels, a section of Spanish titles, some Hungarian and Polish books; dictionaries, grammars, fancy art books; and two long rows of record albums. There were several books on the desk with Chinese characters. "I'm studying Chinese," she said.

The bookcases held double rows of books and wherever a smidgen of space was left open on the edge of a shelf, she had placed some bibelot or figurine or doll. There were a lot of dolls and stuffed animals perched everywhere, dressed in the startled pinks and aquas of cheap carnival prizes. They were as honored, it seemed, in this tabernacle of culture, as the books. On one wall there was a reproduction of a Vermeer girl looking, as they often do, out an open window to an unseen landscape. There were framed autographs, one from a famous French actor which was inscribed to Ružena. ("He came here to study before the War," she said. "I met him when we were students.") A big, cumbersome desk was set diagonally in one corner; it took up about a quarter of the room with its large swivel office chair. A large glass lay over the top and under it Ružena had crammed postcards, pictures of dogs and cats with bright ribbons around their necks, and a number of cartoons. There were family photographs as well, framed and placed on the top of the desk and on bookcases: her son, the son's wife, the two grandchildren, nestled between stuffed dogs and dolls with full skirts of stiff net. There was a television set as well — a large one — propped on an end table, and a record player on the floor in the corner near a cabinet with glass panels full of china and wineglasses and homely porcelain figurines.

Along one wall, propped up on a day bed that took up another quarter of the little room, was a very old woman who was wearing a pure white nightgown and a flowered scarf tied under her chin. She was covered with fresh white sheets and several blankets and an old, intricate quilt in dark colors. Her hair, which was pulled back and knotted in the ancient feminine way at the nape of the neck, was absolutely white. She had no teeth, just the abrupt indentation, the line of the mouth, above the old woman chin. She was the archetypal *babushka*, the granny from the fairy tale who looks both witchlike and angelic. Her skin had the finest wrinkles imaginable; it was beautiful skin, as my grandmother's had been.

Mounted right behind her head on the portion of the wall left open above the day bed was a large bright poster of Snoopy, the dog in Peanuts. The caption was in German or Czech, I can't remember which, but I kept meaning to ask Ružena what it said. As always, Snoopy was thinking, not speaking: the little white clouds of cartoon thought rose from his head to the expression of whatever it was he had in mind.

Ružena was talking in Czech, kissing her mother, rearranging her bedding, introducing me, pushing me over to be kissed and gazed at. The old woman hugged me as if I were a lost daughter; and she did *gaze* at me — she looked hard and long, sighing and cooing theatrically, happily, approvingly.

The granny was dying, Ružena said. Any day, any hour. It was driving her (Ružena) crazy. I said perhaps I shouldn't have come, perhaps I ought to leave tomorrow? No, absolutely not; I must stay. I made the granny happy: to see an American was a happy thing. I made the granny happy. I must stay.

I slept that night on a mattress Ružena put on the floor right next to the granny's day bed; it was the only free space in the entire crammed room. I could have reached up and held the old woman's hand. Ružena slept in the tiny kitchen, also on the floor. When we were all in our beds, there wasn't a place to walk in the entire apartment, except for the narrow strip of hallway and the cubicle of the bathroom.

I slept badly. The granny made strange, end-of-the-world moans and throaty noises. The death rattle, I thought, horrified; she's going to die with me crammed right up against her. I wanted to say something to her, but we had no language between us. My lessons with Mrs. Beranek hadn't progressed past my saying I liked roast pork and dumplings and my hat was in the house where my father also was. She didn't seem to be awake, anyway. But all night long, just as soon as I would drop off to sleep, I would awaken, startled by her deep, lonely moaning. This must be the end, I would think frantically, and then the next time I woke up I would be astonished to find I'd actually fallen asleep after thinking that.

Sometime just before dawn, I woke up to Ružena's quick voice. She was saying something in Czech, very annoyed. She was standing by the granny, leaning from the hallway into the living room. She seemed to be scolding her.

"I'm telling her stop it, stop it," she said to me when I rose up from my bedroll on the floor. "That *ah-augh, ah-augh* — she has to stop it." And she shook a finger at the old woman, who scowled and looked cranky as if she were a naughty child who was playing an annoying game, not someone old and desperate and dying. She turned on her side and moaned again. Those grandmother moans.

"She's driving me crazy," Ružena said and hit her own head with her palm. "Crazy, I'm going crazy. She has to *do* something." And she padded back to her bedroll in the kitchen. I didn't wake again until morning.

We went back into Brno the next morning after breakfast in order for me to change some traveler's checks into Tusex crowns for the friend with the sick baby. Tusex crowns are the government's way of getting hard (Western) currency. They can only be purchased with hard currency and are used to buy a variety of consumer goods and luxury items unavailable in regular stores. "I can pay you later, Ružena said on the train. But I told her I was glad to help. I didn't want her to tell me any more about the friend and the baby who needed medicine which, Ružena said, could only be bought with hard currency coupons. I just wanted to give her the money.

She never specified an exact sum. I said, "Twenty dollars?"

"Whatever you want, whatever you want," she said, turning away, as if she would not stoop to ugly details, as if the entire transaction were my idea.

I changed the money legally, at a government office, and gave her the Tusex coupons. She thanked me over and over, assured me that I would be paid back, and then suggested we walk around town before the train took us back to Slavkov. We couldn't leave the granny alone for long, she said. I wondered at leaving her alone at all.

We walked to the open market area where Ružena said loudly, in English, that everything was too expensive. Then she repeated it in French; *"Trop cher, trop cher,"* she said angrily, contemptuously to the bemused vendors, using her arsenal of languages, as if to prove she was not of them. She sometimes spoke to me in German or Italian, though she knew I could only speak English and some halting French. She steered us quickly through the other shoppers, up a narrow street, down an alley. There were a lot of people on the streets. She stopped everywhere, admiring merchandise, scoffing at prices. She said she wanted, *very much,* a set of kitchen utensils she had seen in a shop — would it be all right if we stopped to look at them?

She led us to a dark little shop which, like many stores in Czechoslovakia (I'd noticed this in Prague), was utterly without charm. There was none of the flirtation of retail shopping, none of the coquetry of style as we know it in the West. Depending on one's personality or mood, this is either depressing or a relief. I had felt both sensations since I had arrived in the country, mostly relief, glad not to be a consumer. (This is not, of course, the effect on the Czechs, many of whom are as bedeviled by the phantom of consumerism as Americans are by the fact of it: they want things very much. Not only things, but services. One day in Prague Jaromil and I had been walking across the Charles Bridge; he said he had long wanted to write a poem about the bridge. I was pleased to hear this — and surprised, because he didn't seem to go in much for memorializing his city; his irony didn't seem to allow much romantic sentiment. I was glad to see it was there all the same. "Always when we go to the Charles Bridge," he said, "we see the tourists. They are looking at the statues, they are maybe taking pictures of the river, they look up at the Hrad. They are thinking, oh history, oh beautiful, oh the baroque buildings. But we are walking along, frowning [he began acting the part as we walked across the bridge where, indeed, tourists from the Music Festival were snapping pictures]; our heads are down. We're not looking at the statues or the river or the castle. We're just trying to figure out how the *hell* to get the electrician to fix the wiring in the house or how to get our name on the list for an apartment. We're thinking, thinking, how to get this or that."

One day, he said, he had been going across the bridge, the tourists studying the saints and the view, when he saw coming toward him from the Malá Strana side a marvelous sight, a triumphant sight: a young man, his step light with elation was walking, whistling, carrying a toilet with the help of another joyous friend. "They are happy, their months of plotting and scheming have paid off," Jaromil explained. "At last they have it, the toilet they have sought here, there, all over." This was the poem of the Charles Bridge he wished to write, he said, though as yet he had not succeeded in getting it right. "I must write about that toilet," he said, obviously gripped by his material which, I saw once again, was not my own.)

Consumer goods are sparse and the way of marketing is drab compared to the West. Conversely the baroque detail of the architecture, of the unplanned jumble of Malá Strana is crammed and satisfying in a way that the modern line of design, especially in an American farmland city like Minneapolis is not. I had not yet felt anything but satisfaction about the Prague architecture, but my relation to the marketplace and consumer goods was more complex — that old demon Style — and so sometimes, as on this occasion with Ružena in Brno, I was depressed by the low-key, probably quite sane, Socialist market. I wanted a wicked phony boutiquey department store for Ružena and me to explore. Maybe I was homesick.

The place she had led me was like a general store; it was doing a brisk business. The utensil set consisted of an aluminum spatula, a slotted spoon and a large fork, packaged in a plastic wrapper. It looked inexpensive and ordinary. Ružena was in seventh heaven. She couldn't *tell* me, she said, how *long* she had wanted exactly this set of utensils. She was stunned, it seemed, by the handsomeness of the black plastic handles and the shiny aluminum; the uniformity of each object delighted her: a set. I realized she wanted me to buy it for her.

She didn't ask me to buy it. She didn't say she would buy it herself. She just admired it until I found myself buying it for her. She was even happier — ecstatic would not be too extravagant a word — with the utensils than she had been to get the traveler's checks changed. It made me feel good to see her so happy. But I also felt a little alarmed, as if something was getting out of hand. But that, I decided, was a mean attitude: the utensils cost less than five dollars, and as for the traveler's checks — I *wanted* to help. We left the shop. Ružena pulled the utensils out of their package as we walked along, pointing out the wonderful qualities of spoon, spatula, fork. Never had there been such marvelous objects.

Then she wanted to stop at the Tusex store, where Western goods can be bought for hard currency. I stopped in several such stores in Prague. They have a wacky quality to them because they are a parody of Western consumerism. In the rather small room where Ružena had brought us there was a car on display (for an astronomical price), boxes full of garish stuffed animals, glass showcases stocked with watches, diamond rings, bottles of whiskey and Western liquor, and other boxes full of cheap wind-up toys from Japan.

Ružena jumped around from case to case, nudging people out of the way, peering first at the diamonds, shaking her head, then lurching over to the stuffed animals, then to the hair dryers and waffle irons for which she seemed to have a love-hate relationship. Then, abruptly, she was ready to go.

"All this," she said, jerking her head derisively at the store as we walked out, "this is awful. I buy nothing, *nothing* here." The whole thing, she said, was evidence of the way everyone in the country was driven to petty greed and a mean graspiness, for one had to save and scrimp in order to afford the coveted Tusex items. Even scrimping wasn't enough; inevitably, everyone dealt on the black market if they wanted to have nice things.

She said she never bought anything here. I didn't ask her about her own rows of record albums, or about the dolls and stuffed animals. I didn't ask her about anything. I felt alarmed again, as if I were in the presence of one possessed. We spent the rest of the time before the train left going in and out of stores, Ružena yearning and longing for everything she saw in the windows, sometimes lurching into a shop with me dragging after her, to ask the price. And always going out again, shaking her head angrily, bitterly, when the clerk told her. She window-shopped like someone in a nightmare; the joy of the matching spoon, spatula and fork seemed entirely forgotten, faded by the brighter allure of things that were still out there in the drab little shops, behind the forbidding counters, and unreachable, as if they were intelligent, perverse beings, holding themselves aloof.

We spent part of the afternoon visiting the museum of the battle of Austerlitz in Slavkov. We looked out the beautiful leaded windows of the museum (a palace where Napoleon had made his headquarters) to the rolling landscape that had been the battlefield. It wasn't good farmland now, Ružena said. They still find mortars and other battle leftovers in the fields. I said I found that impossible to believe. "Still," she said, "it's true."

She pointed out the direction of the battlefield and spun me through the museum itself so fast that I learned nothing. None of the displays was marked in English, and she said there was too much to translate. She said it was a lousy museum, anyway. She said this so loudly and kept talking so long that the guide lecturing to a group of schoolchildren asked her to be quiet. We crept out of the place. Or, I crept. Ružena stalked. It wasn't worth the visit, she said. "What am I doing living in such a place?" she said, very weary.

We walked back through the dusty, homely town — a village really. Ružena stopped at a shop that sold jewelry and clocks; it was some kind of repair shop. She wanted to buy me a ring, she said. I said absolutely not.

But we went in (because she was already inside), and she talked a long time to the clerk, a woman her own age, explaining who I was ("a young American, a student," though she knew I wasn't a student), and inquiring about the amber ring in the window which she wanted to give me. I would have to pay, she said in an aside to me; she had left her purse at home. Did I mind paying?

Somehow or other, I got her out of there without buying — without my buying — the ring. In Brno, I'd already bought for myself (at Ružena's insistence) an overpriced folk-art mug. I was beginning to think I had no spine at all; besides, I didn't have much money left.

We walked back to the apartment along the dusty street where we met no one. She told me she was going crazy from living in such a lonely place, a place without culture. Such a town was "only for the animals," she said, waving her hand at the empty street. She didn't like the clerk in the jewelry repair shop either, she didn't mind telling me.

Then she told me a long intricate story about her attempts to get an apartment in Brno. Back at the apartment she showed me the correspondence, absurd and Kafkaesque, from the housing authorities who maintained she must stay where she was. I was a writer. Did I have any suggestions about how she might write to them?

We spent the evening watching television with the granny who, to my surprise, was still alive. Like many Czechs, Ružena has an (illegal) booster that allows her to pick up a Vienna television station on which it is possible to get "real culture, real movies," she said. But this night we watched a program from Prague, a special entertainment for the trades union convention that was meeting in the city. It was boring, a homely display of amateur "talent." Ružena was contemptuous. She finally snapped it off.

She wanted to see my clothes, she said. That would be better entertainment. She wanted me to show her everything in my suitcase, item by item. She admired a scarf I'd bought in London so much that I gave it to her.

"Oh no," she said softly, "you are young. You keep it." But she held it for a long time and then draped it carefully over the opened suitcase, as if on display. Then she showed me her postcard collection which she kept in two cardboard boxes at the bottom of a bookshelf. If you couldn't travel, she said, it was good to have these pictures. They gave you an idea.

The granny was tired, so we all went to bed early; I next to the granny, Ružena in the kitchen. I was exhausted. If the granny moaned that night, I didn't hear her.

The next morning, when I woke, Ružena was talking to a friend, Eva, who had taken the night train from Prague — in order to meet me, Ružena said. They were drinking coffee in the tiny kitchen. Eva hadn't slept, hadn't eaten, had come on the train from her construction job and had waited in a chair at the Brno station for the local train to Slavkov. She had arrived at seven in the morning at Ružena's door. To see me.

She was frightening to look at. She wasn't deformed in any way, but she was very strange. Her skin was coarse, her nose must have been broken sometime in the past, her lips, which were heavy, seemed to have been split and healed in an odd, menacing expression. She was heavy, square, muscular. Her neck was as thick as Ružena's thigh. Her voice—a friendly, eager voice (Ružena had to translate)—was deeper than most men's, and her laugh was alarming. She wore her hair primly, though; it was carefully curled, with waved bangs flat across the forehead. This was somehow more strange than her tough look.

The conversation between Eva and me was conventional, courteous, a little shy. I told her I was amazed she'd come so far to see a stranger; she said she was amazed that my mother let me travel around all by myself.

"I don't like her," Ružena said to me in English. Eva sat drinking her coffee, content and unsuspecting. "She can't understand," Ružena said breezily, when I looked alarmed. "No culture," as if not knowing English were hard evidence.

She said Eva had been put in a concentration camp as a young girl. (Eva sat there drinking her coffee happily, not knowing, apparently, that she was being talked about.) She was fifteen or sixteen, and had been active in a resistance group. "She had all her—all the *woman things* taken out," Ružena said. "They did experiments on her. That's why she has a man's voice. That's why she looks this way. Then, afterward, nobody wants her." She said this, it seemed to me, a little contemptuously, as if, in the end, it was Eva's fault that she hadn't risen above this misfortune.

"I don't think you should talk that way in front of her," I said severely. I had decided the night before to show a little more backbone with Ružena.

She snorted and went back to Eva, talking in Czech very cheerily. Eva had a sunny disposition. She laughed and thumped Ružena on the back when she gave her more coffee. Ružena thumped her back. Then she said, turning to me, "See what I mean? No culture."

I said good-bye to the granny, who was sitting under the Snoopy poster. She looked elegant and so old in her flowered babushka and white hair that she seemed past illness, past pain; she seemed to have entered some abstract region of death where dying was just a matter of sitting very still, and waiting regally — reigning over one's own disappearance. She kissed me. She ran her hands over my face as if she were blind, though she wasn't blind. Ruzena said, "She says she will miss you very much now. Every day she is missing you now." Then the old woman sank down in the bed, turned her face to the wall, and curled her body slightly. She put her hand over her forehead, as if shading her eyes. She must have been in pain after all. She didn't look at me again.

It turned out that I'd bought — or Ruzena had given me — quite a few things, which I had to pack. Two bottles of Moravian wine (my purchase, at Ruzena's insistence), several sweaters (Ruzena's presents — she insisted), several records of Czech music (ditto), the Moravian folk-art mug. There was, as well, a baroque china clock, the kind that goes on a mantle, which Ruzena wanted me to have.

There had been a great deal of discussion since my arrival about this clock, its value, its excellent craftsmanship ("a reproduction, but a *good* reproduction"), her good luck in being able to find — and afford — such a handsome (not that she wanted to brag) gift. I had made a lot of the clock too. I was touched. But I was also, by this time, apprehensive. I didn't know why. I just wanted to get away.

Ruzena wouldn't let me pack any of these things. Eva, she said, would carry them all — with special attention to the baroque clock — when she returned (unencumbered, as I was, by a suitcase) to Prague the next day. I should not be bothered with all these packages. I might break something. Did I want to break something?

I had already packed one of the bottles of wine. Ruzena was frantic at the thought of its breaking. Did I *want* it to break? Did I want to *ruin* my clothes? She said I absolutely must not pack the other bottle; that was courting disaster: they would knock against each other and smash open. She urged me to unpack the first bottle. She would make a wonderful, well-packed parcel with bottles, sweaters, clock and overpriced folk-art mug. Leave it to her. She would send me more sweaters. Later, when I was back in America, she would send me feather ticks and feather pillows.

She was almost begging. Finally, we set it up that Eva and I would meet the next morning at the Slavia at 10 A.M., and there the wonderfully packed parcel would be handed over, at a time when I could attend to it properly and hold it in both hands.

I left it to Ružena. We all went into Brno together on the train, leaving the granny alone. They took me to a student bar and we ate fancy cakes and coffee and drank little glasses of slivovitz. We toasted friendship; we said, "Until next time." I was crazy to get away. Eva bought me a scarf that said Brno on it and had pictures of the town landmarks stamped on it. She also bought me a recording of "Ma Vlast," her favorite music, she told Ružena to tell me. I took these gifts with me; Ružena didn't demand to take them for the package.

We almost missed the Prague train. We ran down the platform, Eva carrying the suitcase, Ružena running frantically ahead to locate the correct car. We hugged and kissed. Eva heaved the suitcase easily up on the train, and she and I hugged too. "I'll see you tomorrow," I said in English, and Ružena repeated it in Czech. At least, I assumed she did. *"Ano, ano,"* Eva called up to me from the platform. Yes, yes.

And then they were on the platform and I was in the compartment with the window pulled down, waving good-bye. I felt, suddenly, very affectionate toward them, now that I was leaving. I blew kisses. They blew kisses and waved and laughed. The train pulled away and they became smaller, very small, gone. Good people, I thought. I was sorry, after all, to have made such a short trip.

Eva never showed up at the Slavia. I arrived fifteen minutes early and waited three hours. I ordered coffee and cake, I stared up at the Hradčany, I watched the trams go by, watched the other tables in the Slavia fill and empty and fill again with new customers. I wrote in my notebook. I wasn't surprised she hadn't come.

I went back to Zdenka's. "No baroque clock," she said, raising her eyebrows when I came in. "I'll make tea." I had spent the evening with her at a concert the night before when I got back from Slavkov. "I didn't want to say anything," she said, "but I knew she wouldn't be there."

"There may have been a mix-up with the translation," I said coldly. I had never really expected Eva to show up either; maybe that was why I'd brought my notebook to the Slavia: to have something to do. But now, when Zdenka said it, I was full of loyalty and didn't want to go over to the other side — as I thought of it. I didn't want to be cynical. Beyond that, I didn't want to consider the nuttiness of the days I'd spent with Ružena. For some reason, I just wanted to let it go. I wanted to assume all this was normal.

I talked the entire thing over, eventually, with Zdenka and, later, with Jaromil. "She's not a professional," Jaromil said. We were walking in a pine forest outside of Prague, in what Kundera calls in one of his novels (ironically), "the romantic Czech countryside." Jaromil and his wife agreed: she wasn't a professional. Zdenka had used the same term. A professional was someone who worked the Western tourists, those from "outside," as Zdenka called the rest of the world, to whom a black market and the details of making one's way through the Socialist coil were scary and unreal.

"She just sounds crazy," Zdenka had said. Jaromil said yes, Jaromil's wife said yes: Ružena was probably just a little crazy. "And lonely," Jaromil said. "She sounds lonely."

Both Zdenka and Jaromil thought certainly there was no friend with a sick baby: one thing nobody had to worry about in this country was medical treatment. Medical care and drugs were virtually free. "As for the clock," Jaromil said, "it's probably this way. She wants to give you a clock. She wants you to have a present. But later, when you are really going to take the clock away, out of her sight, she *doesn't* want to give you the present." He thought the whole episode was amusing, which relieved me: I wanted to laugh it off. "More Kafka," he said, with relish. And we laughed.

Later that night, at Zdenka's, she and her friend Milan agreed, it was Kafka. But Zdenka wanted to report Ružena; she wanted her full name, which I wouldn't give her. "These things are not supposed to happen," Zdenka said. "I ought to report it." But she let it go.

Milan said I was naive. Not about reporting Ružena; that was my affair. But such things happened all the time and I was naive to be confused. Americans are a naive people, he said. Any Czech would have been wise to a woman like Ružena, to the instability and the petty, frightened greed. I didn't have eyes to see, he said. I was a baby when it came to life here. Things had fallen out, it seemed, exactly as he would have expected — badly, stupidly. He seemed reassured of his own rigorous, unsentimental viewpoint.

Zdenka went into her bedroom. She came back with a strand of wine-colored glass beads, cut in intricate facets, with a beautiful silver clasp. "This is for you," she said, handing it to me. "It was my mother's. Very old, something Czech. Something to take the place of — Kafka." She laughed, and put her hands behind her back and would not listen to my saying it was too lovely to give away.

"Take it," Milan said. "Who knows what she'll take out of your suitcase when you're not looking." We all laughed at that.

Later that night Zdenka told me that Milan had been in prison for fourteen years. He had tried to hide his cousin, who was active politically in the early fifties, and had been sentenced along with him. Milan himself had never had any time for politics; he said he didn't understand what it was all about. "But so many people went to prison," Zdenka said. "Even me. For over a year. But what did I care? I was young; I could sleep anywhere."

Then she told me, with the same courtesy and diffidence Jaromil had used for the same subject, that she hoped I would be careful about him. For some reason, she said, Jaromil (whom she had met when he and his wife had come to pick me up one day) made her nervous. I questioned her closely, but it was no more than that. Like Jaromil's warning about her, it was clearly done as a kindness to me, perhaps because she agreed with Milan about my naiveté. And I realized, looking at her beautiful brown eyes, so like Jaromil's, what countrymen they were in their watchfulness.

❧

I kept thinking about Ružena. She was important because she was inexplicable. She keeps coming back, like an unsolved problem. I'll never know what it all meant — the compulsive gift giving, the crazed window-shopping, her shoe-box apartment crammed with "culture." It was the perfect altar to East and West, Europe and all the classic books, America and the carny dolls and the pop records. It's all one thing to her, one broken world she is determined to mend, to put together in that gimcrack apartment in Austerlitz where the archetypal granny of the Czech myths lay dying under the poster of the bemused Snoopy. Beethoven and Snoopy, Schiller and the Beatles. There, at the edge of the great battlefield, Ružena is putting it all together. It's the work of a lifetime.

Of course she's nutty. She's crazy with loneliness. Her husband, the soldier, is long dead; the Czech granny is dying; her son lives in the West. All she has, I suppose, as a connection with the world she wants so much, are the languages she accumulates as obsessively as her books and records and postcards and the stuffed animals and dolls.

Ružena has lost her grip, but I like her better than the woman in the airport who kept saying, while she told us of her daughter's exile, "Actually, we've been quite lucky." That's what Jaromil means when he says so delightfully, "Kafka, Kafka!," every time something crazy happens. He means, here is an ap-

· 274 ·

propriate response. Here is a person who, out of the broken details of her existence, has tooled a replica of all the loss and waste and terrible longing for life that underlies the grayness of this country. Anyone or anything that comes within the reach of this longing — an American with traveler's checks, a package of uniform kitchen utensils, an amber ring, anything, anything — must be swirled into her great, scavenging work. What more can be asked of a life, after all?

9 ❧

*I*T IS POSSIBLE to claim that the greatest poet and the greatest prose writer of this century (Rilke and Kafka) were born in Prague. Both were German speaking (though Kafka became proficient in Czech and took an interest in Czech literature which, in its national importance, he identified with Jewish literature), both not only stand monumentally above the fiction and poetry of the century, but are embodiments of what it is to be an artist in the modern world. People who never have and never will read a word Kafka wrote know and use the word *Kafkaesque*. And Rilke, certainly, is the archetype of the modern poet, lost between a painful, romantic hermeticism and the noise and metallic squalor of modern urban life. They were both men obsessed by, in rebellion against, their fathers. They were men who, as artists, were torn apart by the feminine nature of art (as they saw it) and the crushing masculinity of the machine age. Neither of them could abide Prague. Kafka, of course, had less success in escaping either Prague or his father than Rilke did. And his very imprisonment there caused him to know it and study it intimately, and finally, to love it.

Rilke left early and returned rarely. He wrote this letter to his wife from a hotel on Václavské náměstí on November 1, 1907, when he had come to Prague to give a poetry reading:

> Will one be here someday and able to see even this, see it and say it, from one stage of existence to another? Will one

no longer have to bear its weight, the immense significance it took on when one was little and it was already big and growing out beyond one; in those days it used one in order to feel itself. There was a child, and all this felt itself through him, saw itself mirrored in him huge and fantastic, became haughty and ominous toward his heart. All this may no longer be. Degraded below itself, come back again like one who has long done violence, it is somehow ashamed before me, exposed, confined, as if it were now meeting justice and retribution. But I cannot rejoice to see badly treated that which once was hard and overbearing toward me and never condescended to me and never explained to me what difference is decreed between us, what hostile kinship. It makes me sad to see these house corners, those windows and entrances, squares and church roofs humbled, smaller than they were, reduced and altogether in the wrong. And now in their new state they are just as impossible for me to master as they were then in their arrogance. And their weight has turned into the reverse of what it was, but how much, place for place, it has remained weight. More than ever since this morning I feel the presence of this city as something incomprehensible and confused. It should either have passed away with my childhood, or my childhood should have flowed off it later, leaving it behind, real beside all reality, to see and express objectively like a Cezanne object, incomprehensible so far as I am concerned, but tangible. But this way it is ghostly, like the people who belong to it and to me from earlier days and who bring us together and speak of us in the same breath. I have never felt it so oddly, my aversion was never so great as this time (probably because meanwhile my disposition to see and to take everything I look at with an eye to my work has greatly developed).

How smug he is under that lyrical sadness, the artist sticking it to the insensitive hometown. He has the pleasure of returning to the scene of his insignificance — returning as *somebody*. There probably is no more powerful documentation of the bourgeois character of old Prague. There is no elegiac sadness in this

Rilke, who is so thoroughly identified with the elegy and the lost past (it takes an effort of the will to keep one's idea of Rilke from slipping clearly out of the twentieth century into the nineteenth, in fact; it is always amazing to think that he rode in an automobile).

No, *this* Rilke, in spite of "not rejoicing" in the diminishment of the city's power, is quite pleased underneath it all. Pleased to have escaped the bourgeois hearth, the pall of convention, the flat hand of the father. He escaped the patriarchal gloom of Prague as Kafka did not; he separated himself from it, he went to Germany, to Paris, finally to Switzerland. "My aversion was never so great": the condescension of the escaped provincial on a visit home. All of which suggests he could not *see* in spite of his desire to "express objectively like a Cezanne object," Prague itself. It could not be metaphorical for him. It could not be touched lovingly, like something truly in the safe past. However, the date was 1907. It was not time to be elegiac yet.

"A small nation's memory is not smaller than the memory of a large one," Kafka wrote in his diary, "and so can digest the existing material more thoroughly. There are, to be sure, fewer experts in literary history employed, but literature is less a concern of literary history than of the people, and thus, if not purely, it is at least reliably preserved. For the claim that the national consciousness of a small people makes on the individual is such that everyone must always be prepared to know that part of the literature which has come down to him, to support it, to defend it — to defend it even if he does not know it . . . It is difficult to readjust when one has felt this useful, happy life in all one's being."

And yet the literature of the recent past, for those countries that fought the Second World War in Europe, is not one which makes the people of large or small countries happy to bear its memory. This entire century, seen a certain way, has been devoted to chaos, the fragmentation of experience, even of perception. There have been two dislocating, merciless wars in Europe;

there has been the great ideological attempt to draw things together sensibly again. But in the end, Jaromil is right: only the details count.

"In the last analysis, nothing exists except miracles." A statement of Kafka's. His friend Johannes Urzidil wrote a book about him and about Prague, *There Goes Kafka,* after the War. Because nothing exists except miracles, he says, "Kafka devotes a scientific scrupulosity to every detail — even to the fleas in the fur collar of the doorman which — and Kafka knows this — when imposed onto the background of a gigantic soul problem, appears as irony . . . This irony is the tart fruit of compassion for the creature, whose individual peculiarity irony exposes to an ever new and insoluble tragedy."

Another way of looking at things in this century is that thought has been broken over the tension between psychological reality and history. All poets, even those who are apolitical by their own declaration (but they have to declare it), strain over this matter. The intensely private, even self-absorbed discipline of psychoanalysis and the devastation of the political or historical world have represented two related but conflicting themes in the century's literature.

Freud and, later, more mystically, Jung, held out the evidence, through the dream, of a consciousness which, as the American poet H.D. said, "proclaimed all men one." H.D., coming to Freud between the two wars (and she was conscious of his Moravian background and the significance, metaphorically, of his coming from the heart of the heart of Europe), is one of the clearest examples of a poet, an American, who was attached to European culture by deep affinity. She went to Freud in Vienna to heal the "personal war-shock" of the First World War. "My sessions with the Professor were barely under way," she writes in *Tribute to Freud,* "before there were preliminary signs and symbols of the approaching ordeal."

She and Freud shared a love of antiquity and he often showed her his latest additions to his collection of statues and ancient sculptures. "The Professor said that we two met in our love of antiquity," she writes. "He said his little statues and images helped stabilize the evanescent idea, or keep it from escaping altogether."

Prague does this for me; its architecture, its streets and covered alleys ground my mind in a reality that is complete, or at least seems complete. Perfection, I could at last discover here (why is it necessary to travel for insight?), perfection is, precisely, everything. That is, it includes the broken, the dusty, failure, death.

This is the fascination, the reason I came back. The allure is fundamentally poetic. Here, in this part of the world (it happened elsewhere of course, but for our culture, it happened here), the imagination was wounded. The image-making faculty was assaulted. It was asked, it was forced, to take in *terrible things*. Nothing after Dachau, after Auschwitz, after Terezin and Lidice, can ever be lyric in the same way again. And yet we are born strangely unscathed, we can't help it, each generation as lyric as the last or the next. I have sat in auditoriums while poets — American, Israeli, Polish — have said that the only response to the horror that is our immediate heritage is silence, the bowed head. In my heart, I have disagreed. I have wanted the old metaphors, rose gardens, those "bowers" Keats was always writing his knights into and then, inevitably, out of again. I have disagreed with the poets I listened to in the auditoriums, disagreed out of an innate urge to utterance but also because of something else, more elusive.

It is true that the imagination was wounded by the history of this century; we have known that obliquely almost from the first. What is the good of finding, through the dream, that "all men are one," only to share a nightmare? But the other truth is more slow in revealing itself. The imagination was enriched by this terrible history. Who denies this (I have denied it) denies the power and truth of every concentration camp story, every life broken over the ideological passion of Socialism in both

East and West. The relation between horror and creativity, between horror and faith, was suddenly illuminated by the mass destruction of our world: as Kafka saw after the First World War, as H.D. saw.

This is a much harder truth to encompass. I was going to say it is harder for poets but there is no distinction between the poet and the citizen at this point. For the poet is simply the representative of the population. It does not matter, strangely enough, if the poet is published in huge editions and is consciously the representative of "the people" as in the Soviet Union (think not only of Mandelstam, think of Whitman), or if the poet publishes in tiny, unread magazines, as in our country. The work gets done.

The gigantic significance of World War Two and its civilian quality, the insane calm of its "solution," seemed to call the rational mind itself into question. It was as if horror and madness, all the desperation of spiritual struggle which used to be the business of only certain people, artists primarily, had been "popularized" like science or some other abstruse study. And suddenly, "everyone" became a protagonist. The ugly, crazed twentieth century wanted saints; that is, people conscious of the individual life in relation to the world, people who live purposely.

This makes the poet (H.D. chose the ritualistic word *scribe*) central. The reason H.D. was hushed was that she went beyond documentation. Those who were there are harder to hush: after all, they have a right. But H.D., in London during the blitz, was not documenting. She was trying, as poets do, to *make something* of it.

Interestingly, the taboo of silence has been enforced most absolutely in works of imaginative writing, especially poetry. There are plenty of histories: biographies of Hitler constitute a discernible category in the publishing world.

People may be uncomfortable with the documents of the period but they read them with fascination. But poets, who must *make something*, are told — or tell each other — that here is the place of silence. Here, at the heart of horror, voice must stop. The string quartets, the music in the camps remains one of the grislier details. People say now, if one frets over an impoverished American TV culture, that, after all, Mozart and Goethe did not stop the Nazis. It is hard to know how to respond to that.

There is a distinction to be made here between those who do defend documentation "so it will never happen again" and what I am talking about. To make something from the horror is different. It is, to our ethical nature, more appalling. H.D. was not only elegizing the bombed London; she said that London bombed was London opened, exposed: dangerous, dangerous ground.

"The 'fallen roof leaves the sealed room open to the air' is of course true of our own house of life," she wrote to Norman Holmes Pearson about her long poem *The Walls Do Not Fall*, quoting passages from the poem. "Outer violence touching the deepest hidden subconscious terrors, etc. and we see so much of our past 'on show,' as it were 'another sliced wall where poor utensils show like rare objects in a museum.'"

She found, she said, in wartime London what she had found before in Egypt: the life of myth, of relation. Only there it had been foreign, smudged, quite literally mummified, hers only by effort. Now, horribly but resoundingly, this truth was hers intimately, vast with significance. "Egypt? London," she wrote in the same letter, "mystery, majic — that I have found in London. The mystery of death, first and last."

"I suppose," she said to Pearson, "this book is 'philosophy . . . Protection for the scribe' seems to be the leit motif . . . And exactly the place of the scribe in the mysteries of all-time — his 'job' as 'householder,' his exact place in sequence, in the pattern, again his 'job,' the keeping-track of the 'treasures' which contain *for every scribe which is instructed, things new and old.*" (The italics are hers.)

A lot to expect of poetry and of oneself. I do not think H.D. is a great poet; I am moved more by her effort, by the poignant attempt than by her poems which often seem too self-consciously mythic, the eye too poised for the eternal, not, as Jaromil said, prized always on the detail — not the detail's "significance," but the detail, period. But the attempt is there.

With Kafka, who was a genius, the matter is even more absolute. How strange that young boy, Gustav Janouch, must have felt when he and Kafka were walking through Prague. For Kafka told him astonishing things, things the young boy — but not Kafka — was going to live through. "The war," Kafka told him while they were walking — of course he meant the First World War, there had only been the one so far — "didn't only burn and tear the world, but also lit it up."

10 &

I WENT TO the ghetto toward the end of my stay. Or what had been the ghetto. I wanted to see the famous Jewish cemetery again where Rabbi Loew was buried. He was the man who was supposed to have fashioned the golem, the magical robot who went berserk one Sabbath when his master forgot to remove the animating shim from his mouth at sundown. I had made my wish at Rabbi Loew's grave in 1975 and it had come true: I had returned. And soon I would be leaving again.

The whole ghetto area has been mapped out for tourists in a plan that directs you from synagogue to synagogue (there are several, all very old), to the cemetery and to the museum of Jewish artifacts in one of the synagogues. This museum, the guide pamphlet says, was intended by the Nazis to be a museum of an extinct race.

In a way, it *is* a museum of an extinct race. Certainly no one could say that the few, mostly elderly figures (other than tourists) who enter the synagogues represent a Jewish community of any significance in Prague, especially when one considers the Prague of Kafka's time, a time that recent.

The synagogues seem to be turned over entirely to tourism during the week. I found a middle-aged woman standing outside each synagogue with a ticket punch to mark my four-crown ticket (one ticket lets you in to all the sites on the guide map). I handed over my ticket, had it stamped by the wordless women who, each the same, waved me into the appropriate door, using their ticket punches as pointers.

I asked the ticket-punch woman at the sunken door of a small medieval synagogue if I could attend a service. She had already punched my ticket, and had waved her arm automatically toward the low door in the ancient building which seemed half-sunk into the ground, like an archeological dig. She didn't look at me; she just punched and waved.

"Jewish?" she asked, looking at me for the first time.

"No," I said.

"Stay away then," she said, not ever looking at me again. "What do you want, troubling them. They don't want you." She said it crabbily, with deliberate rudeness.

I waited a moment, my ticket still held out slightly toward her, that foolish harmlessness on my face, the perpetual expression of the inquiring tourist: the look of the idiot. Forget the Jewish Sabbath service — it wasn't that I had asked for. I wanted that heavy, badly dressed, very annoyed woman (an annoyance that antedated me) with swollen ankles, to *like* me. I smiled at her. "Of course. I shouldn't go," I said as if reprimanding another self, trying to insinuate my more enlightened, more authentic self upon her, a self who knew the right thing.

"It's their religion," she said sullenly, not giving an inch, not looking at me, waving again, with clear impatience, toward the sinking little door with her ticket punch.

It was very dark inside and very cramped. I wandered around, peered into the narrow slits on one side from which the women, segregated, observed the service. I put a coin in the gray metal speaker box and hit the button marked "English," and listened while a female voice, too loud, too cheerful, boomed in the holy room. "You might think," the voice said coyly, "that those tiny slits were hard to see from and that the women don't get very good seats. Not so!" the voice cried. "You can see everything from there, and hear everything too."

The voice was still calling out dates and statistics when I left.

The ticket-punch woman was gone, the street was empty. I began to feel an emotional backlash against her now that she was gone (to lunch, I supposed: it was noon). Bravely, I didn't care if she hadn't liked me: I didn't like her. And was it so awful to have inquired about a service? Hadn't I been invited by Mr. Henle in my poetry class at the St. Paul Jewish Community Center to attend a Friday night service with him? I'd even been introduced to the rabbi.

I was walking toward the cemetery with these thoughts in my mind, teetering on the edge of repudiating all this otherness, all the willful sorrow of this place, its pride in its wounds, the remorseless superiority of that woman. That woman who knew things I did not know. Who, I sensed, knew me. Knew me and dismissed me. And was justified in dismissing me, I felt with great, soupy pity for myself.

Walking along toward the cemetery like this, I must have been frowning when Anna first saw me. For she was suddenly *there*, without warning, an apparition, as if she had dropped by helicopter in the empty, silent street. She was in front of me, very near, before I'd noticed her: a slim young woman who looked so much like Audrey Hepburn that I made some sort of startled cry, partly because someone was there, partly because it was Audrey Hepburn, my old heroine, there in the street with me.

"Are you lost?" she asked in French, looking at my guide to the ghetto (there had been no English editions available that day and I had taken a French one). "Can I help you find something?"

"The cemetery," I said, though I knew where it was. It was her ordinary friendliness that I wanted.

She said she was going just by the cemetery and would take me there. The little kiosk outside the cemetery which had pamphlets and postcards for sale was closed for the lunch hour and there was no ticket lady at the gate, which was closed and locked.

"Oh, you'll have to come back. They've closed it up," she said with wonderful early–Audrey Hepburn earnestness. She had the gamin haircut too.

I said I thought I'd go to lunch myself, would she like to go with me? She only hesitated a moment. Then she said she knew a spot, a real student spot so I wouldn't feel like a tourist anymore, as if this were understood as something to avoid. A person who understood me.

This encounter began another series of walks — a much shorter series because I was to leave in a few days, with Anna, the Audrey Hepburn look-alike. Except for that first lunch, we met in the evening because she was a student and didn't have much free time. We only met three times, and we spoke always in French because it was the only language we had in common, except for my stray bits of Czech. It was strange how she, like Jaromil (although I didn't mention him to her), felt best walking. It wasn't, I'm convinced, that she was afraid to be seen in conversation with someone from the West. We did stop at *vinárny* and *kavárny* now and again. And although she sometimes whispered and sometimes looked around, she talked and talked. Her French was much better than mine. I think we walked because, like Jaromil, like me, like the Swedish medical student and the Amsterdam telephone operator, for Anna the city was more than a backdrop, more than the landscape against which life passes. It was palpable presence, it *was* the life. In itself, it was what she wanted to tell me. So we walked.

The first night we talked about having children; I told her I couldn't decide. She astonished me by saying she was married and had two children. (She was twenty-three.) The idea of deciding whether or not to have children seemed to strike her as mildly strange, not the sort of thing one *decided*. I asked her whether there was a women's movement in Czechoslovakia. She said there was, in a way. But apparently it was part of the Socialist program and as such was not a new idea, not a force as it is in the West.

(Zdenka had said, when I asked her the same thing, that they didn't have time for such things. I asked her if homosexuals were harassed. She didn't seem to know, and mentioned vaguely a hotel where they were said to hang out. "And lesbians?" I asked. "Lesbians!" she said, and laughed, as if this idea had never occurred to her. "I suppose they must be somewhere; I never thought about it." Then she said, "We work too hard. The women here — we work too hard for sex, either way. There's no energy to be a lesbian or not a lesbian." She said it, laughing, but she clearly felt such issues were marginal matters — not just homosexuality, but talk about sexuality of any kind. Anna, though very different personally, obviously felt the same way: this was a national assumption; it seemed outlandish to them to talk of sex in terms of politics.)

Anna and her husband lived with her mother and father — a bad arrangement. The two men argued all the time. Anna's father had been a Communist in the thirties; he had worked in the resistance, had narrowly escaped imprisonment, even more luckily escaped being hanged later in the fifties. I sensed he had once been rather important. Now he was retired. The son-in-law blamed him for the miserable state of the country.

"Your husband is an anti-Communist?" I asked.

"It isn't like that," she said. For a moment I felt the slightest barrier come between us, something related to the dismissive fury of the ticket-punch woman at the synagogue, to Jaromil when I'd asked him about the possibility of our being followed. They regarded me from such a distance! But Anna was young and she had patience.

Her husband had been a student during the Prague Spring of 1968. That, for him, was the beginning and end of everything. He and his father-in-law blamed each other, she said. That was the trouble. Her husband blamed her father for refusing to believe in psychology, for instance; he blamed the older man for trusting the Russsians, for thinking economics settled everything, for not caring about *consciousness*.

The father wanted to be left alone. The soft-headed foolishness of 1968 had only made things worse: that was his point. And for 1968 he blamed his son-in-law and his sort, the arty undergraduate with big ideas. Which, I thought, is exactly what I was in 1968. But my generation — which did not extend itself, after all, to this other protesting student — has not paid for its ideas, or few have, as the same Czech generation has.

"Sometimes their arguments, they get so furious, and the flat is so small," Anna said. "I beg them to stop, beg them." Then, for a time, a cruel silence inhabited the apartment, and the two men fell silent, brooding, and blame pervaded the atmosphere even more brutally without words. Then one of them broke the silence and they stayed up all night in the kitchen arguing and insulting each other all over again. Anna and her mother, one in the living room on the makeshift couch-bed, the other in the bedroom, waited for their husbands to come at last to bed. "It is so hard to console them," Anna said.

She was terribly thin. She didn't seem to eat at all. I would order a meal, and beg her to have something, but she only drank coffee or sometimes, rarely, a beer. She was lovely, her thinness, even though it was nervous thinness and she obviously lived an anxious life, worrying about her status in the French department at Charles University, worrying about her husband, about whether they would ever find their own apartment, worrying, worrying, worrying — even so, she had a beautiful lyric face, and wonderful clarity of expression. She was uncanny because she was very intelligent, acute even, but this quality was coupled with her beauty and an innocence, a guilelessness, that is usually associated with children. Yet she wasn't childish, or even exactly childlike. She was a woman, a mother, someone with heavy responsibilities, which she seemed to take as a matter of course.

Her essential quality was purity; there was something clear, undeflected about her, simply about her presence. She was one of those rare persons who, when we are near them, draw out some dormant ethical passion, a deep desire to be the best person we can imagine, as if goodness alone mattered. Like the city itself, afflicted by scars and experience, she seemed untouched, full of matchless wonder and the ability to see clearly.

She told me about her shell collection, a small collection. It was difficult to get really good shells, she said, or good books on shells. Such things were expensive and hard to find in any case. But she described a wonderful conch that her husband had given her the year before, pink as a blossom and ridged with fascinating crenulations which required frequent dusting. I asked her if she could hear the ocean in it.

"Yes," she said. "But of course it isn't the ocean."

David, her husband, collected rocks. His collection was larger than hers, and he had become quite an expert about semiprecious gems as well. He knew a lot about garnets, the gem of Bohemia.

Like Ružena, everyone in the family collected something. Anna's father collected stamps. I had noticed earlier that a stamp shop on Na Příkopě, a major business street that intersects Václavské náměstí, was usually crammed with customers whenever I passed by it. It was there that I had bought, in 1975, the stamp of the Hradčany that I pasted on my notebook. The entire country seemed to be collecting things, anything. A way to order the world, to feel you own not only a bit of the world's goods, but something of its beauty and order. Over some portion of the worldly chaos you exercise a serene and benevolent order as you catalogue and chart, organize and log the stamps, the rocks, the shells, the mess of stuff before you. Anna and her father had each, apparently, made a sort of peace with their longing through their collections. Anna wanted "more than anything," she said, to travel, to see the ocean. To see Paris, to see London (all the museums! she cried) — she and David talked of it constantly. So she collected her shells, that most un-Czech natural object: Czechoslovakia is a land-locked country, and although Shakespeare gave Bohemia a seacoast in *A Winter's Tale,* it isn't there.

Her father, the old internationalist, had his collection of stamps from all over the world, his tidy rows of beautiful nations, peaceably leagued within his binders. Anna said he had a little pair of tweezers that he used to pick up the stamps, moving them carefully into their correct slots in his books, examining them with a jeweler's eyepiece.

But David's collection of rocks and stones struck me as grimmer, less an outlet than a metaphor of his frustration. If so, he had his reasons. Anna told me his story as we walked around the dark city. That first night she hardly bothered to point out anything to me. We simply threaded back and forth the tiny streets below the Loretto church in Malá Strana where the lamps are still lit by gas. The light they cast didn't illuminate our way so much as cloak it in a lustrous, buttery haze. I could smell lilac everywhere. Aside from the Kampa, the "little Venice" where Zdenka lived, there was no residential area I walked that was more mysterious, entirely composed of winding streets built on hills, the houses old, sunken, some beautifully preserved, with ancient back gardens smelling heavily of lilac and chestnut blossoms. It is an area that was often photographed by the great Czech photographer Josef Sudek who died in 1976, having devoted his life to two major subjects: the city of Prague and light, the quality of which he attempted to capture in his city studies and luminous still lifes. His other great subject — if a work of such depth and comprehension can be divided — was the gardens of Prague, which he photographed in all their tangled beauty. He had been a famous Prague figure ("It's hard to believe," Jaromil had said, "that we shall not see him again here") who dressed practically in rags and used an ancient, very simple camera, and had only his left arm, having lost the other in Italy in the First World War. It would be possible to feel one knows Prague and to love it simply by looking at his photographs. Anna and I walked — I like to think — where he had walked many times before us.

We met at the Loretto where the chimes were ringing somewhat out of tune. Anna had said we must hurry to meet the lamplighter or we would miss him. In fact, we did miss him. Or perhaps we were wandering around the area as he was because we walked once down Novy Svět ulice (New World Street), a tiny lane, before the lamps were lit; later, on a second pass, they were shining. But we never saw the lamplighter, though he must have been near. Neither of us minded. Anna seemed to feel she had done everything possible as a tour guide simply by bringing me there. She didn't talk about the area or point out its charms. She just nudged me along, pointing our direction up or down a lane, letting the lane do the explaining. We walked over and over the area, without stopping, gathered together under that buttery light that Sudek somehow charmed into his pictures, a light that drew everything away from angularity and the margins of definition and into its own warm, imprecise, but accurate curve. The streets curved, even the tiny houses were so old they were rounded at the edges, the plaster over their brick or stone seeming to frost them almost to softness.

Anna worried about David. He was my age, she said, very handsome, a wonderful father, a sensitive man. But he had been thwarted — we spent a long time defining this quality, my French making a word like "thwarted" ethereal and impossible (she brought a French-English dictionary the next day). At the time of the Prague Spring he had been a student of sculpture. Everyone had great hopes for him; he had been encouraged by his professors, had even been invited to give a show at a prestigious gallery at that early age. He got involved — Anna didn't say how — in the cultural life of the Dubček era. Like everyone, he was wild with rage and broken hope when the August invasion had occurred. Some of his best friends left the country; the woman he was to have married dropped him; things became difficult at the university.

He was sent as part of a labor force to Slovakia where he worked on construction sites. He hadn't been arrested and was not "sentenced" to this work, but sometime in 1969 his "case" had been "reviewed" and it was decided — or suggested (either Anna didn't make it clear or I didn't understand) — that he needed a period of work in the countryside to round out a narrow education.

He worked high in the air, on scaffolding, doing work he knew nothing about, although it had been pointed out to him that he was, after all, bringing art to people: the building was to be a folk-art museum and center. One day he slipped from his position on the scaffolding and just missed falling to his death by grabbing a crossbar. It was a miracle he was able to hang on at all.

But the accident had caused permanent damage. His career as a sculptor was over — the doctors and his professors agreed. And perhaps his morale was broken too. I never met him and never fully understood what the damage had been to his arms, but this fall had ended his career.

Then he had met Anna and they married. He became a musicologist and worked at an institute involved in the preservation of manuscripts. At the moment, Anna said, he was putting together a bibliography of fourteenth-century church music.

As for herself, she said when I asked, what was there to say? She was specializing in French literature; she wanted to translate one day. She wanted more children. David said they must wait, though, and David was right. They had to get an apartment of their own. "And sometimes," she said, "that means twenty years. You get on a list and then you wait. And wait."

We had circled the area below the Loretto with its gaslamps almost three times, wandering the silent streets, occasionally passing a house with the blotted noise of voices inside: a tavern that hardly announced itself, a local pub. We saw no one. To call Prague a dream, to call it a fairy tale, as other people also have, is to be entirely accurate. Like a dream, like the figures in fairy tales, the city and its objects reach out slightly beyond themselves, beyond mere presence. Like the presences in dreams and fairy tales, Prague is *animate*. Even its silence, its stillness, lives. In dreams we are pursued by avenging brooms or find ourselves gazing into growing teacups, as if they were opening flowers; the trees of fairy tales sometimes speak, even logs will yawn. All of this is both natural and supernatural. In Prague, as I walked with Anna (and with Jaromil, but more so with Anna who did not fill the silence between the city and us as much as Jaromil — kind, tour guide Jaromil — did), the streetlights, the cornices, shadows and even the thickness of the stones of the houses had the dreamlike quality of perfect stasis and dormant life. Kafka, Jaromil would have said — did say in his way. Perhaps that's part of what "It's Kafka, it's Kafka" meant: everything lives, even the stones — and how odd and how "normal" that is. Especially the stones, David's object, which have seen every-thing — the fruit markets and chestnut vendors, the massacres, the street fighting, the passing of this terror and that joy. The fact that the stones don't speak does not, as we seem to know when we are in such an ancient place, mean that they have nothing to say.

These are the icons of geography — how we light our tapers before them! That is what tourism is, debased maybe, but still there. Every charter flight is filled with pilgrims, no matter how piggish tourists look, no matter how piggish we are. Of course we're idiotic and unattractive (and ignorant, my grandmother's old adjective): how rarely we find what we wanted, how seldom we can even acknowledge what we are seeking.

The animate life of objects, the sense of a spirit within, is often the essence of nightmare, the thing that turns dream to terror. There is dread in such life. We want a little death around us, we want silence to be truly empty of meaning, and the ancient stones to be, really, just rocks, without history, certainly without breathing life. We want, in such moods, the streetlights to burn harsh and electric with severe definition. Not these melting Prague gaslamps with no end to the filmy trickle of glow, no exact limit between light and dark. We want to be modern, we want to forget, we do not want to be baroque. It occurred to me as we walked what a fatuous idea it is that form follows function: form follows itself.

I was able to think all these things, walking with Anna, yet listening to her, when she spoke. We wandered, that first night, in what felt like a neighborhood, a *quartier*, a place of effortless integrity. She said that she loved it, that the beauty made all the difference. And I felt, beside her, the waste I had made of that word, which she spoke so purely. And then, because she was pure and was *what she was*, I didn't feel ashamed and didn't speak of it. I didn't need to.

It was very late when we parted. We'd lost track of the time.

Suddenly Anna was all efficiency, an entire agenda of duties came between us. She had five pages to translate, she had the baby's clothes to wash, she had promised to help her mother clean cabinets the next morning before her classes. She jumped on the number 22 tram and waved from the lighted square of her window. The tram pulled away from the stop and I saw her open her book and begin to read.

Anna was Jewish. She told me about her family's history during the Nazi occupation — the ones who had perished (whom she had not known; she was born after the War), the strange and unlikely methods of escape and self-preservation, the weight of sheer luck in such lives.

We were walking again, as we had the night before, in the little streets below the Loretto. We had met on the other side of the river, and had stopped at a *vinárna* where I ate a whole plate of Hungarian salami with bread and pickles. Anna, as usual, ate nothing. "I haven't been hungry for years," she said. She drank a little wine. I was still hungry after the salami, but Anna was thin and beautiful and so I stopped with the plate of salami. The real truth was that I had a stash of chocolate bars in my bedroom at Zdenka's. I thought of them with elation.

Anna and I walked across the 5 Mai Bridge instead of the Charles Bridge. We stopped by the Hall of Artists which is crowned at the front with busts of various composers placed high above the entrance. Anna pointed out the head of Mendelssohn. During the Nazi occupation, Heydrich, the hated governor of the country, had insisted that the bust of Mendelssohn, who was half Jewish, be taken down from the company of the greats. "He asked the Czechs," Anna said, "which head was Mendelssohn's. And they said, 'Oh, it's that one over there. The one with the big nose, of course.'" And so the Nazis ended up detaching the bust of Richard Wagner from the building.

I had heard the story before: it's in various guidebooks. But I liked having Anna tell it, pointing in the dark proudly, a

thin figure with a lyric face, making history by transmitting
a tale of the land to a stranger. As Jaromil had done at the old
town hall clock. Civic pride seemed a primary emotion and I
felt it myself for St. Paul whose streetlights, I had decided the
night before, compared favorably with Prague's. And, truly
civic-minded, I noted were nothing at all like those of Minneapolis.

Anna told me about her two aunts. Both had been in concentration camps; they had lost husbands and children and their
own parents. And countless friends: everything, in other words.
Both of them had remarried; both lived in Prague. One aunt was
an inspiration, Anna said — so brave, so cheerful. The other
was a complainer, a moaner and whiner. She never let you
forget.

Anna was impatient with the complainer. In fact, it struck me
that perhaps her only impatience, in a life filled with what seemed
to me unusual burdens and responsibilities and frustrations, was
reserved for this woman. She was annoyed by this aunt, she
said. What good was it, all the complaining?

I said maybe the aunt couldn't forget.

"But what *good* is it?" she said. She said it with anger, not
with sadness — she who had been, from the moment I met her,
so understanding of everyone. Anna who worried about the old
Russian woman in the basement flat near her own flat to whom
no one had spoken since 1968, but whom Anna had spoken to
out of simple charity. Anna with her mother and father, her
husband, the thwarted artist, who picked fights with the broken
internationalist, her two children: willing to give attention to
everyone, to be fair, to sympathize with that Audrey Hepburn
earnestness. She had been made skinny by sympathy; the lyricism
of her face was bred of acknowledging daily the difficulties of
this person, that person, the other.

For the complaining aunt from the concentration camp, however, there was . . . nothing. Her face was hard, set tight
against the woman. For the cheerful aunt, Anna went into a

small rhapsody of admiration. But the other one she would not forgive.

It was Ružena's impatience, nonsympathy for Eva whose *woman things* had been taken out by the Nazis. It is the impatience we have toward those who have suffered irremediably. They annoy and try the nerves of even the most loving person. Maybe these people (I was about to write, *these creatures*) present us with the powerlessness of love or any *feeling* to transform the wounds that events have made. What good was Anna's love to this woman? Not good enough, and therefore a blight upon the present. This was something that Anna, to whom sympathy and duty were primary, could not endure.

It was late and we had again lost track of the hour. We walked back to the Kampa together. Anna seemed to feel she should return me to Zdenka's, as if she were responsible for me. The courtesy of Czechs is deep, unbudgeable, full of implacable absolutes. Zdenka was already asleep, the flat dark, when I arrived. I had a key, but I'd never used it before. The lock was old, the key was old. (Zdenka had said something about *coaxing* it when she gave me the key.) I could not get the door open. Anna tried. ("I know these locks," she said sagely, at home with her crumbling city.) The lock stayed locked. The street, always quiet and mysterious as the Kampa is, was even more eerily silent, the mist from the river catching in the chestnut trees near the park, the streetlamps burning vaguely. We heaved ourselves against the door, making dull, useless noises that didn't wake Zdenka and didn't affect the lock. We tried small, delicate movements with the key as if we were safecrackers. Nothing. We stared at each other in the misty light. And then, as if out of the mists, behind us but alarmingly near, a man's voice said something in Czech. The tone was severe, peremptory. Anna swung around before I did, aflutter with explanation, in barely concealed terror. I felt it and caught it, even though as I turned and saw that the man — who was hardly more than a boy — was a policeman or soldier (I never could tell them apart) and therefore, presumably, not going to harm us. I had once had a very similar problem in St. Paul when I had locked my keys in my car; a policeman had gotten it open for me, had even, like a street kid, offered to show me how to hot-wire the ignition.

But this was different, apparently. Anna and the policeman were talking; he ignored me, frightened off, she explained to me later, by my being a foreigner. He spoke only Czech. While she talked to him, pointing to the door, alternately seeming to plead and to command, I stood to the side, wondering why I was terrified. We had done nothing wrong. "Try the key again," she said quickly aside to me. And I realized we had to get it open. "I don't have my card," she said, quickly, desperately, as if this explained everything and I must get that door open. I was becoming desperate, terrorized without knowing why. I had no idea what she meant by her card, an ID card I supposed. But my terror was simply the accumulated nervousness I'd gathered in the past weeks, the terror of strangeness, the knowledge that couldn't be kept off any longer that I didn't know anything about anything in this crazy misty city I kept trying to claim.

I put the key in the lock. I have no idea what I did, I believe I *willed* it to open, proving perhaps that terror has its own gifts. It opened smoothly, easily. I felt giddy with disbelief. Anna began gushing unnaturally to the cop — "Ah, at last, ah, it's open, well, so we'll just be going now . . ." This seemed to be the ingratiating, stealthy message. She too was willing something to move, to do what she bid it: an act of survival. Finally the cop left.

Then we were in the dark little hallway of Zdenka's flat, holding each other, panting like fugitives who had miraculously not been sniffed out by the police dogs. I still had no idea of the nature of the terror, only that it was terror and Anna had been changed by it so that she was not Anna, was not a personality, had become briefly and effectively a cringing but wily animal — a deer, how like a startled deer those dark eyes were and the cords of her neck with the gamin haircut — an animal that for all its innocence would not be found by the hunter.

But she wasn't even like a deer, not even a bird. She was a leaf — whatever thing that is most insubstantial but that shakes most violently. Her heart was beating so hard and she was shaking so much that she seemed, as I held her, to have no body at all, just the double rhythm of her heart: shudder-crash, shudder-crash. We stood there in the dark for what seemed a long time. I was much the bigger of the two of us so it seemed that I held her and she clung to me. I had only one clear thought as I held her: *I am not good in emergencies.* Later, this thought smeared itself into the messier world of my emotions and I felt remorseful and eventually depressingly guilty that I, with my magic American passport, had exposed Anna to danger, possibly to jail even. ("Remember," said an American guidebook I had in my suitcase, "you have an American passport. Your friends do not.")

But I only felt these things later, after Anna had gone safely away. (I walked her to the tram and this time she did not argue that *she* should deliver *me* to my destination.) And so, I saved her at least from my apologies, my gloom over my carelessness, my American guilt. At the moment, as we stood there in the hallway of Zdenka's dark apartment, so dark we could hardly see each other, I felt nothing at all. For the first time in that city I had wanted so desperately to see ("observe perpetually") there was nothing to see. We were in the blackness. I held in my arms this small creature who was not even, for me or for herself, a person just then, but the essential impulse of life relayed, as percussion in the timpani, through a taut skin. She was, entirely, rhythm. Shudder-crash, shudder-crash. I had never held a woman so long, so closely.

I followed this rhythm I held as if I were tracking, not thinking, just feeling it next to me, attached to the beat, the terror that must always, no doubt, have been there behind the red trance of the Schmidt Brewery sign that I used to watch form and re-form itself as I sat, the happy teen hypnotee, drawn to the beat but never knowing why. Only now I held the thing. And it was human, my kind. Rhythm was not simply assurance, not just "finding one's voice"; it was this other thing, this shudder-crash, the language before language. Terror. The desire, the positive need, to be safe. I just wanted her to be safe. For good measure, I wanted her to have some self-righteous ideas, a frivolous, harmless greed for pretty clothes, a wasteful affair behind her perfect husband's back — isn't that how we live and don't we feel that these things and the right to have trouble with a key at our own door constitute freedom? What I wanted in the dark hallway was for Anna to stop shaking and become a person again.

She soon did. She laughed, "Oh," a long still-rhythmic, still-without-language *oh*, "that was close!" And laughed, squeezed my arms as she pulled away. And then, as we walked to her tram she explained the seriousness of being found on the street without one's ID card. Her husband had warned her over and over. And because of the hour, she would indeed have been detained at police headquarters, until the authorities on the day shift could contact her family, her husband who would have been sick with terror when she didn't come home and didn't call. And there would have been a fine, a heavy penalty. Luckily, the cop hadn't asked for the card, but she was convinced if the lock had not finally turned, if we had not quickly proved our right to be in that place, he would have asked. It was the next step.

The tram came soon. We embraced, we said we would write. There would be no time for another visit. I watched, waving as the tram pulled away, and saw that as it left, she again pulled out a book from her bag, using the time profitably, not sitting, not just dreaming, not even collecting herself.

11 ✿

IN 1968 PRAGUE was a busy place. It was easy to obtain a
visa into the country or a passport out. Many stories about
the August invasion center around attempts by vacationing
Czechs to return to the country, and of foreign tourists to leave.
Ironically, it was easier to get out than for Czechs to reenter during the first days of the invasion. Probably at no time since 1948,
perhaps since before the War, had there been as many foreign
visitors from the West in the city.

Jaromil and I were taking our last walk through the city
when he told me this. It was evening, early June. I had been
in Prague almost three weeks, long enough for the lilacs to have
bloomed and rusted away. It was summer, another season. We
walked across the Charles Bridge, and took the stairway down
to the Kampa, the little island of Zdenka's flat, the "little Venice."
We walked back and forth along the retaining wall by the river.
I was asking my last questions. I wanted to know what the city
had been like before the August invasion in 1968.

"It was a different city from now," Jaromil said. "The big
thing was, everybody was out at night, walking around, talking.
They didn't go home. Not just in the bars, getting drunk like
now. We had visitors from all over. People came to us." He
stopped talking and looked out from the wall of the Kampa,
across the Vltava to the National Theater which is one of those
great monuments, like immigrant churches and cathedrals in the
United States, to working people's reverence for art. The theater

was built during the Austrian rule, as a national cultural shrine (it has the imposing design and heavy look) for the Czech people. The funds were raised by collections everywhere, in the villages and countryside. When, almost immediately after it was at last built, it burned to the ground, the money was raised again and the theater rebuilt. As we looked at it, the building, which is across from the Slavia and the Writers Union, had been closed for extensive repair and renovation for seven years. I had never been inside.

The trams on the other side of the river were giving off blue electrical sparks occasionally on the overhead wires and rattling on their tracks by the embankment near the Slavia. The Kampa was deserted and dark. The horse chestnuts by the wall were almost past blooming, as they were in the U Fleku courtyard. On the sidewalk mounds of the paper-white blossoms with their dashes of red had piled up. To the left, we could see the Charles Bridge, almost deserted. Its blackened saints looked like abstract shapes meant to express alarm or some harsh post-expressionist angularity. They seemed bizarrely modern, as if the bridge wasn't being guarded by saints, but was hurling out disjointed gestures from what were, by daylight, simply stone draperies.

"When the foreign visitors left, how did you feel?" I asked. "After August twentieth. Was it lonely?"

"Lonely? I don't know about lonely," he said. "I stood here in the fall, right here on the Kampa, looking across the river. The troops weren't around much anymore; they had withdrawn out of the city where they caused too much animosity. All the tourists were gone, of course. It was like this — very silent. I remember thinking, 'Well, now we are alone again.'"

He turned and smiled at me, and held his hands out, palms up, and shrugged, the Czech shrug, the eloquent gesture a mime would use. It was, literally, a *refined* gesture: it took the paradoxes of tragedy and comedy, of helplessness and intelligence and found this movement to express them all.

Now we are alone again. He said this, smiling, as if the city were alone again the way a family is after guests finally leave, guests who have stayed too long and been too much trouble. Perhaps his is the idiosyncratic, offhand bravery of a man who finds the melodrama of his country distasteful, finds it *too much*. It may not be the typical response to Prague's evening silence and its ironic isolation in the heart of Europe. But it felt, at the moment, normal. He was not acting normal; he *was* normal, natural, at home. He stood there in the dark, looking out at the river, at the bridge with its blackened saints, and he seemed to invite the astonishing beauty of the city, and to ward off tragedy effortlessly, simply by his love of what lay before him, the piled-up detail of his city's history. I do not think he was sad.

On my last day, I went for a walk in Malá Strana. I'd said good-bye to Zdenka and to the shy, proper Elena when they went off, together, to school and clinic. Zdenka forgot her bag lunch, and Elena came tearing back to get it, her careful English suddenly forgotten in the flurry not to be late. "Food, food," she kept saying, pointing to the bag. "Mother, mother." I understood and we laughed; we had never really been able to talk to each other; there was no language.

I walked around the flat, touching the furniture, the faded art nouveau couch which was as deep as a bed. The rooms in Prague apartments had charmed me: bedrooms could have been parlors, parlors bedrooms, no room seemed assigned just one, solitary meaning. Partly, this was a matter of space, but not with Zdenka, who had a roomy flat. The couch in the living room looked like a bed, the bed in her room, covered with dozens of pillows and even a carpet like Freud's couch, could have been a divan in a belle-epoque salon. I stood for a long minute in front of the china cabinet where Zdenka kept her mother's collection of Bohemian crystal, the garnet-red and mist-white cut glass for which the country was once so famous. I picked up a sugar bowl, incised with a thinly colored picture of a picnic, the women wearing absurd, wide hats and balloon skirts, a small dog, head cocked, in the corner, the whole scene framed with grape vines and bunches of gray grapes, all incised as if with a feather. Careful work, I thought, and put it carefully away.

I left my suitcase at the tobacconist's just on the other side of the Charles Bridge, where I also left the key for Zdenka to fetch on her way home: I could see exactly that far, and no further, into the future of her life once I left.

Then I walked in Malá Strana. I ended up in a terraced garden, tucked under the Hradčany, overlooking the city. Kenth, the Swedish medical student, had showed it to me. He had developed the habit of sending me a postcard, always a garden, whenever he was in Prague. It was the only time I heard from him. I had bought a card at the tobacconist's. ("Prague in Spring": flowering trees) and I sat down to write him a card:

> Kenth! It's still here, lilacs and
> roofs, steeples and gold. From
> the Castle garden!
> > All best,
> > Patricia

It was a warm day, full of sun; there was a breeze so it wasn't too hot. I sat on an old bench, in front of a statue of a nude goddess. She held the heavy fall of her hair away from her head in one hand; in the other, she had a big bunch of grapes. She was blackened with age and had the spectral, beseeching quality of statues. But she was behind me and I didn't look long. I looked down, through the garden, to the view below.

The garden was terraced. It was hardly a garden anymore; it didn't seemed cared-for. A wild rosebush was next to me, and there were various bushes, vines and other flowering trees, but for the most part, the place had simply been let alone and gone nearly wild. There were many lilacs, that bush that blooms best from its oldest branches. But the blooms were rusted, finished with spring. The grass and weeds were uncut, the stone staircases and gazebos overlooking Malá Strana and the city had been allowed to crumble. It looked very Italian, especially the cream and coral villa at the bottom (the office of some institute or other) which had a wall fountain whose lion's head dribbled like a very senile old fountain. The sound of the water falling against the old stone created the illusion of a cave, a cool cavern within which water was running steadily, timelessly, making its slow, hypnotic mark on the stone, on the ear, on the brain. There seemed to me no more restful, perfect sound. It was the equivalent of silence, only it was full, not empty.

There was a haze over the city, even though it was sunny. Mist, fog, city haze, fine rain, anything that fills the landscape — these things open the memory. Details forgotten, casual conversations lost long ago in a backyard when someone was smoking a cigar and someone else said, "Now, how far is the nearest star?" and everyone, together, looked up at the night sky as if at a tool whose use had been forgotten. I was thinking of home, how, when I got there, I must write about flowers after all. So what if they were "poetic"? It ran in the family: my father in the greenhouse, my grandmother in her garden. I will write about my grandmother's garden, I decided. If I could even remember it. I was worried about accuracy: everything seemed dark.

There, through the glinting city haze, I could see at last the double spires of the Týn Cathedral. One was covered with scaffolding for restoration; when I had stood in the Old Town Square, looking up at it with Jaromil, I hadn't been able to see the spire. But in this garden, so far removed and high above it, I could see it clearly through its lace of pipes and boards. Many other spires were scaffolded too, the inevitable dressing of ancient cities. From several of the gothic towers, huge cranes were suspended in modern patterns. They added to, rather than detracted from, the view — the strict modern line lifted like a chin from the medieval face.

Everywhere, especially in the near range just below me in Malá Strana, the red-tiled roofs with their blackened ripples formed a pattern of waves. I thought of Sudek, the romantic photographer of Prague, trooping around the hills and gardens with his heavy, nineteenth-century camera, his right arm lost in the First World War, crazy to the end for gardens, the city gardens of Prague. "Sudek," Sonja Bullaty, his former assistant said, "was not afraid of lyricism." Without the language (what is it to be able to order a beer in Czech? Not speaking the language, certainly), my relation must be his: the pictures, the views of Prague, the old sepia album, only finally real, spread below me not as a book but as the city itself. And here was the "romantic light," golden, polluted, stinging my eyes a little.

The birds were louder in the garden than any other sound. I could hear a faint underbuzz of traffic and the clacking of the trams — one of those mechanical sounds that is old-fashioned and harmless and seems to partake of nature. Also, at intervals, I heard voices, but never in English; especially the high, inquisitive voices of children. But mainly and, most diligently, the birds. They twittered, they cooed, some said only one long word at rare intervals; others could not stop scolding, warning, insisting.

I beat my fist in my hand and promised, right out loud, that I would live here one day: sheerly for the beauty. I wanted this beauty, these broken gardens. A pointless promise; Prague isn't Paris or London — there is no way for an ordinary American to live here. Prague would be the dream city of the expatriate artists if they could get their hands on it. But that is impossible.

I shrugged. It was perhaps my only Czech moment. I shrugged. I could not have what I wanted. And for the first time I sensed what is behind the shrug because I had made the gesture myself, involuntarily. Behind it, also involuntarily, is the force of memory. This beauty, I thought, I will remember it. I left the garden and went down into the city.

Afterword

W E HAVE an extra day," the voice on the telephone said brightly. "We thought we'd do Prague." In the years after *A Romantic Education* was first published in 1981, I was to receive this call again and again. Friends or friends of friends, even complete strangers, checked in: did I have any tips on where to stay, what to see? Actually, these callers rarely were making trips *to* Prague. In the 1980s Prague was not a destination; it was a detour people wedged in on the way to or from (usually) Vienna. Sometimes Prague got scratched when they discovered that Czechoslovakia wasn't part of the Eurailpass system.

In any case, I had few tips to give. I couldn't be sure the restaurants I knew were still there, and I'd lost touch with the people I'd met — not because it was impossible to keep in contact with them (the mails, though slow, generally worked), but from a failure of imagination. I couldn't seem to believe in their reality once I was on the other side of the Iron Curtain, that most apt of political metaphors.

As my visits to Prague receded into the past, my friends began to look like *tableaux vivant* from a world whose otherness had become dreamlike and mythic, and not simply geographic. I turned the people I met there into cameos who moved briefly through a bad socialist-realist movie. Just as they could not travel west of their own border, I could not move them into the future, and finally, not even into the present. I never forgot them — not Ružena and her baroque clock, not the manic Zdenka and her motherly daughter Elena, not Anna, the Audrey Hepburn look-alike. But our letters finally faltered. They were frozen in their seemingly unchanging world, the inaccessible "over there."

My trips to "Zlatá Praha" — Golden Prague — during the pewter-gray seventies were visits to the far side of the moon. They did not partake of tourism. But I couldn't claim they were great explorations. They were journeys into a myth about history. After my return home I never imagined I would go there again. I never imagined I could.

Worse, as time went by, my own interior pictures of Prague had faded. They blurred and became as indistinct as the nineteenth-century cityscapes my grandmother had cried over in her Prague album in St. Paul. I hung up the telephone from the inquiring calls of travelers feeling vaguely oppressed. It wasn't that once again I had proved myself to be no expert on the subject — I'd never claimed to be an expert. And it wasn't that I was losing Prague all over again, in my memory.

The problem was, *I wanted* the city, the whole country, to blur over and fade away. My grandmother may have cried over her romantic pictures of Prague, but she had never wanted to go back once she left. And now, strangely, after my headlong rush to embrace the place, neither did I. I began working on a book about Italy.

But I kept up my mildly obsessive file of newspaper clippings and magazine articles. I had a fat file of notices about "dissidents," about protests and human rights violations, punctuated occasionally by travel pieces urging the seasoned European tourist to "try" Prague, emphasis on its "untouched" medieval beauty and its "unknown" Art Nouveau architecture. These travel pieces extended a flattering dare: only the game European traveler (someone a cut above the tourist) would go to Prague. But for this rare bird — check the sidebar on restaurants, it's not a complete consumer wilderness over there.

In time, when people called to talk about Prague, more and

more they called to tell me, not ask me, about the place. The atmosphere they described was stagnant, numbingly controlled: politically and culturally, it was the same world I had visited in 1975. I was chilled as much by the stasis of the situation as I was by the reports of repression. I believed the changelessness. It felt permanent. After all, mine was a postwar life; I never knew a world that wasn't divided in half. The Cold War, more than Vietnam (and more than I knew), was my real war.

As the 1980s clicked by I kept clipping, and I kept up on the two literary lions — Kundera and Havel. Kundera made of Czech history and of exile an international metaphor; his view of history was bleak, ironic, attached to that permanence of experience which I too felt and which was part of the listlessness that made me wish to avoid the place. Havel, on the other hand, remained rooted in place, often in prison. His personal voice attained, over time, the authority of public morality. In its philosophical purity, that voice made him more icon than author. I admired Havel. I believed Kundera. I believed in hopelessness and exile. These two worlds framed the historical myth the Czech lands had offered me in my visits there.

Then — as if in a movie's magical jump-cut — it was suddenly November 1989, and Prague snapped into startling focus. The fade of my memory (which was a form of narcotic, a depression) cracked from sheer brittleness, just as the regime did. What had seemed unthinkable only weeks, even days, before was suddenly real and — this was the fascinating part — revealed itself as inevitable. Of course anything that ossifies turns to dust, blows away. Wasn't it obvious all along? Yet for weeks nothing but amazement filled the newspapers and the TV screen — and my own heart. We couldn't get enough of this death. In Prague this collapse was soon accorded its crown, drawing all its alarms and astonishments, its power shifts and reversals, into the fateful name from which there was no turning back: the revolution.

I tore whole front pages from the *New York Times* for my file.

"Dissident" began to take on an antique ring in the Czech context. Havel, who had become etherealized by his faithfulness, was — unbelievable! — president of the republic by the end of December. His foreign minister's first pressing task: to find someone to cover his shift at the brewery where he'd worked as a stoker since signing Charter 77. The Velvet Revolution, they were calling it. Even the political jokes coming from Kafkaland were goofy, not grim. Heard the one about the Czech revolution? It's so peaceful, even their martyrs don't have to die.

So I returned. Not, as it turned out, during the heady months following the revolution, but a year and a half later, when the euphoria had drifted like laughing gas away from the Czechs, and was being breathed deeply by Western visitors who clasped the Czechs to their pounding capitalist bosoms, telling them everything was going to be great — give it a year, give it a couple of years.

But the Czechs were already turning back to ironic type. They were beginning to see that Socialism, behind its Iron Curtain, wasn't the only regime with a hard heart. The fabled market economy was proving to be surprisingly heartless too, in effect saying in its bright liberating voice, you're on your own now, comrades.

❦

Now, a decade after the Velvet Revolution — a term disdained by most Czechs whose economic problems hardly suggest a luxurious fabric — I go to Prague every summer to teach and simply to live, and I can speak of "my apartment in Malá Strana" (a sublet from a friend). I have what I thought I could never have, what no American could ever have — the chance to live in the beloved city as if it were Paris or London, as if it were "the West."

Which it has become. The Americans I meet now in the city, the tourists and those, mostly young, who are living the ex-pat life, regard me with a certain wonder. "You saw it *before*," they say with undisguised envy. They interrogate me closely about this Czech life "before."

Before what? Well, before us, for one thing. Before McDonald's and KFC, before the fevered hordes of summer tourists in Reeboks and tee-shirts coursing over the Charles Bridge buying trinkets. Before currency exchange offices on every corner and the *International Herald Tribune* for sale at any kiosk. Before skinheads and Czech and Asian "mafia" enforcers, before teenage hookers on Na Příkope. Before Prague became "the pickpocket capital of the world." Before good French restaurants (before bad ones), before blues bars and bagels ("The bagel is American bread," I recently overheard a middle-aged Czech woman explain authoritatively to her inquiring companion as the 22 tram passed Bohemian Bagel, a busy American hangout on Ujezd).

And what were the treasures I had been privileged to see before all of this came to be? The Charles Bridge empty in the middle of the day, its sooty saints gazing on the vacancy before them? The great yawning piazza of Old Town Square devoid of crowds, minus beer gardens and boutiques crammed with lead crystal for the tourist trade? Was my peculiar cachet based on the homely fact that I had been around to see dour faces in drab clothes standing in line for wizened carrots? And why does the image of all the neglected and crumbling real estate of the Cold War years bring on such waves of wistfulness among the ex-pats as they regard the astonishing (but predictable) gold rush of Western consumerism overtaking the city?

The city was literally flaking away for decades. Someone said if the revolution hadn't come when it did, the whole city would have simply collapsed, and Prague, which survived the Second World War almost unscathed, would have fallen in peacetime from sheer neglect. "A month later," one of my Czech friends said, "and I mean it — buildings would have started collapsing."

Indeed, one of the most striking distinctions between Prague *then* and Prague *now* is the astonishing renovation of the historic (and touristic) center. What was gray and sooty becomes, year by year, ever more pastel, the just-frosted fondant pastels of Central Europe reasserting their eighteenth-century hold — Schonbrunn yellow, the Bohemian Rozemberk rose, the Mozartian lime-green of the Estates Theater where *Don Giovanni,* as the Czechs love to recite to visitors, received its premiere.

Not only the color of buildings has changed, but the entrepeneurial rush, especially in the center, has created a new kind of Kafkaesque unreality. An article in a Prague paper reported that the elderly, worried about their imperfect memories, were checking into clinics in unprecedented numbers because they would go to bed with a butcher shop on the corner, wake up to find a boutique full of Lycra gym clothes, only to discover a video rental in the spot a month later.

Prague is undeniably more vibrant, more dynamic and exciting — more fun — than it ever was during the Cold War. Restaurants and bars buzz on every block. The Czechs, in full entrepeneurial flower, have translated their menus into four or five languages. The English translations are cause for much merriment among Americans (who of course couldn't speak Czech to save their lives). They trade stories of finding appetizers such as "smoked language in sweet and sour sauce" and "sea crap," and "salmon rose," and main courses innocently labeled "roasted chicken spit" and "stuffed turkey cock."

I understand the envy of the ex-pats when they quiz me about "before." There is an element of shame in their envy, the shame of recognizing the crude imposition of the familiar American market culture on the tatty but nervy native Czech life of only a decade ago which survived like a human *samizdat* of subtly linked friendships, social customs and assumptions, lifted eyebrows and mumbled jokes, interpenetrating the brittle carapace of the corrupt Socialist regime.

It is as if, for the new earnest visitors from the West, Prague is a stage set — the improbable dream of the baroque city where Kafka and Rilke walked in exultation and anguish — but the purpose of the stage set eludes them. They worry that they have arrived "too late," and have expatriated themselves to a theme park. They sense that the life of the place is something quite other than the charms purveyed by the rouged-up tourist center, beguiling though they are.

The city presented different barriers to me after the revolution. I was used to Prague being unreachable — that was how it became such an eloquent metaphor in my mind. But suddenly it had become another place you could rack up frequent-flyer miles getting to. I hated to admit it, but even as I first thought about returning for the first time in 1991, I felt complicated about the freedom the country had won for itself. Was it possible I couldn't take liberation? I worried that I had committed that worst of poetic sins: fallen for my metaphor instead of cleaving to its real body.

In the end, I was drawn back to Prague in 1991 by someone else's story. It was in the Minneapolis paper: Josef Mestenhauser, a professor of international education at the University of Minnesota, was returning to Prague to receive his law degree from Charles University — forty-three years after his 1948 escape from the country. He had been two months away from graduation when he was arrested, and had managed to break out of jail. He made a dash to the West, his hand on the revolver in his coat pocket all the way to the border.

He had never returned. His name, he later told me with more wonder than anger, had remained on the active wanted list, a twenty-five-year prison sentence awaiting him, right up to the Velvet Revolution in 1989. Now the new government wanted to offer university degrees to those students who had been victims of the former regime. It turned out there were a lot of them, young men in 1948, retirement age now, scattered around the globe, mostly in North America, some in Australia and South America, a few in Western Europe. Sixty of them gathered in Prague for the ceremony in late April 1991, less than a year and a half after the regime collapsed, almost a lifetime since they had last been there.

"Why should I complain?" Joe Mestenhauser said when I asked him about all those years, cut off from family, exiled from his native land and language. "It's been a good life."

But not, I thought, the life you must have thought you had coming. His family, like Havel's, had been part of the liberal intelligentsia; after university a job was waiting for him in the foreign service. His family was acquainted with the Masaryks. Joe's name was on the ballot for a seat in parliament in the 1948 elections, which were never held. This was the class — indeed the liberal leadership and cultural world — dismantled and scattered by the 1948 coup.

In the end, I threw my trip together in under forty-eight hours (no visa requirement anymore). I felt safe following Joe Mestenhauser's trail: here was someone who was bound to be knocked for an even bigger loop when he encountered post-revolution Prague. He wasn't making peace with a metaphor, after all, but with an unlived life.

❧

Ruzyně airport retained its Cold War aspect when I first went back. The Golden Arches hadn't arrived yet, and the airport had the stripped-down look of a hangar, just as I remembered it from the seventies. It was small, disorganized, without duty-free shops. A drab outpost. Compulsory exchange of money at the "official" (that is, inflated) rate was a thing of the past — no more uniformed currency officials with shiny money changers strapped on like ticket sellers at a carnival, and no checkpoint on the way out to be sure visitors had exchanged the requisite amount of hard currency. Yet there was something odd about arrival.

A brisk young ticket agent led everyone from our flight (about thirty people) across the tarmac, past the aimless young soldiers who didn't return our glances, into the building and along a corridor. Without a word of explanation, she stopped in the flight gate's waiting area and shut the glass door to the corridor that led to the main terminal. It was an old door, and the glass rattled in its sash. I thought she would turn to announce something, but she kept her back to us and just stood facing the dingy glass of the closed door. We stood there too, as if we were in a bus shelter, waiting to be picked up.

It was a strangely vacant five minutes. Nothing happened, and no one seemed to find this annoying or odd. Except me, the only American in the group. I wanted to get into the city, but I was peeved even more by the fact that nobody else seemed perturbed by this unexplained delay. I turned to a Dutch businessman. "What's going on?" I asked.

"Oh," he said, "we must wait until the other passengers have gone by."

"What other passengers?"

"The next departing flight," he said. Then, seeing that the blankness did not clear from my face, he smiled. "There's no risk anymore, of course, but the form remains. They do it out of habit, because that's the way it's always been."

Passengers leaving the country — "going out," as the old lingo had it — were always kept from those coming in, those from "over there." Safe from the taint of blue jeans and rock and roll, from all of our happy sins and grim delights. And, as we in the West liked to flatter ourselves, kept from the taint of our freedom. *No risk anymore, of course, but . . .* I turned again to the glass door, to the olive-drab back of the uniformed guide who would liberate us when the coast was clear. Metaphor hound that I've always been, I took this glass room to be a lens. It was trained on one of those almost invisible moments, a defining instant between two eras. *The form remains.*

※

The holding room behind the glass door, the military guide, and the entire Cold War backwater look of Ruzyně have all vanished since those early postrevolution months. Now when you arrive in Prague, you are delivered, as everywhere, into the anonymity of international travel, its bland and reassuring order, its invitation to shop. It is, of course, ridiculous to mourn the loss of an ugly, dirty, maddeningly inefficient airport. This is especially true when the airport, underused because its citizens were going nowhere and foreign travelers had no reason to come, was a sad emblem of the country's unwilling isolation.

But while I can advise the wistful ex-pats to get up at 5 A.M., assuring them that they will see the Charles Bridge as I first saw it in 1975 — empty and beautifully brooding, there is no way ever again to see grotty little Ruzyně as it once was and to feel its irony. It sent the clear message that you were not a traveler but an interloper, a stranger in what was a strange land, someone who had wandered into the secret territory of the Other. After the revolution, for a few brief years, the airport provided that eloquent reminder: *the form remains. . . .* Now even that reminder is obscured.

Which only proves that I'm as susceptible to nostalgia as the romantic ex-pats, although for different reasons. The first day I saw the Charles Bridge again, tears spiked my eyes at the sight of the happy crowds, the buskers and the vendors, the sheer *brio* of it all. It was a carnival, this place I had come to love for its lonely splendor, its gray solitude. *You may not cry,* a stern inner voice commanded as I watched the circus. Gone the solitude and isolation of the 1970s; impossible now to walk across the bridge, between the blackened statues of saints, and feel that old sentimental irony: *alone in Mitteleuropa.*

The city belongs now — belongs again — to the world. Like Venice, Prague is a city that deserves its tourists. It will never be alone again, and to mourn that would be to mourn human avidity. The Cold War was the anomaly. It sustained a tense international illusion that made us believe — at least two generations of us — that the world really was divided into two heroically opposed adversaries. The end of that peculiar soot-gray Cold War melodrama doesn't deserve tears. To weep for the loss of such isolation is not only nonsense. They are the tears of the greedy Western consumer who cries to see other people having their chance to be free — and greedy — too.

※

I arrived for that first annual trip to Prague after the Velvet Revolution in spring, during the city's signature season, the same season I had first encountered it in 1975. It is also the season the world associates with the city: Prague Spring, when the window on the West was briefly cracked open, and then slammed shut. The events of 1968 came to signify all the broken hopes that gave the city its Cold War allure. For its Cold War grimness did give the city a kind of black-leather-jacket glamour. In the midseventies, Prague's bleakness did not look, to a child of a heated-up Western consumer culture, like all bad news. It looked like what was missing, the exotic and tantalizing Other. Going there was a trip through the imperial American looking glass, down the Socialist rabbit hole. The most golden thing about Prague then was its silence. Loneliness was its chief allure, radiating a sullen romance bred of cigarette smoke and satire.

My original visit to Prague, in May 1975, coincided with the week the American troops left Saigon. I had originally sought out the city in books during my generation's youthful immersion in national shame, the long anguish of the Vietnam War. Prague — and Czech history — were real to me, but they were also touchstones, charms I might finger to convince myself I belonged not only to the big country that devastated the little country, but to the little country of my ancestry holding itself in moral aloofness from another crushing giant.

That is probably why, in its dark political night when I first came to know it, Prague was beautiful to me. I was entranced. I accepted utterly its national anguish — required it, even. As a young American aggrieved by the Vietnam War, I suppose I wasn't, after all, looking for history, but for that more dangerous elixir: purity. How sentimental it was possible to be, contemplating Prague's weird isolation in the center of Europe, its gray beauty, its moral presence, as I stood in the Kampa under a flowering chestnut tree, the flimsy white blossoms stained with red falling all around me, as I stared down at the dark Vltava, the cool blue of my American passport snug in the zippered pocket of my backpack.

※

The Velvet Revolution was decisive, of course. It provided the thrilling sensation of a melodrama well concluded: the evil leader and his henchmen are driven from the castle; the poetic hero is released from prison to reign in their place. When I followed Joe Mestenhauser's triumphal return in 1991, every encounter trailed its bit of political eloquence, a magical reversal: so you *can* go home again! This was the period when everyone was dazzled by the surprise finish — forgetting that no moment in history can be an ending. Time keeps forcing history forward into new plots.

For a few years after the revolution the bleak past was safely framed and was definitely "the past," a treasure trove of ironies to be inspected, often with relish. This retrospective spirit was still in the air when the *New York Times* travel magazine sent me in 1992 to do a travel piece on Prague ("We just realized we've never done anything on Prague," the editor said, caught in one of the West's Rip Van Winkle moments as Eastern Europe was "discovered").

Maybe the separation of Czechoslovakia into the sovereign states of Slovakia and the Czech Republic in 1993 marked the real end of the Velvet Revolution. This ethnic division was observed in the West with mild relief or even admiration — at least the Czechs and Slovaks weren't butchering each other in the manner of the Balkans. A civilized divorce — this was the image even the Czechs came to accept in time.

By 1995, when I went to Prague for an extended stay as a Fulbright Fellow, the past was — well, passé. I had been awarded the Fulbright based on my proposal to interview Czech writers about their relation to the revolution. What had it been like to be a writer "before" — and what was the difference "after"? I was asking the ex-pat question.

But I was asking it too late. Nobody wanted to talk about before and after. "We talked our heads off the first two or three years," a glamorous fortyish woman told me as we sat up late, drinking red Moravian wine in her attic apartment around the corner from my Malá Strana sublet. She had worked with Havel at the revered Theater under the Balustrade and, I was sure, had stories to tell. "I've told them all a hundred times," she said. "I'm sick of it. We're all sick of it."

The Western press, and the West in general, kept up its romance with the "dissidents" much longer than the Czechs did. You didn't have to be anybody, the glamorous director said, to be interviewed about life before the revolution. The Western press craved liberation stories. "They want us to be brave dissidents — forever," she said.

During my Fulbright residency, I came to realize that if I asked a writer the "before" question, I would not be invited back. Not simply because people were sick of telling their stories, but because they held in contempt those who could only rehearse their history in the familiar either-or oppositions of the Cold War.

For some people, of course, the question about what they did "before" was awkward. Even as early as 1991, when Joe Mestenhauser had received his law degree, things had been tense in some quarters. The ceremony had turned out to be a politically sensitive event. It had been planned during the heady early days of the revolution. After the revolution, most agencies and institutes — governmental, academic, and public organizations of all kinds — had indeed been purged of old Communist loyalists, just as my *New York Times* clippings reported. However, this had been done only at the highest levels; heads of agencies lost their jobs, but the people just under them and the rest of the administrative staff typically stayed right where they were. In some cases, they simply moved up and filled the vacancies left by their former bosses. The rituals of restitution and reconciliation distressed these old-timers.

These people were often as much a part of the old regime as their purged predecessors. It wasn't only a question of ideology; the frustration was with a habit-ridden, corrupt bureaucracy. Subdirectors of agencies and associates of various programs might *say* they were all for reforms, but procedures didn't change, nor did people feel confident that this was simply a matter of waiting for life to catch up with history. My first moment at the airport, waiting behind the glass door, flashed to mind: *the form remains.* Those who landed on their feet in the old regime managed to do so in the new one. Corruption wiggled nimbly past ideology. And in the new order it wasn't just privilege and perks to be had; there was gold in that free market revolution.

Joe Mestenhauser had heard rumors, for instance, that one of Havel's advisors was a man who had been directly responsible for putting him in prison. Havel was formed, Joe felt, by the experiences of 1968 and had little imagination for the lessons of 1948. In any case, if the country hoped to work together, too much honoring of past victims, dissidents, and those long gone from the country ran the risk of aggravating old wounds and could endanger delicate coalitions.

For many people, including Joe, the question of past actions touched a more fundamental fact: with few exceptions, everyone in the country had been part of the system. It was impossible to *live* in the country in the forty-one years of the Communist regime without engaging, to some degree, in what *someone* could define as complicity.

From the first days of the revolution, Havel had urged the country away from retribution; he had the moral authority, as one severely victimized by the regime, to make his position matter. Perhaps common sense also told people that forty-one years of a system that required people to bend and twist like pretzels did not bear overly close scrutiny. People born in 1948, for example, had been educated, married, and employed in that system. They could hardly be called "complicit," much less "guilty." They had simply existed in an environment.

I first came upon these complications about "before" at a dinner with Joe's family after he received his law degree. We were in Mělnik, in the vineyard region outside Prague. Joe's brother Zdenek and his family were gathered for a Sunday dinner: his wife Vlasta, their daughter Marcela, her husband Pavel, both in their thirties, and their two small sons. As a girl, Marcela had refused to join the Young Communists ("They say she's like me," Joe said. "Stubborn"). She ranked so high in the state scores, the officials were forced to admit her to university anyway. She was on maternal leave from her university position (a generous three years — the up side of Socialism, Joe said. And indeed, this Socialist "right" became a perk that was whittled away a few years later in the new order).

Pavel was a fellow at an institute devoted to ecology. The whole question of how people conducted themselves in the past, he said, was complicated. For instance, the chief of his institute, a Communist, had refused to punish those in his department who were active in 1968, as he was instructed to do. Eventually he was forced into retirement. Pavel's point: membership in the Party alone couldn't be used as a measure of judgment. "Some Communists really were idealistic," he said, "and they did good."

Things could get crazier. At one point during the Communist years, Pavel had publicly criticized the official Party line on ecology, which he considered benighted. He did it knowing he would be punished.

But he wasn't punished. The authorities assumed he was knuckling under to his boss, who held a similar view and who was on his way out. They were unable to perceive independence of thought even when it presented itself. Maybe, Pavel said, they meant to reward him for something more essential to the system than ideology: toadying to a higher-up.

At the end of the meal that day, Joe took me out to see Zdenek's garden. It had a view over the countryside, some of the property given over to vineyards, and in the distance, the confluence of two rivers. A beautiful vista. The garden was filled not only with spring flowers but with plots for vegetables, berries, and grapes. Several cold frames were set into the earth where leaf lettuce was already up. In the corner there was a rabbit hutch, the new babies quivering on fresh straw. At the edge of the property a lean-to had been made into a greenhouse where Zdenek started seeds and wintered-over delicate plants.

"This is what they did all those years," Joe said, gesturing to the yard.

"What?" I said.

"Cultivated their gardens." As a result of Joe's defection and their father's known opposition to the regime, Zdenek had been denied a university education. He'd managed well enough, and was retired now, but Joe shook his head. "I would never have blamed him if he had, you know, denounced us somehow. But," he said, looking into the romantic wine country beyond, "he never did."

⁂

Anna, a Czech physician I met in 1991 through American friends living in Vienna, saw the Cold War cultivation of country gardens differently from Joe Mestenhauser, who felt painfully the diminishment of his brother's life — as well as its unassuming courage — in those carefully tended rows of vegetables. Anna believed that this seemingly apolitical immersion in a bucolic idyll had been a secret weapon against the old regime.

She took me to an exhibit of work by the Czech romantic painter Josef Mánes at the St. Agnes Monastery near her apartment on hidden-away Kozi ulice (Goat street), not far from the crowds of Old Town Square. We walked around the beautifully restored cloister rooms, looking at scenes of the idealized Bohemian countryside, the Kokořin mountain landscape I had walked with Joe and his family the year of his triumphal return.

The old Czech village life was gone, of course, Anna said. Modern life would have affected it anyway, with young people going to the cities, but it had been systematically destroyed after 1948. When the Communists outlawed private ownership and turned family farms into cooperatives, they also instituted a program of village amalgamation which, she thought, was more devastating to traditional life than the end of private ownership itself. Little shops and small post offices were closed, and whole clusters of villages were forced to use a single market area. The delicate web of relationships that made the village so important in Czech life was trashed — forever it seemed.

By the end of the 1950s, many of the village houses were vacant. During the sixties, Praguers started to buy these dilapidated houses — sometimes they were little more than huts, but some were magnificent 300-year-old farmhouses with walls three feet thick, and had spring water drilled deep from cellar cisterns. They repaired these places and used them for weekend homes, where they grew flowers and vegetables. Joe had been thinking of this, no doubt, when he said *they cultivated their gardens*. There was no question, Anna said, that this urban flight had an escapist aspect, a safe haven from the regime. Some intellectuals had been critical of the "hut mania," she said, seeing it as an abdication from political struggle.

But she was convinced the weekend houses had a beneficial effect, even functioned as a kind of passive resistance. For it wasn't only the notion of private ownership that the country had to learn all over again; the concept of the *local* was, from the point of view of governance, perhaps even more important. One of the most heralded new freedoms since the revolution has been the right to a passport, to travel outside the country without permission. Anna herself has managed to go on cut-rate camping trips to the American national parks (the classic tourist trip for Czechs who hunger for American vistas but have little interest in American cities).

Treasured as this new ability to travel is, perhaps the right to stay put, systematically denied by the forced collectivization of the 1950s, was an even deeper unconscious need. In Poland during the Communist years agriculture had retained a largely private structure; even in Hungary farming had always been partly privatized. In Czechoslovakia, however, everything was taken over by the state. The huts were the only breathing space people had.

"Paradoxically," Anna said as we stood before one of Mánes's idealized nineteenth-century village cottages, "these city people began to bring back the old Czech country spirit." It wasn't a return to the Czech fairy tales of Božena Nemcova — the romantic conception of the village was, she admitted, a nostalgic dream born of industrialization. But this spontaneous national urge for even the tiniest foothold in village life had a political impact: villages erased by collectivization had been reconstituted. And people had a place to care for, often one with some long-standing family connection, a place for which they, not some distant commission, were responsible.

"That had to be good," she said, looking with satisfaction at the glowing Mánes cottage, deep in its unreal woods.

Conversations like this, unrushed and speculative, made me realize with some astonishment that I had friends in Prague. I was returning every year not simply to see the country, but to see my pals — besides Anna, there was the translator Petra, one of the surprise millionaires, her life suddenly changed forever when private property was returned to its original owners in the "restitutions" that continue to be sorted out, and her family found themselves in possession of a magnificent building on Old Town Square — the equivalent of discovering you owned part of Rockefeller Center. At the other end of the scale were the sculptor Jiři and his artist wife Šarka, who lived, it seemed, on nothing but a radiant faith in art. And there was Vlasta, the meditative weaver who worked like a diligent fairy-tale spinner, alone in her studio with its bower-of-bliss garden tucked under the Hradcany.

Thanks to them, I became part of a group of linked friendships that included art conservators, painters, musicians, and writers. Typically, these people, middle-aged and well educated, had not been "dissidents," but neither had they been Party members. The Cold War had been rough in the usual ways for them as intellectuals and cultural workers, and simply as citizens. But, except for Petra with her surprise restitution, they were living the old way, making do, patching together a life in the new economy that actually provided a less secure safety net than the repressive old regime had.

Anna, for example, was a selfless, old-style intellectual, naturally gracious, passionate about books, grateful for an opera ticket, completely absorbed as she stood before a painting in a museum. Not consumer material, as she had not been toady material in the former regime. She was repelled by the new economy, the market fever. It was a question not only of a different life experience from that in the West, but of different values as a result of those experiences. Poverty didn't necessarily engender an envy of wealth. These people had their way of life and were sticking to it.

These friendships proved to be the chief difference between my own Prague "before" and "after." I no longer had Czech "contacts" as I had in the Cold War years. I had — I have — Czech friends. I had never managed to sustain a friendship with a Czech before, and my shame over that was now given its proper place, framed as an inevitable aspect of the Cold War, and not solely a personal failing. I was an American. And even an ordinary American was not safe material for friendship in those years.

I could see that Anna's life was, in some ways, much tougher after the revolution than it had been before. Prague's historic center, where she has lived for decades, belongs now to a microeconomy governed by tourism, and she cannot go to the neighborhood pubs or *kavarny* that have always sustained much Czech social life. She cannot afford tickets — once laughably cheap — to music or theater. "In the old days," she said, "we entertained at home to feel free, to say what we wanted. Now we stay at home because we can't afford the price of beer. Everything's for the tourists now."

Anna turned herself into my postrevolution guide. She took me in hand, determined to find a table on a busy night at a *real* Prague *vinárna*, she said, not a tourist trap. She led me to Vyšehrad, where she bought me a guidebook to be sure I found the memorials to Karel Čapek and Dvořák in the cemetery. Every year she nudged me deeper into the culture — and complexity — of her country.

She had a heavy schedule at her clinic and was fighting a losing battle to maintain her position in the new health care system (one thing from the old regime, at least from a public health standpoint, that didn't need fixing). She had an absurdly low salary, but she helped her daughter, a university student, and also had the care of her elderly father, whose apartment was a few blocks away. She was long divorced, and lived in a fourteenth-century building with her terrier, Dyn, who greeted her return every night with demented joy. Anna was in constant trouble with her neighbors about Dyn. "He barks," she said, looking at him glumly. "But," she said, appealing to logic, "dogs bark."

She made it her project to get me out of Prague into the Bohemian and Moravian countryside. We went to Třebon and south Bohemia, the beautiful lake country of my grandmother's girlhood that startled me by looking so like Minnesota (with castles). We hiked the Beskedy Mountains. We traveled to north Bohemia and pondered the relics of the 1945 Czech post-War fury that had forced the "Sudetan" Germans to abandon their historic homes and flee for their lives into defeated Germany. We visited several spas, each year watching the elegant old structures and grounds at Karlovy Vary and

Mariansky Lazny color up, as the villas in Prague were, with fresh paint.

Once we made a day trip to Terezin with an American poet who, like me, was teaching in a summer program in Prague. The town, about an hour from Prague, had been transformed into a "model" ghetto during the War. It had figured in Nazi propaganda and been used to mislead the International Red Cross. Outside the town, an old fortress had been a concentration camp where Jews and political prisoners, especially Communists, had been tortured and murdered.

The American poet was Jewish and had been drawn to Eastern Europe in part because it was the land of the Holocaust. One strand of tourism to the region, in fact, has been quite distinct from the carnival spirit of the Charles Bridge. Pilgrims to the concentration camps have a shockingly crammed itinerary from which to choose now that the Iron Curtain has lifted and the land of the concentration camp is revealed.

Terezin is sometimes called "the children's camp" because of the rich archive of poems and drawings that survived — though so few children did — from the ghetto. We expected to see a well-documented exhibit, curated with the sophistication of the Holocaust Museum in Washington. After all, the old regime had been enthusiastically anti-Nazi, and there was a long Czech tradition of mistrust of the Germans.

But the museum in the town was only getting started, thanks to an international Jewish drive committed to documenting the ghetto. The exhibits were modest, heartbreaking, but rudimentary. "Is that all?" the American poet asked. It did seem a little threadbare, considering the entire town had been, in effect, a concentration camp.

We went on to the fortress. Here the museum had been carefully outfitted, apparently long ago. Portraits of (mostly young, virtually all Communist) Resistance fighters were lined up in rows. All of them had been tortured and murdered in Terezin. None of them was Jewish.

The poet regarded the scene for a long moment, frowning as he read the antique curatorial texts with their exhortations to the valor of the Communist freedom fighters. Then he turned to Anna. "Hey," he said with stage amazement. "Look at this. It turns out no Jews died in the Holocaust. Only Communists died. I can hardly wait to tell my folks."

※

Every weekend we piled into Anna's two-cylinder Polish Tuzka with Dyn, and hit the road. It was like touring in a Mixmaster, putt-putting along in the beat-up yellow Mr. Magoo car, narrowly missing disaster as BMWs and Mercedes flashed by, powered by the mad aggression of the newly rich. We had many close calls. The free market bullies nearly forced the little car into the ditch; they shook their fists at us as they hurtled past. Clearly, to them, *we* were the hazard, tooling around in our ridiculous Socialist excuse of a car. We were the dead-end past; we didn't deserve to live. It felt that nasty sometimes. Finally, eight years after the revolution, Anna gave in and managed to get a second-hand VW-made four-cylinder Škoda. "I couldn't take it anymore," she admitted.

We stayed one July at a fairy-tale hunting lodge recently opened to the public. Like many such choice places, it had been reserved in the former regime for Party members. We ordered wild boar and drank thimbles of Beckerovka. Dyn moaned tenderly over his delicate dish of boiled bones under the table (the Czechs, like the French, maintain a civilized hauteur about American rules against dogs in restaurants). We were sitting next to a beautiful old hunter-green tile oven. I noticed a small figure, a bronze statuette, stuck in the back of the stove, consigned, it seemed, to a dark corner of hell. It looked like Lenin. I asked the waiter about it.

"Yes," he said, nodding, as if at a common weed. "It is Lenin. We found him in a cabinet when we opened the lodge. We decided this is the place for him — in the stove." He didn't laugh, didn't work the joke. It was a deadpan Czech moment, the sort of gesture I had come to love in the Cold War years.

"Perfect," Anna said, mopping up the last of her *knedliky* with blackberry sauce, gazing with satisfaction at Lenin in his hotbox, and with admiration at her countryman. In spite of her own troubles, she, like our other friends, had no desire to go back.

Another year we made a tour of the Moravian wine cellars ("an older wine culture than France," Anna said, allowing herself a moment of civic pride). We even went in search of the blighted territory in the north, evidence that the Czechs (as indeed most of Eastern Europe) are at least twenty years behind the West in environmental policy. She wanted me to see everything. But mostly, we visited her friends north, south, east, and west, dipping off main roads, following turns and improbable trails to their summer cottages, the beloved *chata* every Czech lives for or wishes for, the little residences Anna believed had been part of the unlikely glue that held the country together during the Cold War.

We spent Sunday after Sunday sitting in the musty coolness of old cottages or country houses, drinking red wine at wobbly tables covered with a patched embroidered linen, gathering black lilac (for tisanes) from garden hedges that scribbled themselves into flowery meadows where beehives were stacked like filing cabinets. We moved beyond the margin of the meadows and hiked into the charcoal-dark woods, bestirring ourselves to hunt for mushrooms, cackling over our plush finds like happy witches returning to our gingerbread cottage for dinner and a long night of talk as dusk gathered itself in violet folds.

One thing about the threadbare Socialist regime, grafted onto the old Czech bourgeois heritage: it supported a culture of time wasting, which is the essence of friendship. It felt old-fashioned, deeply relaxing as little in contemporary life is. The country had been sustained by its relish for friendship, a life of little consolations — coffee and homemade berry coffee cakes baked in ancient woodstoves, served, crumbling, on chipped china. And the people you wasted time with were, by definition, people of your sort, not because of economic status or even profession. They had the same moral code, the same view of life, so akin it didn't need to be argued. It was as if during the Cold War, especially after 1968, they really did let themselves eat cake — and it helped.

Anna thought that the notorious Czech male pattern of marital infidelity was the dark side of this Cold War life of small satisfactions: ambition, outside the Party (and even within it), was impossible. At least a man could display his prowess as a lover. It was a theory of repressed ambition emerging as libido instead of, in the standard critique of the driven American overachiever, stifled libido coming out as workaholism. But wasn't this the general attitude toward sex in Europe? I asked. What about the French? — the Iron Curtain didn't explain them. But Anna maintained that infidelity was different here, just as alcoholism was: it wasn't wholly personal, but partook of the lethargy of a numbed, controlled culture.

I became addicted (what an American word) to these lazy weekends in cottages all over the country and the long evenings in Prague flats. I hardly spent a night alone at home. The kitchen suppers at Anna's, her "salons" at which people played music or sang, and the garden picnics in Vlasta's bower of bliss below the Hradcany — they were all part of the conspiracy of deliciously frittered-away time. A genius of ease presided, and we talked late, late into the night, the afternoon tea in blue-and-white onion-pattern Meissen cups giving way to glasses of homemade wine, and finally, in the dark of evening as the crickets came out, small lead-crystal shot glasses of *slivovice,* the distillation of plums bringing the bright day to its finish in a burning transparency.

I came back to Minnesota exulting about these long-into-the-night days, the sheer joy of companionship from these parties that refused to end, that weren't exactly "parties." My friends were not part of the economic gold rush, "the Klondike" as the Czechs themselves call the raw free marketeering of the country. They live as they lived before, getting by, entertaining each other. I was trying to explain to Jarda, my Czech (now American) friend whose Malá Strana apartment I sublet, how much I loved this quality of Czech life. I noticed his frown deepen as I carried on.

"Then can you tell me," he said severely, obviously warming to a pet subject, "why you — all these Americans — go to Czecho, and you come back saying how you love this Czech life, you love Czech drinking and talking all night long. Then people invite you over for dinner and — you look at your watch, it's eleven o'clock! Oh-oh, everybody better go home! Can you explain this?"

I could not. I could not even explain why it had not occurred to me that it was, after all, possible to do these simple things in America — wasn't it? It was not an Iron Curtain, but some more filmy cultural scrim that made it all seem impossible. I could only shrug, bowing my head, momentarily baffled, and plot to return again the next summer for more.

※

There was one person from the Cold War years I hadn't lost touch with. Yet I lost him eventually too, and more painfully — the man I called Jaromil, who not only was a poet, but stood for The Poet in my reflections on Czech life.

The pseudonym with which I outfitted him now seems quaintly cloak-and-daggerish, but it was a cloak-and-dagger time. I carefully provided all the people in this book with false names and occupations, which no doubt promoted my sense that they were characters and not quite real. Nor did I tell everything I knew about Jaromil; it seemed essential to protect him — and myself too. I fancied myself a small player in the Cold War cloak-and-dagger drama, having smuggled some of Jaromil's poems out of the country. I had rolled them (cunningly, I thought) into emptied tampon tubes, which I replaced carefully in the Tampax box and brought safely across the border. I sent the poems to an editor whose name and address Jaromil had given me.

At first I kept in touch with Jaromil. He replied promptly — not long letters but courtly ones, a bit elfin, as I remembered him. While I was still writing my book, perhaps a year after he'd shown me around Prague, he came to America as a visiting poet at a college in the Midwest. I arranged a reading for him in Minneapolis, and showed him around St. Paul ("This is the house where Scott Fitzgerald was born!") as he had shown me Kafka's Prague. It seemed a dream — to have one of my Czech friends visit *me*, visit my country. "Just act normal," Jaromil had always said as his political watchword, sidestepping the hard choices Kundera and Havel had battled over as they defined the lot of the Eastern European intellectual. Jaromil's visit to America was one of those "normal" things that seemed, in the Cold War, extraordinary, a miracle even.

I sent him a copy of *A Romantic Education* when it was published. I waited eagerly for his response. Nothing came. I flattered myself with a cloak-and-dagger explanation: the police had confiscated the book. I sent another copy. More silence. I wrote several letters over the next year. Nothing in reply.

He may have come to the United States again as a visiting scholar, but he never contacted me. It occurs to me now that my correspondence with my other Czech friends ended when Jaromil stopped writing me. It didn't seem that he had simply fallen silent, but had disappeared — and my fragile web of Czech connections dematerialized with him into the bin of history, another deathly *tableau vivant*: The Poet of "the Other Europe," as Philip Roth called the whole region during the Cold War — gone forever into a silence that began to seem native to the place.

Another, more canny instinct told me Jaromil had simply dropped me, but I had no idea why. I wrote the American editor to whom I had sent the smuggled poems, and inquired obliquely. He professed ignorance. The loss of Jaromil, like the loss of Prague itself, became one of those numb absences that punctuate a life, that have no apparent reason. Not a great tragedy, certainly, but a vexing mystery. Like the missing tooth of the old saying, it was a loss I could not keep away from; I kept returning to it, wondering what I had done — if I had done anything. Or perhaps there was something I *hadn't* done.

Five or six years later a literary scholar I knew through a friend went to Czechoslovakia on a Fulbright Fellowship. I heard he had met Jaromil. I wrote him. It was the first time I had confided Jaromil's identity to anyone. I was afraid, I told him, that Jaromil was angry. I didn't know why, but I was convinced I must have written something to upset him. But what could it be?

"I'm sorry to inform you," the Fulbright Fellow wrote back from Prague, "that your fears were correct." Jaromil had told him I had been "unkind" in my book. He did not elaborate. He said that was all Jaromil had been willing to say.

This tatter of information sent me into a stew of self-castigation — and confusion. I had been unkind. But where, how? I couldn't get the word "unkind" out of my head, as if it had been slapped on a billboard, the righteous judgment of The Poet. I read over the passages in the book about Jaromil, looking obsessively for signs. I gave the book to several friends and asked them to give it to me straight: where had I been unkind?

They found me not guilty. Get a grip, one of them said. You're a writer — writers always offend people. That's part of the job.

But I couldn't claim that kind of writerly pose. I had been far too well-intentioned, too earnest to pretend I didn't care. And the personal ethic binding me to the people I had met in Prague demanded that I not harm them. Hadn't history betrayed them enough? I had no desire to "use" anyone, inevitable as that is for any writer. At least, I didn't want to misuse anyone.

My American friends let me off the hook. I had always associated the give-it-up shrug with the Czechs, but now my American friends were shrugging: what's the big deal? But I kept coming back, as if to an elusive scent, to one passage in the book, the description of my first glimpse of Jaromil. He was "dapper," I had written, and he wore "astonishing shoes . . .

red, the deep polished red of two candied apples." These shoes, I wrote, had "raised heels, and the toes were rounded and a little bulbous. . . . It was clear they were meant to be very stylish."

I went on. "No adult with a Ph.D. and even the most harmless sense of his own importance would wear such shoes in the United States." Yet Jaromil did — and not, I noted "in the witty, self-conscious way that stylish people sometimes dress in the West." The shoes were not a joke. "He was dressed," I wrote, "to meet an American."

I followed this description of him with one of myself "wearing a flower print skirt, the sort of thing that is called a peasant skirt, suggesting that it is worn by milkmaids in happy Central European landscapes."

In these descriptions I had tried to evoke the foolishly romantic image I bore of his country with my costume (the peasant milkmaid) and the equally comic one he conveyed of America with his disco shoes. Hardly enough to break a friendship. And — the argument I kept making to my imagined accuser — hadn't I made myself a comic figure too in my milkmaid peasant skirt? I decided finally that like so much I had left behind in Prague, this too would remain an unfinished story, something I would never understand. Another occasion for a Czech shrug.

But the word "unkind" continued to flash its ugly neon in my fretful thinking, and the red shoes popped up like poisoned apples in my mind. I was consoled by common sense: this business about the shoes was all too trivial, too silly. It couldn't be *that*.

※

At the end of my 1991 visit I told Anna about Jaromil, about our early friendship, how I smuggled out his poems, how he visited me in Minnesota — and how he had dropped me. It had been over twelve years since I had seen him. Somehow, the act of telling Anna this history made me face the fact that I could, after all, call him now. That I must. I couldn't hide any longer behind my metaphor. He wasn't just The Poet. He was a person with a job and a phone number. All I had to do was pick up a telephone.

I put it off from day to day.

Finally, the day before I left I decided I had to call. I wanted to know — and of course didn't want to know — what my "unkindness" had been. I dialed the office number I'd kept all these years. Jaromil answered on the first ring. He recognized my voice before I could say my name.

"Patricia!" he said in his quick, almost breathless way (I remembered his voice too). "Where are you?"

I told him my Malá Strana address. He said he had a meeting with a visiting English scholar, a translator and his wife, at the Palffy Palac in half an hour. It was two blocks from where I was. "I can give you fifteen minutes," he said. "Tomorrow I go to Turkey. I am always traveling now. But come to the Palffy, there's a restaurant on the second floor." I felt I had been summoned, even though I had called him. The fifteen minutes felt like a courtly reprimand, a preliminary rap on the knuckles.

He was remarkably unchanged when he came through the Palffy doorway into the dark inner courtyard where I stood waiting. Dressed, as always, in a dapper suit, his tie in a Windsor knot. He was hurried, radiating the cheerful rush of a successful man with places to go, people to see. He mentioned my books immediately, and said with wide eyes as we walked up the staircase to the restaurant, "You have done very well for yourself — books, awards — haven't you?" It was not unkind, to use the word I now associated with him. But it was not a friendly remark. And the tone was coolly ironic.

I was disappointed to discover that the English translator and his wife, a gentle elderly couple, were already sitting at a table. I wouldn't even get my fifteen minutes.

But to my surprise, he introduced me to the English couple, with a booming bonhomie, as a writer who had included him in "a well-known book" about Prague. "She called me Jaromil," he said with comic wonder, as if this were his greatest literary trophy. "She made me a symbol of Czech poets." The white-haired translator nodded encouragingly and his wife cooed a bit: I had honored Jaromil, they gathered.

I was startled, shocked really, to see how casually all my care could be tossed off. I murmured that I had never disclosed publicly who "Jaromil" was. I felt slightly foolish, as if in giving him a false name all those years ago I had not protected him, but had disobeyed his principal dictum: *just act normal*. Maybe *that* had been the unkindness?

So, why not let this be the moment, because it is the one he chose, for me also to discard the cloak-and-dagger pseudonym of the Cold War. He was Miroslav Holub, not only a poet well known and even revered in the West, but a research immunologist whose identity as a scientist gave him a special cachet in literary circles. He was a man who had managed to move on both sides of the Iron Curtain, the great twentieth-century divide, but he also represented an even more abiding dichotomy, the struggle of the modern mind between the poetic and the scientific. He seemed to move effortlessly between these two opposing worlds too. It had been my sharpest disappointment, years ago when I was working on this book, that my commitment to obscuring his identity had made it impossible to make use of his double identity as poet and scientist.

"Yes," he said to the English couple, "she made me famous in her book." His eyes were round with wonder. I remembered well the particular style of his almost imperceptible dead-cold irony. Only now it was trained on me, not on "the system."

"This is your chance," I said, plowing ahead anyway, "to set things right. There's going to be a new edition of the book. I can make changes. You can tell me what I got wrong."

He didn't look at me as he threw up his hands in a dismissive flutter. "No, no!" he cried, turning airily to the English couple. "You write what you want. It's fine. It doesn't matter. You write what you want. It's a free country — isn't that what you say?"

※

It was an oddly clean moment. I knew I had been slapped, but there was no sting. Later, when I walked out of the big, drafty Palffy Palac, leaving Miroslav with the English couple, I realized I was free, though I still had no idea what my offense had been. If he were regarding the situation from afar, Miroslav — or my old Jaromil — would no doubt have labeled the scene pure "Kafka," as he used to crow when he observed some Cold War absurdity.

He decided to keep me in the dark, even to keep me at arm's length. With that choice the integuments of friendship were unbound, and the simple truth revealed: we weren't friends. He hadn't bothered to get angry with me — I wasn't worth it. Finally, the thing could rest.

When I returned to Prague the following year, I told Anna about this epilogue to the mystery. She listened with the alert canniness of one used to diciphering codes. She nodded: made sense, she said. He didn't want to do me the favor, the honor, of acknowledging I had wounded him. She didn't like his poetry much, she admitted. Too cold, too detached. Kundera had always disappointed her too. Not because of his politics. "He hates love," she said. Kundera was writing in French now, I told her, not Czech. He had exiled himself twice over. She shrugged. "He prefers Paris," she said. "They make much of him there."

By the time I returned to Prague as a Fulbright scholar in 1995, Havel's wise early counsel about not pursuing the Cold War history of individual citizens had been forgotten — or disregarded. A "list" had been published. The Czech Republic is small enough that publication of such a document could poison the entire intellectual life of the country. Legions of people in all walks of life were outed as — but that was the question. What *did* appearance on the list mean? The names had been taken from files in the secret police archives; from the moment the list was published outraged counterallegations claimed that these were simply people the authorities had tried to coerce, not necessarily people who had agreed to collaborate by informing, often in absurdly minor ways, against friends and colleagues. Indeed, some of those on the list were well-regarded dissidents with impeccable credentials.

Miroslav's name was on the list. I was mystified. He had always professed contempt for the former regime. And he hadn't been able to publish in the country. But at lunch one day, a Czech writer friend of mine who had spent time in prison during the Cold War and who worked on human rights issues (and was not on the list), was almost gleeful. Miroslav, he said, had been the worst kind of opportunist. He had been canny enough not to join the Party, the former dissident said, because he knew that would compromise him in the West. But he was willing to cooperate quietly in order to have the right to travel. All that mattered to him was his status in the West. "We always knew what he was," the man said with disdain. I understood "we" stood for all the "real" Czech writers.

But he's invited to read all over the world, I said. "Of course," the dissident replied, exasperated. "Of course he travels now." It was the only way he could have a literary life at all. Miroslav was nothing in the Czech Republic, he said, nothing in his own language. People knew what he was.

But what had he done to get on the list? No one seemed to know or say. It was all too vague and gossipy for me, the kind of character assassination that, once started, develops a life of its own. I mentioned a writer whose name had appeared on the list and whom everyone agreed was wrongly, absurdly, accused. And how much of the venom against Miroslav was bred of simple jealousy? After all, he enjoyed a rare international reputation; his works were translated into English — the great hurdle to an international identity for a writer from a "small language." "Look," the former dissident said, "you don't understand what it was like. Maybe — just maybe — once in your life, if you were lucky, you might somehow manage to travel. But if you traveled to the West the way he did all the time, you were in their pocket."

At the end of my Fulbright residency, I gave a reading at the American Center. To my surprise, Miroslav was in the audience. He seemed eager to see me. He wanted to have lunch and even waited patiently until I was free to find my calendar so we could make a date.

My friend, the former dissident was there too. "Did you see," he said after Miroslav had left, "how nervous he was when he saw me here?"

I had not, but I had my own thoughts: Miroslav seemed — there was no other word — chastened, or at least subdued, not the buoyant writer-on-the-go he had been at the Palffy only a few years before, fitting me in for fifteen minutes between his English translator and his flight to Turkey.

But I didn't trust my observation: how much of it was bred of my own imagining? And though I might not trust the gossip, I was no doubt absorbing it like the poison Havel had warned it would be.

More important: who was I to judge? When I talked to the American director of the summer program where I taught, his position was clean as a whistle: "Listen," he said, "We're Americans. We can't begin to understand the complications of this situation." His position: don't take a position. He invited Miroslav to give a reading for the summer program — a form of "acting normal," as Miroslav had always advised.

The former dissident said, "You see, only the Americans ask him to read."

But Anna, always my Czech moral barometer, said, "Why not?"

Being on the list did not, it seemed, consign a person to oblivion. Apparently the list was another Czech hell made of nuances, another Cold War onion that could not be peeled to its core but only to its ultimate nothingness. As the director of the summer program had said, an American couldn't begin to grasp it. But I began to wonder if even the Czechs could be trusted to hold on to all their complications.

※

By 1996 I was speaking not only of "my friends" and "my apartment" in Prague, but of "my translator." Czech writers might yearn for the wider audience that translation into the "world language" of English promised, but I had always wanted to creep in the other direction, into the provincial embrace of Czech.

Translation has an honored place in Czech intellectual life, not only because it brings world literature into the home language, but because it has traditionally provided steady work for intellectuals. This literary work was especially important for banned writers and others thrown out of their professions after the Prague Spring.

That was how my translator, Eva, came to translation. During the "normalization" that followed the 1968 invasion, she was fired from her job as a producer at the main Prague radio station. She was middle-aged, broke, unemployable — and fluent in Bulgarian and English. Eventually she found her way into an office job as a court typist when a sympathetic friend discovered a loophole that allowed him to hire her as a "temporary worker" without going through the standard background check. They kept renewing the contract every three months until she retired eighteen years later. But at first she had only translation work to bring in any money. Even after she got the court job she kept taking on manuscripts because she discovered she liked the work.

By the time I met her in 1996, she was in her seventies, a still-beautiful woman, elegant, yet down-to-earth. And still translating. "Excuse me, Patricia," she said once, intent on her research, "but are you able to explain the meaning of the word 'bimbo'?" She was working on a novel by Ed McBain, one of her regular authors. "I always like to have a book going," she said. She lived in a fourth-floor walk-up and didn't stop to rest as she made the climb. "All my friends come up huffing and puffing," she said. "They can't believe I live here."

It was only by a lucky chance that we met. During my Fulbright residency, in 1995, Anna had called one rainy April day, and said that we had been invited to Jiři and Šarka's studio. They were the sculptor and painter who lived, it seemed, on nothing, radiating wonder and generosity as if they were more angels than artists. They had a surprise for me, Anna said. My Czech radar pulsed instantly: cake!

We sat in their studio overlooking the river embankment, surrounded by Jiři's spectral stone figures, mostly grieving Madonnas, and we drank Moravian wine, gazing out the long, grave windows to the Vltava below. It was raining hard, a miserable gray day. The studio was cozy, and we drank the red wine out of chipped glasses. I wondered idly about the cake.

After we had discussed Jiři's latest figures and had talked the afternoon toward night (no cake), Šarka, responding to some private timer of her own, suddenly jumped up and said it was time for the surprise. She went to the tape deck, the one extravagance in their modest lives, and slipped a cassette into the player.

I looked out the window at the beautiful miserable day. I was ridiculously happy, wrapped again in the curative Czech time wasting. A romantic melody came out of the cassette player. Then it faded under, and a lovely voice, a woman's cultivated reading voice, began to deliver a story. My Czech is bad — bad enough that I shouldn't really speak of "my Czech" in spite of my lessons, my language tapes, my good intentions. I speak English with Anna, a sort of homemade French with Šarka and Vlasta, with bits of Czech tossed around like decorative glitter. Anna translates for me most of the time.

I had no idea what the woman on the tape was reading, but it didn't matter. I liked the lovely low voice, the drift of words falling inside with a constance akin to the steady rain outside the window. I had developed a habit of silence in Czech social situations, unburdened by my bad Czech from any responsibility to keep conversation going. It didn't occur to me that I would understand anything on the tape, so I didn't try.

Then, like a spark ignited at the base of my skull, some fugitive riff or rhythm penetrated: I understood in an instant that these low purring sounds, these rises and falls of expression were — *my words*. It was the passage from *A Romantic Education* about my grandmother's Sunday dinners. I looked up, staring like someone who has seen a ghost. My friends were regarding me steadily, smiles spreading slowly across their good faces. Tears sprang to my eyes; their eyes were bright too.

"Potato!" I cried madly. "I heard her say potato!"

"It's a very good translation," Anna said. "Perfect."

We played the tape three times, and cried, and drank some more wine. And then there was cake, after all.

When, several weeks later, we finally tracked down the translator, and I called her, Eva said in an alarmed voice, "Oh dear, I hope the radio station paid you. I hope you aren't upset we used it without permission. No one knew where you were." They had no idea I was in Prague. She was afraid I might take legal action.

"No, no," I said. "Don't worry." I tried to explain to her, but how could I tell her what it meant? I didn't feel she had translated my work. She had translated me — not simply into a language, but into the family. My Czech friends finally heard me talking effortlessly in their impossible language. Though its life span was tethered to a tape loop, my Czech, at long last, was flawless.

%

The Prague summer of 1998 was steamy, the hottest on record according to Eva. I spent it in the pattern I had developed over the years, part of the time committed to the Prague Summer Seminars program and writing in my little Malá Strana apartment, the rest of my days visiting my friends.

But it started out with a scare: to my surprise Eva, who had no car, met me at the airport. Every year it was Anna who picked me up, strapping my luggage on top of her little car as if I were a long-lost traveler who had returned home rather than an arriving visitor. But Anna, Eva said, had had a stroke. We took a taxi into town.

She's only fifty, she's too young, I wanted to protest. But in another way, I wasn't surprised at all. The lazy time-wasting days I luxuriated in were not her daily round, not her real life, no matter how much she relished her salons and promoted our trips to country cottages. She laid out these bucolic days and the intimate Prague soirees for me like an extravagant bouquet she had gathered for free in her native place. They were her composition, a kind of living testament describing, as no description could, the hidden pulse of Czech life, the life that had beat beneath the grinding humiliations of the Cold War and now continued to throb under the fevered free market life that had supplanted it. This, she kept insisting, is it, the real It.

In fact, she worked three different jobs, racing from clinic to office to hospital, on her feet running from five in the morning until midnight. She had finally been forced out of clinical work she loved, shunted into a bureaucratic backwater as the old health care system fell to pieces. She was too old to take on the huge debt required to shift to the new private practice physician model and too young to retire.

She sewed her own clothes or bought them in thrift shops (she had a flair), put up her own preserves and had devised a million careful ways of cutting costs and stretching money ("Don't leave the car in gear," she cried once when I was driving and we were going down a slight hill. "Put it in neutral. Saves petrol").

Her salary wouldn't support a graduate student in the United

States, and she had the daily care of her ancient father, who sat in his apartment around the corner, blind and hopeless, dying by inches. She had to help her daughter get through university, and she was afflicted by a magnificent generosity that caused her to help everyone else who crossed her path. Including me.

The stroke, it turned out, was a warning; she wasn't paralyzed. She was home from the hospital, on medical leave, feeling all right, though a little unsteady. When I visited her the next day she wanted to begin planning the summer field trips. But for once, I called the shots. We would confine ourselves to day trips, and I would drive.

It was because of this change in our usual pattern that I was in Prague when Miroslav Holub died on July 14. He had had various circulatory problems in recent years; I had noticed the last time I saw him that he limped slightly, favoring a leg. Still, it was a sudden death and took people by surprise. He had been scheduled to give a reading in the Prague Summer Seminars program two days later.

Instead, on that day, Anna and I took the tram to the crematorium where his funeral service was held. It was a stifling day, and we were late, rushing through the plaza that led to the corporate-looking temple where we could hear taped music playing. The plaza was landscaped with bright flowers wilting in the heat, and was punctuated by massive granite bowls from which eternal flames shot up like fires from the chimneys of a smelting factory.

Inside, more socialist-realist decor. A long white bas-relief of idealized workers was hoisted above the center dais. Apparently it was meant to depict life's stages; the last panel showed all the figures with their hands covering their faces. The space — not a room, not a hall or auditorium but some indeterminate architectural container — was vast, and in spite of its essential blankness, gave off an aura of confusion. Was it a warehouse? Or a temple to a supremely anonymous space-age god? It was neither church nor funeral parlor, but a kind of meta-location refusing the comforts either of religion or of American-style undertaking.

In a way, it was just the place for a Czech like Miroslav to be sent off. Unlike the super-Catholic Poles or their own former countrymen, the Slovaks, the Czechs have a long tradition of disbelief; they chafe under the moist consolations of organized religion. Well over 90 percent of them profess to be atheists, and Miroslav, fervently rational and a mordant ironist, was in this and much else Czech to the core. His "absurdist wit," as the *New York Times* obituary called it, was the flip side of his inevitable trust in scientific method. These composed his faith as well as his world view. No choirs and stained glass for him.

Anna and I crept to the side of the huge space, and leaned against a pillar. The benches, whose pew-like style contributed to whatever churchiness the place had, were not full. But as the aunts on my mother's Irish side used to say when they counted the house at a funeral, the crowd was more than presentable.

The coffin was hoisted high on a draped pyre before the massive center doors which would receive it. Masses of flowers covered the steps leading to the dais. Some of the flowers were festooned with broad ribbons bearing the names of medical institutes and literary organizations. A large arrangement of gladiolas was displayed prominently; its ribbon carried in gilt lettering the name of the literary organization devoted to human rights which was headed by the former dissident, the man who had said so bitingly that Miroslav had been in the pocket of the secret police. The dissident, I noticed, was not there. It was summer, someone said later, and "nobody" was in town. At any other time of year, I was told, the place would have been filled.

There were two brief speeches, one from a medical colleague, another from a man representing the dissident's literary organization. Anna said they were standard eulogies, nothing special. She seemed to approve of this. "We don't like a lot of fuss," she said, another "we" that spoke for the nation. Then we sat for a long, surreal time while the full rendition of *Boléro*, said to be Miroslav's favorite piece of music, played itself out from the tape deck to its weary crescendo.

Then silence. Then the creaking of the pyre as it moved away on its electrical track. The big center doors opened, received the tottering box, and closed slowly, with a slight grinding noise.

The Czech obituaries were respectful. There was mention that during the "normalization" period after 1968 Holub was branded as an "ideologically disoriented" writer. I could imagine Miroslav's wicked relish of this priceless apparatchik lingo.

The obituary in *Mlada Fronta Dnes*, the centrist daily, noted that he had officially repented his "mistakes." The writer, Josef Chuchma, said that "the price he paid for this self-criticism was not negligible: the loss of civil and artistic credibility." Meaning, of course, credibility in his own country. It was the view of my friend, the former dissident.

Things were simpler in the West. The obituaries in England and the United States (which were translated into Czech for a separate story in *Dnes*) were reverent. Ted Hughes called Holub "one of the half dozen most important poets writing anywhere." Seamus Heaney said his poetry was "too compassionate to be vindictive, too skeptical to be entranced." The *New York Times* obituary noted that after 1968 Miroslav had become a "nonperson" and "any mention of his work was forbidden." Nothing was said of his "repentance" after 1968 or its meaning, nothing of his appearance on the notorious list after the Velvet Revolution.

When I got back to the States, I sent the Czech and English obituaries to a Czech friend who has lived in America since 1968, a man whose opinion I trust and who, coincidentally, is also a scientist and a writer (of fiction, not poetry). "Holub was an intelligent person," he wrote back, "who collaborated with Communists from the very beginning of his writing career." It was the harsh view I had heard from the former Czech dissident. "His two books, *Angel on Wheels* and *Living in New York,* were written, *clearly,* with the idea to please Communist ideologists, ridiculing 'capitalists' and denigrating everything about the U.S. I remember my disgust, that a scientist and poet I knew could lower himself so. He did everything to facilitate his possibility to travel.

"Remember," he wrote, "it was in the time when the possibility to travel abroad was the highest possible reward for loyalty. This might not be understood well in the U.S. It was understood well in Czechoslovakia. It would require a great power of imagination to put yourself in the shoes of somebody who reads, studies, and knows that he/she cannot, ever, see anything or anybody past the western border."

Holub, he said, "understood this and what to do. Carefully, so he could still move around without being branded a flaming Communist. Very smart but not smart enough: he was never part of social groups you would respect. This is certain." My Czech-American friend was invoking, as Anna often had in the past, the inner web of trust and decency that "real Czechs" had honored and recognized throughout the former regime.

But, I couldn't help wondering: had Miroslav harmed anyone? He harmed the truth! I could hear my friend and the former dissident cry, outraged. Anna's view, based on a long talk with a respected translator who had been a dissident herself and who knew Holub: Miroslav probably did no real harm, his name on the list wasn't evidence of anything in particular. The West was hopelessly gullible, everyone agreed, but neither was he the worst of a bad lot.

On and on it could go, I knew, the assessment which was not so much a judgment as an anguished attempt to read history before it could be written. Josef Chuchma's obituary in *Dnes* had ended on a note Anna liked: Today, he wrote, it was still "too recent and painful" to judge the "Holub case."

"He had to put the facts down," Anna said of the *Dnes* obituary. "But he doesn't beat him up." This, she felt, was the way to handle a life lived in two opposing worlds as it passed, finally, into the oblivion of the third, waiting for history to make the only judgment that will matter.

As for "the likes of me," as my grandmother used to say — I understood finally that I had no business judging any of it or any of them, not Miroslav and not those who excused him or vilified him. The Czechs may want to be part of "the West," but they know the West — me with my blue American passport — can't be part of their tangled history, their inner family. I may have "my Malá Strana apartment," but I'm forever a tourist on the bridge, dazzled by the scene.

The last time I saw Miroslav, in 1996, we met at Ganey's, a second-floor restaurant near the National Theater, much favored by ex-pats and hip young Czech writers and artists. Like all such places, it served mediocre food, was foggy with cigarette smoke, and let you sit forever over a beer. I thought we were meeting for a drink, but when I rose after two hours to go to my dinner engagement, Miroslav looked hurt. "I thought we were having dinner, walking around the city afterward," he said. It seemed he had time to spare; I felt bad that I couldn't change my plans.

He wanted to talk about something, he said, before we parted. Did I remember how I had written about him in my book?

I held my breath.

The shoes, he said. Did I remember his shoes?

Oh yes.

"You know," he said, the familiar mock wonder of his Cold War eyes gone for once, an abject beagle-like pain in them, "I could never wear those shoes again after you wrote about them. You made fun of them."

I told him I was sorry. I asked if he remembered my peasant dress, how I had poked fun at my own costume too. He didn't seem to hear me.

"I tried to use them just for gardening," he said, not looking at me but down at the table, in the thick of his feeling. "But I couldn't even wear them in the garden. I had to throw them away." He paused a moment. "They were new shoes."

He looked up and I saw — I thought I saw — the fearful isolation of one who couldn't accept his history, who felt he had been pounded for wanting what everyone wants — the world. Western literature has always been fascinated by hubris, the pride of the powerful, of those with special privilege ("it was the time when the possibility to travel abroad was the highest possible reward for loyalty"), those who take a fall. But why have we always assumed that hubris is the sin of pride when it turns out to be the gnawing anguish of fear that fires the pride to begin with? The fear of missing life, of not getting your share.

The big creaking doors that swallowed Miroslav's flower-covered pyre closed not only on a life, but on an age, one that will be dying for a long time to come in the bruised chests of the passing generation that took its worst blows.

Maybe, as my Czech friends say, it is impossible for an outsider to know how to judge such a life or even how to mourn it. But there is still the righteous privacy of personal relations, what Keats called "the holiness of the heart's affections."

As we sat across from each other at Ganey's, I said again that I was sorry. Miroslav lifted his glass. I looked at my old Cold War guide across our golden cylinders of beer, and I toasted this sacred trust which I still believed to be mine, no matter what.